The Court of Last Resort

Carol A. B. Warren

The Court of Last Resort

Mental Illness and the Law

With Contributions by
Stephen J. Morse
Jack Zusman

The University of Chicago Press
Chicago and London

Carol A. B. Warren, associate professor of sociology at the University of Southern California, is the author of Identity and Community in the Gay World; Sociology: Change and Continuity; *and (with Joann Delora and Carol Rinkleib)* Understanding Human Sexuality.

The University of Chicago Press, Chicago 60637
The University of Chicago Press, Ltd., London

© 1982 by The University of Chicago
All rights reserved. Published 1982
Printed in the United States of America
89 88 87 86 85 84 83 82   5 4 3 2 1

Library of Congress Cataloging in Publication Data

Warren, Carol, A. B., 1944–
   The court of last resort.

   Bibliography: p.
   Includes index.
   1. Insane—Commitment and detention—California.
2. Mental health laws—California.   I. Morse,
Stephen J.   II. Zusman, Jack, 1934–
III. Title.
KFC111.15W37   344.794′044   82-1839
ISBN 0-226-87388-9   347.940444   AACR2

For my friends, wise counselors, and for my parents

Contents

vii

Preface

This book is intended for sociologists interested in psychiatric sociology, symbolic interactionism, and critical sociology. It is also intended for those who work in the mental health law area, as attorneys, judges, psychiatrists, legislators, or agency staff.

The purpose of the book is to contribute a study of courtroom decision making in involuntary commitment cases to the growing literature on mental health law, and to set the study within different disciplinary perspectives and theoretical, methodological, and analytic levels. What is gained in scope and breadth of the presentation is sometimes lost in depth of coverage; many important theories and studies have, perforce, had to be omitted—theories and studies that would have been included in a unidisciplinary endeavor.

The research on which the book was based was funded by the National Institute of Mental Health Crime and Delinquency Section, grant RO 1 MH 27846-01, and by the National Science Foundation Law and Society Section, grant SOC 78-0800. Additional funding was provided by the President's Circle of the University of Southern California.

I would like to thank the people who helped me with this book. For assistance in data collection: Elizabeth Thompson (University of Southern California), Phillip Davis (University of Georgia), and Pomphylia Baker. For assistance in data analysis: Elizabeth Thompson, Joann Sandlin (San Diego State University), Virginia Hiday (University of North Carolina), and Patricia Jeffries (University of Southern California). For comments on drafts of the book: Peter Manning (Michigan State University), David Greenberg (New York University), Virginia Hiday (University of North Carolina),

Robert Thompson (University of Southern California School of Law), Jack Zusman (University of Southern California Medical School), Stephen Morse (University of Southern California School of Law), John Monahan (University of Virginia School of Law), Barbara Laslett (University of Southern California), John M. Johnson (Arizona State University), and Sheldon L. Messinger (University of California, Berkeley). For assistance in obtaining documents and statistical data: Lawrence Panciera (University of Southern California), Steven Lubeck (Los Angeles County Mental Health), George Wolkon (Los Angeles County Mental Health), and David Guthman (District Attorney's Office, Los Angeles). For assistance in typing: Marie-Joëlle Tran huu, Linda Landry, Pomphylia Baker, Edna Bell, Rosann Ogden, Bea Shelton, Maureen Barnett, Barbara Biedebach, Wanda Ward, Pat Noble, Claudine Dervos, and Jindarat P. Lau.

In addition, I am indebted to Stephen Morse and Jack Zusman for each agreeing to contribute a chapter to the project. Professor Morse is a lawyer, psychologist, and advocate of the abolition of involuntary civil commitment, while Dr. Zusman is a psychiatrist and an advocate of its retention. I included their points of view in this work both because they possess a scope and breadth of expertise on the legal and psychiatric issues that I do not possess, and because they both have definite positions on the issues. As I discuss at greater length in Chapter 9, after seven years of research and thought in the area of mental health law I am more in favor of retaining than abolishing involuntary civil commitment, but I take that position reluctantly and not as a partisan.

1 The Court of Last Resort
An Introduction to the Study

*T*his study is about decision making in a court of law; about the many processes of social interaction which make up case outcomes. But the court of last resort is a special kind of court, and it involves a special kind of law. Metropolitan Court (a pseudonym) is a mental health court through which persons involuntarily committed to mental hospitals seek their release. Thus decision making in the court is also of a special kind; it must take into account not only the rational world of law but also the irrational world of the mentally disordered.

The purpose of the research is to examine the individual, interpersonal, organizational, and interorganizational elements which enter into decision making. The perspective is mainly symbolic interactionist and inductive rather than structuralist and deductive. But deduction and structural concepts play a part in the theoretical framework of the research through the notions of context and reflexivity.

The specific outcomes recorded as the end products of court decision making are not just the product of situated encounters between clients and decision makers, they take place in a historical and socioeconomic context which shapes and constrains the range of the decisions which participants can make. The concepts I use to organize the research were not simply induced from the data; they were shaped also by preexisting notions I have about the world, which, reflexively, are the product of my own biography and of the sociohistorical context of my work.

The study examines both the ideal (pertaining to consciousness and conceptual categories) and material or real (pertaining to interactions, resources, and vested interests) determinants of decision

1

making.[1] The ideal determinants include mental health law and interpretations of mental illness. The material determinants include both the relationships between actors within the decision making system—such as those between public defenders and district attorneys—and the economic foundation of the system—such as the amount and source of funds available for processing cases or handling mental patients.

The setting of the study is an organization; organizations provide one arena in which to observe the confluence of the ideal and the material determinants of social action. One element of organizations is the set of rules and precedents which constrains the action of members toward organizational goals; the other is the action of members as it is shaped not only by those goals and rules but also by an enormous variety of economic, work-related, and personal factors. Organizations provide a setting for the study of praxis, or social action at the intersection of ideas and material interests.

The Theoretical Perspective

The perspective within which the study developed is symbolic interactionist; the theory most closely relevant is labeling theory. Labeling theory has two major aspects: a theory of the promotion and formation of identity, and a theory of the audience response to deviance. It is the second aspect of labeling theory which relates most cogently to the process of decision making in mental health courts, although the first has some relevance (see Chap. 3).

Rules, Conflict, and Labeling Theory

In Part I of the book, ideas concerning mental illness, and mental health laws, are considered as background factors to decision making. Labeling theory points to both the economic and the power dimensions of laws and ideas, and to the socially constructed nature of deviance labels. The mental health law of California, the Lanterman-Petris-Short Act (passed in 1967 and put into effect in 1969; hereinafter LPS), is a product of political interests on the part of legislative groups (see Bardach 1972). Labels of "mentally ill" or "mad" applied to others are social constructions based on both the behavior and attributes of those others, and on the ideas and laws concerning mental illness which form the sociohistorical or structural context of labeling.

Views of the nature of rule making and rule makers differ depending on whether the structural context of interaction is seen from

---

1. This usage of material/real and ideal differs somewhat from standard philosophic usage.

a functionalist or from a conflict point of view. From a functionalist point of view, rule making and rule makers are simply differentiated parts of a harmonious social system, crystallizing and channeling the collective will into formal rules and sanctions. This is not my point of view. Taking my cue from macroconflict theorists, I view the structural context of interaction as based on economic and political interests, and the ideas of law and mental illness as reflections of the outcomes of those power struggles. At its outer limits, the phenomenon of deviance labeling is a matter of the power to create and sustain the categories through which the social control of deviance becomes possible.

The labeling of deviants by social control agencies is a matter of interaction, but interaction takes place within macrosocial structures—and, in my view, these structures are conflictful. I have given a more detailed view of how I arrived at a conflict view of structure in the Appendix on Method; briefly, as I moved conceptually and investigatively beyond Metropolitan Court to the arenas in Sacramento (California's legislature) and beyond that appeared to shape past and future directions of mental health law, I found those forces to be economic and political power interests. My symbolic interactionist perspective became, and remains, set within a conflict structuralist perspective.

The Organizational Matrix

Labeling theory is also relevant to the question of decision making by those social control agents who must implement laws and make judgments concerning deviants: the gatekeepers of social control systems whose decision making is the topic of Part II of the book. These gatekeepers make decisions in the reflexive context of sociohistorical conditions. The background to their decisions is always the prior layer of decisions that has been crystallized as law or policy by those with, as it were, a higher power. Gatekeepers' decisions also come from biographically shaped self-interest, professional concerns for the intraorganizational group as against other intraorganizational groups, and so on. Both the "upward" biographical factors in decision making and the "downward" policy factors are grounded in the sociohistorical context.

Like Brown (1978), I would argue that organizations are the key link between conflict macrosociological approaches and symbolic interactionist (which Brown calls neo-Durkheimian) approaches to the study of society:

Many scholars have noted the disparity between Marxian approaches to macro societal issues and neo-Durkheimian sociologies of consciousness in micro settings. The first focuses on the real structures of society, the second on the social construction of reality. Theory of formal organizations, largely in the tradition of Weber, is a good place to attempt to link these major but divergent schools. Such linkage might occur from two directions: scaling Marxism down to the level of organizational practice, and scaling micro sociologies up to the level of organizational structure.... "Rationality," "legitimacy," or "authority" are structures of consciousness as well as features of face-to-face settings; as such, their construction can be reinterpreted phenomenologically as the praxiological foundations of organizational life. [P. 366]

Those processes which link the macrostructuralist and the micro-interactionist levels of analysis include, in the mental health system, decision-implementing organizations, such as Metropolitan Court. To the insights of Marx and Blumer, in my view, need to be added the insights of Weber. The application of deviance labels in the course of organizational work is an important aspect of any theory of decision making and social control from a labeling perspective.

Labeling Theory and the Transformation of Identity

The labeling perspective underlines the significance of the ownership and control of the material means of rule making and enforcement, and of the categories through which deviants are interpreted. As such, it is a perspective rather than a theory; a way of viewing the world rather than an explanation or prediction. But there is another aspect of labeling theory which is more theory than perspective and which needs to be taken into account in any discussion of mental illness because of its relevance to this field: the theory of secondary deviation.

The theory of secondary deviation specifies the effects of the labeling process on those labeled as deviant (Lemert 1967). The identity-transformation aspect of labeling theory does not logically depend on viewing the generation and implementation of social control as a process of conflict; it could equally well be that labels are affixed by those in power but that those in power got there in a manner proposed by the functionalists. In practice, however, a more conflict-oriented version of the labeling perspective and the theory of secondary deviation are usually found together.

The theory of secondary deviation predicts that the affixing of deviance labels transforms the views of future audiences in the direction of greater stigmatization of the deviant and, further, that continued labeling promotes the transformation of the deviant's own identity. In addition, Lemert (1967) proposes that this transformation of identity promotes further deviant behavior and an increasingly deviant way of life.

The labeling perspective in general and the theory of secondary deviation in particular have been significant in the development of contemporary legal-psychiatric scholarship. Empirical studies have documented the greater vulnerability to deviance labeling (specifically, mental illness) of persons with attributes that connote powerlessness within existing social structures, such as minority ethnic status (Teknekron 1978), poverty and unemployment (Gove 1975, p. 54), and lack of family (Greeley 1972). The theory of secondary deviation has been used to challenge the use of involuntary civil commitment, since mental hospitalization is viewed as promoting increased mental disorder rather than cure. From this perspective, involuntary civil commitment can be seen as preventive detention or cruel and unusual punishment rather than as therapy (see Chap. 2).

Most important, labeling theory has been used by all the major sociologists writing in the psychiatric sociology area, with the exception of Walter Gove and some of his colleagues, to deny the existence of mental illness as any kind of condition or entity independent of the labeling process. Given an initial acceptance of the labeling perspective, such a position follows logically: persons are labeled as mentally ill, and controlled in various ways, because of a power imbalance between labelers and those labeled. If mental illness labeling is seen as a response to the bizarre behavior of those with undesirable social attributes, and social control efforts are directed at those with the fewest social resources, than all it becomes necessary to know about mental illness is the labeling process that gives it social and existential reality.

The Existential Reality of Mental Illness

As the writer of a book which is in part a polemic—both explicit and implicit—I find it necessary to state that I do not accept the theory that mental illness has only socially constructed and not existential reality. As I elaborate in the Appendix on Methods, I believe that the sociological enterprise is a reflexive one in which the researcher's preexisting ways of apprehending and classifying the world come into play, with the data gathered, to create the study. When I first entered Metropolitan Court, I believed as an article of faith (although I saw it then as sober scientific reasoning, not belief) that mental illness was merely a matter of the labeling of undesired behaviors and persons. I do not believe, now, that mental illness is only a matter of labeling. To not state this belief would be to omit part of the framework which must be displayed in order for the reader to judge this piece of work, just as to not say that I believe social structure to be conflict rather than functionally based would deprive the reader of the opportunity to make a more complete judgment of what I have done.

Today, I believe both that madness is a socially constructed reality brought into being by the processes of labeling and social control and that it has existential reality. Madness, it seems to me, is a reality both for the audience (and thus within a sociohistorical context) and for the mad, and this existential or experiential level of reality is what gives madness as deviance a different character than, say, check forging or taxi dancing.

What kind of existential reality madness is I do not know; I have neither the background nor the knowledge to make a judgment on such matters as the purported chemical or genetic basis for schizophrenia. Persons who do have such knowledge assure me that if I did have it I would still be unable to make definitive statements about the empirical reality of madness. But the experience at Metropolitan Court has left me with an abiding sense of both the social and the existential nature of madness.

Methods

A detailed discussion of the methods used in this study is given in the Appendix on Methods. Here, I want to give the reader a brief idea of how the study was done and the processes I went through to arrive at the conclusions discussed in later chapters.

The major method of data collection was participant observation at Metropolitan Court. This data collection method was supplemented by analysis of court documents, visits to other parts of the mental health law system, and interviews with people at the court and in other organizations which had contact with the court. I became familiar with the interorganizational linkages between the court and the police, jails, state, county, private, and Veterans' Administration mental hospitals, board-and-care homes, psychiatric emergency teams (PET), and several administrative agencies.

I observed in the court and these other settings for a period of seven years, sometimes accompanied by colleagues, research assistants, and students who helped collect data for me.[2] I attempted to

2. In addition to the colleagues and research assistants mentioned in the Preface, I gained a number of insights, as well as considerable information, from some of the undergraduate students in my classes in the sociology of the mental health system at the University of Southern California.

understand the operation of the court in the interorganizational network as any member would come to understand it: through interaction with the parts of the network. The research direction is, therefore, outward and upward rather than downward and inward—from the courtroom to the network rather than the reverse (which would be the approach taken by a theorist starting with conflict or functionalist perspectives or hypotheses). All statements about decision making are ultimately grounded in the concrete interactions of everyday life.

In addition to unstructured data collection methods, I undertook three systematic studies: observations and documentary analysis of 130 court petitions (habeas corpus hearings in which the involuntarily committed seek their release; see Chap. 7); observation, the generation of theory and hypothesis testing related to 100 habeas corpus hearings (see Chap. 7); and observation of 60 conservatorship cases (in which those involuntarily committed for long time periods seek their release). These three studies were the basis for much of the qualitative analysis and for the quantitative analysis in Chapter 7.

In addition to documents provided by the court, which in the main were patients' hospitalization records and social histories, I used other documents where my own research was not adequate. For the analysis of identity transformation in Chapter 3, I used ex-patients' autobiographies. For background material, history, and statistical data on LPS, and the treatment of the mentally ill, I used secondary sources such as Bardach (1972, 1977); Fox (1978); Lamb, Sorkin, and Zusman (1981); and Morris (1978).

The quantitative data analysis in Chapter 7 is a multiple-regression study designed to test hypotheses derived from the intersection of sociological theory with empirical courtroom observation; thus it is an exercise in the testing of grounded theory. The remainder of the book is a conceptual analysis of the many factors which pertain to courtroom decision making at the multiple levels of interest noted above. The Appendix on Method discusses the special problems of data presentation I encountered in writing this book as well as other studies of the court (Warren 1977, 1979).

The Setting

Metropolitan Court stands alone in a dingy, dirty part of town next to the railroad tracks. It was once a warehouse; it still looks like one. Into the court annually come thousands of persons, most of them seeking release from involuntary confinement in mental hospitals, but some of them involved in narcotics hearings, mentally disordered sex offender misdemeanor hearings (MDSO), not guilty by reason of insanity hearings (NGI), and other matters at the intersection of the mental health and criminal justice systems (table 1.1).

The petitioners to the court come from the surrounding metropolitan area and county. In Department 1 of the court, approximately 2,800 persons annually come to petition for a writ of habeas corpus under LPS; to seek release from 14-day involuntary confinements imposed upon them for being mentally disordered, and, as a result of that disorder, gravely disabled, and/or dangerous to self, and/or dangerous to others. In these short-term commitment cases, the judge of Department 1 makes the decision to release or reconfine the petitioner.

In Department 2, hearings are held on conservatorship cases. Conservatorships involve the appointment of a conservator for a mental patient—either a private party such as a relative, or the public guardian—who may determine whether the mentally disordered person shall reside at home, in a board-and-care facility, in a mental hospital, or elsewhere. Mandatory and patient-initiated review of conservatorship decisions are made in this courtroom by a commissioner appointed by the judge of Metropolitan Court. Occasionally, a patient's public defender will ask for a jury trial to determine the petitioner's competency. There are a handful of jury trials a year in Department 2.

Decision-making Personnel in Metropolitan Court

Decisions in the court are made by the judge and the commissioner on cases that come before them. Other personnel who have direct influence on the typical habeas corpus case are members of the public defender's office located in the court, members of the district attorney's office located in the court, testifying psychiatrists, mental health counselors (MHCs), and the patients themselves. The cast of characters making decisions in conservatorship cases is the same, except that the county counsel's office makes the case for the people, and this office does not have a branch in the court.

The judge at the time I was doing the research was a white middle-class male over 60 years of age, who had presided over Department 1 for a longer time than intended by the legislation. He was a Reagan appointee; during his term of office he appointed a series of commissioners for Department 2, none of whom appeared to satisfy him very much. The functions of both judge and commissioner were to hear the testimony and make a decision in mental health cases. They could, but need not, read supportive documents submitted by MHCs and by the staff of the hospitals holding the patients.

Table 1.1
Metropolitan Court Business and Personnel

Department 1	
Business	Personnel
Habeas corpus writ hearings under LPS (involuntarily committed mental patients seek release from mental hospitals)	Judge
	District attorneys
	Public defenders
	Clerk
Mentally disordered sex offender hearings	Court reporter
	Bailiff/sheriff
Narcotic addiction hearings	Patient petitioners
Incompetent to stand trial hearings	Psychiatrist witnesses
Not guilty by reason of insanity hearings	Mental health counselors prepare reports on petitioners but do not appear in court

Department 2	
Business	Personnel
Conservatorship hearings: temporary, permanent, mandatory, and patient initiated	Commissioner[a]
	County counsel
	Public defenders
	Clerk
	Court reporter
	Bailiff/sheriff
	Psychiatrist witnesses
	Conservators
	Conservatees

[a]Rarely, a jury.

At any one time there were generally four or five district attorneys working in the court and several county counsel eliciting testimony. The DAs make the case for the people, gathering their evidence generally from the hospital staff rather than the patients, and arrive at courtroom or plea-bargained decisions in concert with the judge or commissioner, psychiatrists, and public defenders. The fate of patients is sometimes decided in chambers:

JUDGE [in chambers]: What do you want to do about the Coolidge case? [a tricky case involving a mentally ill and mentally retarded person].

PUBLIC DEFENDER: I want to make an issue of it; the law is not clear enough on mental retardation, what to do with an m.r. schizophrenic.

DISTRICT ATTORNEY: We can probably release him if you won't press the issue right at this time. Our office is working on it. Both the judge and the PD agree with the DA.

Patients are required by law to have access to free defense counsel if indigent; during my research time, I saw only one *pro se* defense (self-defense without counsel) and only a few cases defended by a private attorney hired by a patient. The public defenders of the court are scornful of private attorneys, believing they know nothing of mental health law and knowing they are unaware of the informal procedures of Metropolitan Court (see Feeley 1979, pp. 90–91, for an analogous situation in a lower criminal court). I once observed a private attorney make a lengthy, elaborate, and dramatic case for the release of a patient which had been decided in advance by the judge, DA, and PD; they chuckled inwardly during his performance, and outwardly after he had left the court.

There were four or five defense attorneys employed by the court office at any one time during the time of my research. Their job was to interview the patients and possibly the hospital staff in the search for reasons why patients should be released under LPS. The public defenders generally find the patients who have filed writs and interview them briefly before the court hearings begin for the day; they have a list of names which they call and then check them off. Sometimes, for cases which have interest of one kind or another for the public defenders, they may go to a hospital to interview a patient. Patients also make contact with public defenders by telephoning the PD's office from the hospitals.

The public defenders have to talk to the patients, and yet they do not wish to be monopolized by their clients or pestered by other patients not on their list. Like other court personnel, public defenders become expert at either acting as if patients are invisible, or brushing them off:

> I was walking through the hallway with Alan Jones, a public defender, when a very agitated man rushed up to us shrieking, "Are you my attorney? They said I was to see George Allcott. Are you George Allcott?" Alan continued to walk, calmly repeating "no" to the panting, shrieking man, who continued to run after him, touching him, turning red in the face, futilely trying to prevail.

The testifying psychiatrists in the court give evidence regarding the mental disorder, grave disability, or dangerousness of the patients seeking their release. Under the law a patient can call his or her own psychiatrist to make a case for sanity; in practice, the involuntarily committed are indigent and do not use counterexperts any more than they use private attorneys. The psychiatrists in the past generally have been prepared to testify that the patients still come within the provisions of LPS and should not be released; if they thought otherwise, or believed that the judge would think otherwise, they would release the patient after he or she filed the writ in order to avoid a court appearance. In recent months, however, psychiatrists more frequently have been testifying that their clients are *not* "LPS-able"; they prefer the court to have responsibility for the patient's release.

Most of the testifying psychiatrists work at the two large local state hospitals which feed into the court. There are two or three regulars from each hospital who testify in court. Although the law specifies that the insanity testimony be presented by the *treating* psychiatrist, in practice the treating psychiatrists are left on the wards, and these regulars do all the evidentiary work. The public defender's office has stipulated—agreed—that the presence of treating psychiatrists be waived in order that the hospitals remain staffed. Usually, the testifying hospital psychiatrists are somewhat familiar with the patient before the court interview which precedes the hearing; sometimes they are not:

> JUDGE: What is the basis for your opinion?
> TESTIFYING PSYCHIATRIST: My interview with her before the hearing. She refused to talk to me, therefore I would say she is a paranoid schizophrenic.

The court also appoints private psychiatrists, at a rate of about $150 per half day, to do patient interviews prior to the hearings. Three or four regulars, court favorites, usually are to be seen around Metropolitan Court. Like the regular public defenders, the regular hospital and private psychiatrists are regarded by court personnel as the only ones able to fathom and cope with the ways of mental health law and of Metropolitan Court:

> JUDGE: How many previous hospitalizations has this man had?
> PSYCHIATRIST [new to court]: I don't know, I don't have his record with me.
> JUDGE: You people from these private hospitals, you ought to know that you are supposed to bring in the record.

The function of the testifying psychiatrists is to give an opinion concerning the psychiatric and legal status of the patient, to interview the patient prior to the hearing, and to bring in or check on the hospital records that will support the conclusions obtained through the interview. The psychiatrists attach a diagnosis to the patient and present purported connections between the diagnosed disorder and inability to provide food, clothing, or shelter, the suicidal tendencies, or danger to others.

The three or four MHCs employed at court are assigned to contact patients who wish to file writs of habeas corpus. One MHC stays in the court offices and contacts patients who have called the public defenders, one or more are assigned individually to each of the large state hospitals, and one goes out into the more variable and combative files of private and VA hospitals. The one MHC who goes to all the hospitals besides the two state hospitals does a lot of traveling in the geographic sense; all MHCs must travel in the cognitive sense, since they are supposed to be aware of both the legal interests of the court and the medical interests of the hospital:

> As we were driving to the state hospital where she would spend her day, May Allison (an MHC) told me that she felt caught between the hospitals, the court and the patients. The court gives official instructions to contact every patient with the information that they have a right to a habeas corpus hearing. The hospitals feel that the MHCs are invading the medical realm and pestering the patients with unnecessary and unwanted "rights." The patients often do not know what they want, file writs and then withdraw them, or refuse to file and then change their minds.

There are two other types of personnel in the court who contribute to the decision-making process. There are the ancillary personnel who support courtroom decision making by their actions and feedback to the primary decision makers. These supportive personnel include law clerks, bailiffs, sheriffs, police, secretaries, file clerks, and the psychiatric technicians who transport patients to the court and back to the hospitals. Then there are the patients, who often contribute directly to decision making by their testimony from the witness box, and always contribute by the presence of the documents they have generated at an earlier time period.

The Petitioners of Metropolitan Court

The petitioners to Metropolitan Court are, in the main, poor, jobless, lacking family, friends, or community supports, not more likely to be of minority ethnicity than one would expect from the composition of the county population, and not necessarily elderly. They are persons on the margins of society. In the court, they come face to face with the middle-class norms and values that underlie LPS standards for grave disability and dangerousness.

On the Social Margin

A social margin is "all personal possessions, attributes, or relationships which can be traded on for help in time of need" (Segal, Baumohl, and Johnson 1977, p. 387). Most of the people who come to the court have little social margin. They may have no possessions, even no home. They may have no relationships; their relatives and friends have had enough of them. They may be so repulsive or frightening that people do not like to come near them.

Almost all the petitioners in Metropolitan Court are lower class, both in their contemporary poverty and in their backgrounds. Many are black or Chicano, about 25% in the cases I observed, or roughly the same proportion as in the county population (for a statistical description of the sample of 100, see table 7.1). A few are neat and clean; most are not. There is something quite strange or different with the way many of them look:

> A man walks into court, head down, shuffling gait, he cannot lift his head or speak without mumbling. The psychiatric aide next to me whispers that he is a classic case of thorazine side effects.

> The woman who wants to be released looks incongruous among the business suits and dresses of the court's center stage. She shuffles to the witness stand, a towel wrapped around her head, bedroom slippers flapping on the floor, an old chenille robe.

> In the corridors, it is almost always possible to tell the patients from everyone else, at once. Many are suffering from the side effects of psychoactive drugs: drooling, head drooping, tongue hanging out, dead eyes. Some are elderly and disheveled, lost in their minds' worlds which seem so vacant to me, so real to them. Of course I cannot tell the patients who look "normal," because then I think they are not patients. Today there was one surprise; a man of about fifty, neat in a leather jacket and pressed grey pants, short clipped gray hair, crazy as a loon on the stand, with delusions, but otherwise perfectly reasonable. Apparently a stable chronic schizophrenic for 25 years.

"Why," asked many of the students I took to Metropolitan Court, "are all the people in the court so poor and lower class? Aren't there any middle-class people who are mentally ill?" The answer I gave was one which combined labeling and conflict theory: middle- and upper-class people have more of a social margin, therefore they are less likely to be labeled and handled as mentally ill, at least through the state hospital system. But it is also probable that the structural strains of lower-class, poor life in this society can precipitate more mental disorder (see Srole et al. 1978).

Middle-class people are more likely to be seen by friends and colleagues as "eccentric," and the mental illness label held back for a
longer time, than the lower class, although there is some evidence
that deviant behavior within the family is *less* tolerated by the middle
class (Gove 1975, p. 53). Middle-class people, if they are committed
involuntarily to mental hospitals, may be more likely to be taken to
private hospitals; private hospital patients rarely file writs. As one
MHC says, in the private hospitals "when we come in the front door
the body goes out the back door." Money, networks of relationships,
and various other possessions and attributes contribute to the social
margin of the middle class.

A minority of the poor persons in the court once lived in better
circumstances. In my systematic data collection I saw perhaps five
such persons, including a man who was once a psychiatrist, a
woman who was once a doctor, and an 86-year-old woman with
independent income who was hospitalized twice in a three-month
period on grounds of danger to others: she repeatedly became drunk
and hammered on her apartment walls until neighbors called the
police. In a precise English accent she would deny, to the MHC and
to me, that she drank: "I never touch the stuff." Then she would tell
us that the neighbors had the FBI watching her, through her TV.

Middle-class cultural values are heavily involved in what constitutes grave disability, danger, or bizarre behavior; this fact is one
of the reasons given by Morse in Chapter 4 for the abolition of involuntary confinement. Notions of appropriate food, clothing or shelter,
and of inappropriate violence vary with the class and ethnic background of the individual. It might be relatively easy to get agreement
from different types of persons on some widely shared taboos, such
as walking on the street with no clothes on, or unprovoked violence
against a small child, but beyond these commonsense agreements
there would be debates about what constitutes grave disability or
danger to others.

Court cases of danger to others range from violent behavior which
would be adjudged deviant by most people to behaviors for which
the supposed "dangerousness" would need considerable cultural explanation:

> The young man was certified as dangerous to others and self and
> hospitalized after he had smashed through a plate-glass window
> to get at his mother, got into her bed and attempted to rape her,
> then attacked her with a kitchen knife.

> The middle-aged black man was certified as dangerous to others
> and gravely disabled after he was found by police "lurking"
> around a white, affluent neighborhood at 4 o'clock in the morn-
> ing.

Similarly, grave disability cases range from running naked around the streets and becoming dehydrated, from a refusal to take in liquids, to "inappropriately" wearing military uniform, or living in a cardboard shack in the corner of a parking structure.

The notion of danger to self, or suicidal acts and intentions, is not so easy to classify by social class; indeed, petitioners who have been committed as suicidal are more likely to appear nonmarginal. Some are anguished husbands or wives with spouses who have left them; after a stay in the mental hospital they return to their jobs and homes. Others are lovelorn adolescents pining after other adolescents or movie stars:

> A man who did not look like a patient but who had an extremely sad expression was wandering around the hallway. I asked a PD who he was, and he said that the man was a normal middle-class person who had made several suicide attempts after his wife had left him; the PD added, "He is not crazy—they gave him a depressive neurosis diagnosis."

> The 15-year-old boy was committed after he had jumped out of a first-floor window in what was referred to by the psychiatrist as a suicide gesture. He was in love, he said, with [an actress in her late thirties]. The judge did not release him on writ; when I asked him why, he said that he did not like to take the risk of releasing a suicide possibility, particularly an adolescent, on the outside chance that something would happen and he would get blamed. In addition, many of the boy's family were in the court testifying that the child should remain in the hospital.

Policy Relevance

Although the patients contribute to the decisions made in the court by their testimonials or mute presence, their interests are not the major factor in the case processing at Metropolitan Court. As indicated in the earlier part of this chapter, policymakers and rule makers on the one hand, and rule enforcers on the other, have different sets of interests which they bring to bear on their social control–making activities. But some of these interests intersect, particularly on matters having to do with professional and expert judgments about what is best for mental patients. In the area of mental health law, both those who make judicial review decisions in the court and those who apply pressure to legislators or who actually frame legislation have distinct points of view concerning the propriety of continuing to involuntarily incarcerate persons in mental hospitals. In the area of policy controversy and change, as well as in the courtroom, some of the major decisions are made or proposed by psychiatrists using the medical model and lawyers using the legal model of human behavior and social response.

Research on mental health law decision making is not just an academic enterprise, it has policy implications (see also the Appendix on Methods). This is particularly true in states such as California and New York which are at the forefront of developing trends in the area. Since the passage of LPS, other states such as Florida, Nebraska, Wisconsin, and Pennsylvania have modified their statutes in the direction of less and less lengthy involuntary commitment of mental patients.

The provisions of LPS are discussed at length in Chapter 2. Briefly, LPS abolishes the concept of indefinite involuntary commitment of mental patients and provides for a series of shorter-term confinements hedged about with procedural safeguards and with both mandatory and patient-initiated judicial review. Judicial review of 14-day certifications make up the bulk of the data I used to study courtroom decision making. There are several provisions under LPS which allow commitments for periods of time longer than 14 days, depending upon whether the mentally disordered person is classified as gravely disabled (unable to provide for food, clothing, and shelter), dangerous to others, or dangerous to self.

LPS also mandates treatment in the least restrictive setting; a mandate which has been taken to mean that state hospital confinement should not be the automatic choice for patient care. If a less-restrictive alternative is available for a patient who wishes to leave the hospital, then the judge is supposed to release that patient. And at Metropolitan Court the judge often does so, especially if family members are willing to provide residence and care (Warren 1977).

Policy Controversies

Although many states are moving in the directions proposed by LPS, there is by no means agreement on the issues, particularly between lawyers and psychiatrists. As Wexler, Scoville, et al. (1971, p. 12) note of mental health law: "The aims of therapy and constitutional due process are difficult to mold into one statute." The medical model and the legal model of human behavior come into conflict in the process of judicial review of mental health system decisions. Psychiatrists involved in judicial review bring the medical model into the courtroom; attorneys and judges trained in law attempt to make sense of a combined legal-medical model.

Part of the controversy revolves around the issue of whether or not involuntary civil commitment should be retained in some form or abandoned altogether (for the arguments, see Chaps. 4 and 5). Some scholars assert that offending behaviors of all types should be criminalized (Monahan 1976), while others reverse these priorities and insist that even crime should be psychiatrized (Abramson 1976). Related controversies include the adversarial or therapeutic role of the mental health defense attorney (Andalman and Chambers 1974; Cohen 1966; Goode 1975; Shah 1974), and the rubberstamping of psychiatric assessments by judges (Hart 1974; Wexler 1981).

Those who attack involuntary confinement are often lawyers and those who defend it psychiatrists. Lawyers argue that involuntary civil commitment should be abolished because it involves preventive detention for crimes which have not been committed, the violation of due process rights, the entry into the law of arbitrary cultural definitions of inappropriate conduct, and, if danger to others is one of the criteria used to commit, there is a pseudoscientific use of unscientific predictions of dangerousness. Hart (1974, p. 94) summarizes: "The process . . . too often operates as a system that would shock common ideas of fair play and justice if applied in the criminal courts. When the individuals involved are not criminals, but those who have been declared 'mentally ill,' the cry for due process suddenly grows faint."

On the other hand, psychiatrists who utilize the medical model sometimes see legal involvement in mental disorder as pernicious and destructive. A psychiatrist who had just testified in Metropolitan Court said, "These lawyers think they are doing good, but they are doing harm. They spend their time trying to get patients out, but they are still sick, so they come back, but we never get time to treat them. The whole system stinks."

LPS and similar statutes represent an uneasy truce between the growing militance of the anticommitment forces and those who wish to see the continuation of some form of confinement. Those who seek continued involuntary confinement win, by the very fact of its continued existence. Those who seek its abolition win, by the fact of increasing due process, by the least restrictive alternative mandate, and by limitations on the length of confinement. But both sides, while they can be conceived as winning, more often see themselves as losing. Unless involuntary commitment is abolished, the abolitionists will continue to be dissatisfied; unless legal intervention is curtailed, the medical experts will continue to be dissatisfied.

Part One The Law and Mental Illness

In the labeling perspective on deviance, laws and rules directed at the social control of deviants are products of vested interests taken in sociohistorical context. Laws and ideas about deviance are not only reflections of contemporary interest groups' perspectives, they enshrine and crystallize interests which are both just-past and long-past. Ideas about what mental illness is and how to respond to the mentally ill have roots in what Foucault (1965) has called a dialogue with madness that goes back to the Middle Ages. Mental health legislation reflects those groups which are active and powerful at the time the legislation is passed, just as the implementation of legislation reflects the interests of those groups who are currently engaged with it.

Laws and ideas are not only the products of vested interests, they also have an impact on them. Legislation is passed, or ideas are developed, through a process of conflict over interests. Once formulated, laws and ideas take on an independent existence which must be reckoned with in the actions of other groups in conflict related to those laws. The reflexive or feedback process continues: interest groups and interested individuals responsible for implementing the law can also promote changes in the law in the form of new or amended legislation.

In Part I I examine the major elements making up the system of knowledge and legislation within which the mentally ill and the involuntarily committed are interpreted and handled. The four chapters examine the substantive, procedural, and case law, and theories of mental illness, which affect and are affected by the various interests within the mental health law system and within Metropolitan Court.

2 The Law
California's
Lanterman-Petris-Short Act

*T*he law under which mental health decision making in Metropolitan Court is subsumed is the Lanterman-Petris-Short Act (1967; hereinafter LPS) which went into effect in 1969. It was passed at a time when the intersection of ideological, economic, and political interests brought about renewed interest in involuntary commitment. It has been modified a number of times since 1967 by the California legislature. LPS is still the mental health law of the state, although for a number of reasons, detailed below, it may be altered within the next decade. Since LPS was passed, New York and other states have passed similar laws extending the rights of mental patients and limiting the use of involuntary civil commitment (Hiday 1977). The drift of case law is in the same direction.

The Economic, Political, and Historical Roots of LPS

The law made what in theory were sweeping changes in California's handling of the mentally disordered. These changes had immediate roots in the fiscal problems of the state and in the political ambitions of some of the members of the California legislature. They had long-term roots in the historical treatment of the mentally disordered in this country, and in the legal justification for involuntary confinement which came to this country from Europe.

In any proposals for legislative change there are potential economic impacts and thus potential threats to economic interests. These economic interests include state and county or other public budgets, employees of affected institutions, communities in which the institutions are found, and the public insofar as they are attentive to the

21

issues involved. In proposing to reduce the population of state mental hospitals through the passage of LPS, the law threatened the livelihood of employees of those hospitals, and some unions and professional organizations lobbied against it for that reason (Bardach 1972). But the fiscal problems of the state were an important factor in the promotion and passage of the legislation.

Mental health services are a nice target for legislators interested in saving the state money both because of the poor and relatively powerless clientele, and because of the lack of what Bardach (1972) calls an attentive public for mental health—a citizenry interested in, and disposed to be a watchdog for, the rights and treatment of mental patients or the condition of mental hospitals. During the then-governor Ronald Reagan's first term in office in California he proposed to cut severely the mental health budget for both the community mental health and state hospital systems. In the face of concerted opposition from economic and political interests he backed down from the proposed cut of 3,700 to 3,000 mental health workers. A contemporary cartoon depicted the lack of an attentive mental health public and the consequent cavalier attitude of the governor toward mental health: "In one installment in the serialized romance of Sir Ronald and his loyal servant Sancho Nofziger (the reference being to Lyn Nofziger, Reagan's press secretary) *San Francisco Chronicle* columnist Arthur Hoppe had Sir Ronald slay an innocuous creature called 'the Mental Health. This act of specious courage he justifies to the alarmed Sancho by saying 'Fear not loyal Sancho, I know somehow in my bones that around here it never will be missed'" (Bardach 1972, p. 33).

LPS was intended to partially replace the more costly 24-hour state hospital care system with less restrictive and less expensive alternatives, such as board and care homes, day-care centers, and community health clinics. Workers at Metropolitan Court often simply assume that LPS was passed to save the state money:

RESEARCHER: What prompted LPS?
DISTRICT ATTORNEY: The state wanted to save money by cutting down on state hospital treatment.

Persons in the mental health law system have professional and ideological as well as economic interests in passage (or blockage) of legislation. Bardach (1972) traces the passage of LPS to the political ambitions of some members of the California Assembly Subcommittee on Mental Health Services. This committee had earlier been successful in promoting changes in the treatment of the mentally retarded in the State of California. Bardach (1972, p. 101) asserts that, "encouraged by this victory, the subcommittee members—particu-

larly Jerome Waldie—and Waldie's staff assistant Arthur Bolton—
were keen to press their reform efforts into the area of mental illness. . . . they needed, first, a concrete issue around which to coalesce
a large number of interests and, second, a feasible reform program."

The issue that the subcommittee found was involuntary civil
commitment; their attention was drawn to this issue through reading
a number of papers by students of Erving Goffman, papers which
described commitment hearings in the state as perfunctory as taking
only a few minutes. In an example of reverse lobbying, in which
legislators persuade experts and practitioners, the subcommittee developed the outlines of what was to be California's new mental
health law, LPS.

The trend in the new legislation was away from older ways of
handling the mentally ill, and toward newer ones that deemphasized
paternalism and gave new credence to notions of liberty and rights.
But the concepts of "away from" and "toward" imply not only a new
challenge but also a set of old practices which, in turn, are the product of deeply entrenched notions of the involvement of the state in
the lives of the mentally disordered.

The two historic justifications of the state control of the mentally
ill are *parens patriae,* or protection of the citizenry, and police power
or control of the citizenry. Since these themes will be developed in
more detail in Chapters 5 and 6, I will confine myself to a brief
description of them. *Parens patriae* refers to the right of the state to act
as parent or guardian of persons such as children, the elderly, and
the mentally disordered, deemed unable to care for themselves; the
police power justifies the state in depriving of liberty those persons
deemed dangerous to the citizenry (including themselves).

During the decades prior to LPS, in California as in most other
states, *parens patriae* was seen as an adequate justification for the deprivation of liberty involved in civil commitment. Mental patients
were defined as incompetent; the usual standard for their commitment was the need for care and treatment, and confinement could be
indefinite. Prior to the 1860s in California, persons could be committed to almost any kind of institution by almost anyone (Fox 1978).

Early legal protections of the involuntarily committed in California
were precipitated by a series of published exposés of "railroading"
cases in the 1860s (Fox 1978), pp. 39–41). By the 1880s, to be involuntarily committed in California a person had to be found "insane"
by a doctor and, by reason of that insanity, "unsafe to be at large."
Nevertheless, in 1892, "the Napa Hospital Trustees warned that any
'destitute and friendless' person with 'strong eccentricities' was liable to be 'hurried away, railroad speed, to an asylum'" (Fox 1978,
p. 51).

Today, the emphasis has shifted from *parens patriae* to police power; the trend nationwide is toward more concern with danger to others. About one third of the states, like California, use both justifications in their involuntary commitment laws, while the remainder use either one or the other. Intervention in the lives of the mentally disordered by the state is taken for granted; it is a sort of inalienable historical context. But the balance of policy is shifting toward police power, procedural rights and legal restrictions, and away from protection. It is against the background of economic, political, and historical conditions of mental health law that judicial review of involuntary commitment takes place in Metropolitan Court.

The Lanterman-Petris-Short Act

As Brooks (1974) notes, there are three ways in which states handle involuntary commitment; judicial, administrative, and psychiatric. Administrative hospitalization utilizes court hearings but minimizes the adversary element and procedural rules. Medical or psychiatric hospitalization requires only the signature of one or more psychiatrists for long- or short-term commitment. Judicial hospitalization involves legal personnel at all or most phases of the involuntary commitment process.

Prior to LPS, California's mental health law was predominantly psychiatric; now it is a mixture of psychiatric certification and legal review procedures. Figure 2.1 illustrates the process of voluntary and involuntary commitment to mental hospitals in the county, with numbers of patients at each state in the process for the year 1978–79, from 72-hour hold to long-term conservatorship.

The 72-Hour Hold

The first stage of involuntary commitment under LPS is a provision for 72 hours emergency evaluation and treatment in a mental hospital upon the certification of a physician who is a member of designated facilities' attending staff, a peace officer, or designated county personnel that the person is (1) mentally disordered; and (2) gravely disabled (unable to provide food, clothing, and/or shelter), and/or a danger to self, and/or a danger to others as a result of that mental disorder. Patients are brought in for evaluation by police, relatives, mental health workers, and others; in a statewide sample of 250 admittees to California psychiatric hospitals, Teknekron (1978, p. 148) found that one-half of the involuntarily committed were brought in by police, compared with a tenth of those admitted voluntarily.

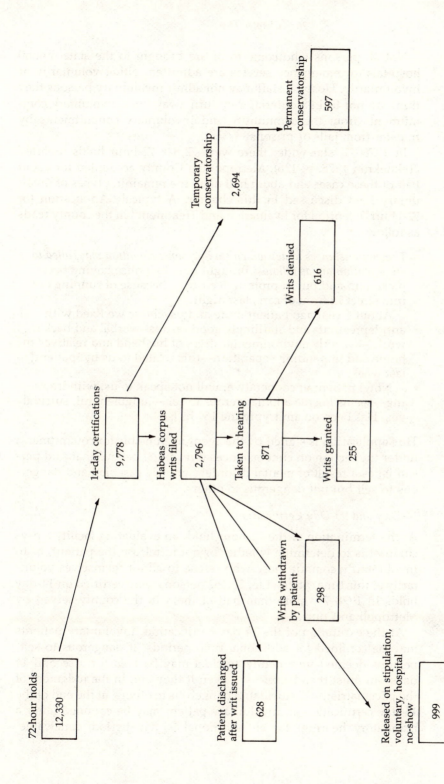

Figure 2.1. The LPS process, Metropolitan County, 1978 and 1979.

72-hour holds

12,330

14-day certifications

9,778

Temporary conservatorship

2,694

Permanent conservatorship

597

Habeas corpus writs filed

2,796

Writs denied

616

Taken to hearing

871

Writs granted

255

Patient discharged after writ issued

628

Writs withdrawn by patient

298

Released on stipulation, voluntary, hospital no-show

999

Not all persons who come to or are brought to the state mental hospitals for emergency service are admitted, either voluntarily or involuntarily. Hospital staff may not admit involuntary persons they think do not fit LPS criteria; they turn away both involuntary commitments from the community and involuntary commitments by transfer from jails or prisons.

In 1976–77, statewide, there were 72,826 72-hour holds reported (Teknekron 1978, p. 128); Metropolitan County accounted for about half of these cases and about half of all the remaining types of involuntary hold discussed in this chapter. A typical "Application for 72-Hour Detention for Evaluation and Treatment" in the county reads as follows:

> *The circumstances under which said person's condition was called to my attention are as follows:* Brought here by police having been picked up and put in protective custody because of running out into street in front of cars, last night.
>
> About 1 year ago patient mute and psychotic we Rxed with antidepressants and startlingly good results—verbal and back to work—Recently environmental stress of husband and relatives in home and impending separation—this related to us by [patient] last week.
>
> Now: patient uncooperative, will not speak to us, withdrawing—seems hostile and dangerous to self—judgment nil, suicidal yes. Has been on amitryptyline 150 hs [*sic*].

This application is signed by the agent responsible for commitment; under the section on circumstances it reads, "I believe that said person is, as a result of mental disorder" gravely disabled and dangerous to self but not dangerous to others.

14-Day and 90-Day Certification

At the termination of the 72-hour hold, an evaluating facility's psychiatrist is to determine whether or not to release the patient, or to involuntarily commit those who refuse to admit themselves voluntarily at this time. Statewide, 22,562 persons were certified on 14-day holds in 1978–79, more than half of them in the county served by Metropolitan Court.

At the expiration of the 14-day certification, involuntary patients may be confined for additional time periods. If dangerous to self, persons deemed imminently suicidal may be held for a second 14 days but must then be released even if they are, in the judgment of the psychiatrist, still suicidal. If dangerous to others, at the end of the 14-day certification an involuntary patient may be confined (after a mandatory hearing) for an additional 90-day period, renewable.

During both the 14-day and 90-day certifications patients may, at their option, file a writ of habeas corpus to seek judicial review and release by Metropolitan Court.

In part because of the difficulty of demonstrating dangerousness discussed later in this chapter, the 90-day certification as danger to others is almost never used in California. Long-term mental hospital confinement for danger to others is a reminder of an earlier era, as in this atypical case I observed:

> For three days, hearings on the release of Justin Harding went on. Harding had been employed by a large corporation in the city as a computer expert. According to company records he lost his job as a result of drunkenness at work; according to Harding, he lost his job because the president of the company, Sean Marlow, was out to get him.
>
> After Harding lost his job, he could not find work elsewhere. He started to write letters to Marlow, asking for reemployment. When his letters were ignored, they became more frequent, and more threatening. Harding threatened by letter to "kill" Marlow, to "get" him, to kill his wife and sons. Once he was seen passing by Marlow's house nursing a shotgun.
>
> Arrested on charges of threatening Marlow, and hospitalized as a paranoid schizophrenic, Harding spent the next seven years confined in either a criminal or mental facility, sometimes escaping, but always continuing his threatening letters to Marlow. He never took action against Marlow beyond the threats. He was finally released from the mental hospital during this three-day case in Metropolitan Court, where psychiatrists testified that he was no longer dangerous to Marlow, was probably no more than a little paranoid schizophrenic, and may never have been: he may instead be an alcoholic or drunk.
>
> Thirty pounds underweight and glowering from under unkempt stringy hair, Harding was released on a writ, only to resume his letters to Marlow. The judge, psychiatrists, district attorneys and public defenders all seemed to agree that the only reason for the long confinement, and the lengthy hearing, was the influence on the proceedings of Sean Marlow.

Conservatorships

If after 14 days certification as mentally disordered and gravely disabled the person is still defined as unable to provide for food, clothing, or shelter, he or she can be certified for a 30-day temporary conservatorship for evaluation and review (see below). A mandatory judicial review is held to determine whether the conservatorship should become permanent. Permanent conservatorships are for one-year periods, renewable by judicial hearing. The conservatee has the right to judicial review every six months in addition to the yearly mandatory review, and the right to a jury trial.

Conservatees may be placed anywhere by their conservators: at home, in a nursing home, a board and care facility, or in the state hospital. In 1975, 228 of the total number of county conservatees were placed in hospitals while 164 were released and the remainder were placed elsewhere. Conservatees may have their property, as well as their person, subjected to decision making by their conservators.

Because conservatorships represent the longest-term form of public control over the mentally disordered, the population of hospitalized conservatees is among the most pathetic of those who come into contact with Metropolitan Court. Some are suicidal youngsters. Many are chronic schizophrenics. Others are elderly persons with chronic brain syndrome (senile dementia) who are unable to function at all. On one of several rides I took with the psychiatric emergency team serving one district of the county I observed the initiation of a 72-hour hold on an elderly woman with chronic brain syndrome; she later became a conservatee and was placed in a state hospital:

> I was to be allowed to ride with the PET team at last, with Joan, the psychiatric nurse, and Tom, the psychiatric social worker. Our first call was to the house of an elderly woman. The referral was from a social worker who had provided housekeeping services and limited care for the woman and now said she could no longer cope: "She pees on the floor, and she bangs into things and bruises herself, and she doesn't eat."
>
> We arrived at a neat house on a middle-class street. There was no answer to our knock, so the three of us walked in. The house was neat, clean, and orderly. In the middle of the floor stood an old woman.
>
> The caller had said that the woman was 89. She was dressed in a clean-looking housedress with gray hair askew; her arms and legs were badly bruised. She did not acknowledge our entrance; she stood smiling and talking softly to herself, staring. As Joan pulled out the 72-hour hold forms, Tom approached the woman and took her arm: "How are you today?" She reacted to our presence and began to talk, a stream of broken words and phrases which could not be remembered or recaptured. As she drifted from Tom's arm she bumped, sightless, into a chair. Joan waved her hand in front of the woman's eyes: "By God, she's blind!"
>
> All the routine questions of the PET workers were left unanswered. We explored the house: neat, clean, orderly, barely a sign of habitation. No dirt or filth; no food. Joan telephoned for the ambulance: "This is really illegal under LPS, but we have no alternative."

We waited 40 minutes for the ambulance as the elderly woman continued to walk around her room, bumping into things and alternately mumbling softly and shouting phrases from fragments of a past life. The ambulance workers hoisted her into a stretcher and put soft restraints on her as she laughed and sang, perhaps delighted at this unwonted attention. The referring social worker's husband came from his house down the road and offered a stream of apologies for what was happening. Both Joan and the worker's husband asked me and themselves, suppliantly, "What else is there to do?" Neither I nor they had an answer. The old woman was taken to the state hospital.

Conservatorships are defined as voluntary or involuntary. When asked by the county counsel or judge, "Do you want a conservatorship?" some patients respond "yes," others "no," while still others are unable or unwilling to respond. Even the "yes" response of some of the elderly conservatees does not come within the commonsense meaning of voluntarism:

A conservatorship hearing was being held to determine whether an elderly man should continue to be cared for in a board and care home, or whether he should be released into the community. The old man, with rotund blank face, nodded, smiled, and said "yes" to everything throughout the hearings. "Do you want to leave the board and care home?" "Yes." "Do you like living in the board and care home and would you like to stay there?" "Yes."

Still other conservatees are in such a condition that they cannot be brought to the courtroom to express their will:

JUDGE: Why is Mrs. Simmons not in court?
COUNTY COUNSEL: She was found on the floor of her apartment, where she had not gotten up for three months. She was malnourished. Maggots had eaten away part of her leg. She cannot be moved from the hospital until her leg is healed and she gains some weight. A neighbor fed her on the floor for three months. She was lying in her own feces for three months.

Some conservatees, although perhaps with some degree of ambivalence (see Chap. 3), protest their conservatorship and seek reviews and jury trials, thus coming within the legal meaning of involuntariness. Finally, a number of conservatees accept or seek actively the services of a conservator and could be seen as voluntary within its commonsense as well as its legal meaning.

Due Process Rights

In Metropolitan Court petitioners are protected by some—but not all—due process rights obtaining in the criminal court. Many of these rights pertain to judicial review. Patients have the right to mandatory yearly judicial review and jury trial in conservatorship cases and to patient-initiated review every six months. In 1976, about 100 conservatees took advantage of the six-month review, and about 80 of these were released by the court.

Patients on 14-day and 90-day certification also have the right to a habeas corpus hearing. In 1979, about 35% of those held on 14-day certification filed writs: a total of 2,796 persons (see fig. 2.1). At the time I did the quantitative research (1974–76), a lower percentage of the 14-day holds filed writs; about one-half of those who came to hearing were released by the judge of Department 1 (see also Chap. 7). The increase in filing was due in part to the stationing of patients' rights advocates in the hospital during the mid- to late 1970s. These advocates make it their business to inform the involuntarily committed of their review rights in case MHCs or other court personnel neglect—in spite of their legal obligation—to do so. One public defender commented: "The patients' rights advocates are not allowed to approach patients during the 72-hour hold, only during the 14-day hold. So the hospitals are releasing patients at the expiration of the 72-hour hold and then picking them up on another 72 hours."

Patients have the right to be notified of all proceedings against them and to be present at all hearings. They have the right to representation by an attorney during all judicial review proceedings, to the services of an attorney if unable to provide a private attorney, and to self-representation (the *pro se* defense). In theory, there is supposed to be a financial review of persons provided with public defenders in Metropolitan Court; in practice, a defender is routinely provided, and I never encountered a financial review:

> I observed a conservatorship, with a public defender, in which real estate property was being disposed of. When I asked the judge why people with money can use the public defender's office, he replied that it costs more to do financial investigations than just to provide the defenders' services.

Until a recent federal district court decision (*Doe* v. *Gallinot*, 1979), which technically applies only to grave disability cases, those on 72-hour holds in California did not have the right to a court hearing related to the emergency procedure. In cases other than grave disability they have no right to such a hearing; nor do they have the right to remain silent without prejudice during examinations to determine their sanity. Patients have no right to the presence of counsel at psychiatric interviews. Hearsay evidence from a patient's record may be introduced into evidence at judicial review, and any past record can be brought up, if these are relevant to his or her psychiatric condition:

> The petitioner was an obese middle-aged man who, the psychiatrist testified, had been in and out of hospitals and prisons. "What was he in prison for?" the judge asked, and the psychiatrist mumbled that she would rather not say. When pressed, she said that the man had killed his father twenty years ago but was not now dangerous to others. He was released.

Both in criminal and in civil commitment cases, the burden of proof is on the state (*Addington* v. *Texas*, 1979); in practice, the person seeking release from confinement must often prove that he or she is not mentally disordered and does not come within the LPS provisions (Hart 1974, p. 121). The constitutional minimum burden of persuasion in involuntary commitment cases is clear and convincing evidence, or some similar standard that is intermediate between the civil law standard of preponderance of the evidence, and the criminal law standard of beyond a reasonable doubt. It should be noted, however, that in re Roulet, the California court applied the criminal law beyond a reasonable doubt standard to conservatorship proceedings. It is therefore possible that if the California Supreme Court considers in future cases the burden of persuasion in involuntary civil commitment cases generally, on state constitutional grounds the California Supreme Court will apply the beyond a reasonable doubt standard to all involuntary commitment. Indeed, in recent decades there has been an extension of criminal-like due process rights to the involuntarily committed through case law in involuntary civil commitment nationwide (*Lessard* v. *Schmidt*, 1972).

Case Law in Involuntary Civil Commitment

As Rubin (1978, p. 33) notes, there has been a proliferation of case law concerned with the rights of the mentally disordered "in this relatively new field of the legal profession." He adds, "No sooner are some suits settled when new actions, often on different grounds and in search of new precedents, are brought. After some initial setbacks, the legal advocates are now consistently winning their cases. The result is the development of a firm body of mental health law." The areas of particular ferment in mental health case law are the right to treatment, the right to refuse treatment, the right to the least restrictive alternative treatment, the right to due process, and the right to mandatory judicial review.

The constitutional and moral basis for concern with these rights in involuntary civil commitment cases is the deprivation of liberty involved in such commitment. In order to deprive a citizen of liberty, the state must be convinced, in criminal cases, that the citizen has committed an offense; a criminal offense is not at issue in involuntary civil commitment cases. What is at issue is either the incapacity of the disordered person (in which case the *parens patriae* doctrine is the underlying justification), or the dangerousness to others (in which the police power is the underlying justification). All the rights noted above are a response to the deprivation of liberty involved in civil commitment cases.

The Right to Treatment

One of the bases for the state permitting the deprivation of liberty attendant upon involuntary civil commitment is that such commitment facilitates the treatment of a patient whose decision-making capacity is flawed and who cannot therefore properly understand the need for, or properly consent to, treatment. Without treatment, involuntary commitment cannot be distinguished from preventive confinement. But the right to treatment has been an issue in mental health law only since the 1960s, with *Rouse* v. *Cameron* (1966) in which Judge Bazelon, drawing on an article written six years earlier by Morton Birnbaum, noted that a constitutional case could be made for the right to treatment.

The first test of the constitutionality of the right to treatment came in *Wyatt* v. *Stickney* (1972);[1] this case also illustrated the intersection of economic and legal issues. The case began with the plaintiffs attempting to prevent budgetary dismissals of state mental hospital employees, and gradually became an indictment of Alabama's mental hospitals as providers of treatment to the involuntarily committed. Eventually the judge issued a detailed ruling prescribing the measure necessary for bringing the state hospitals up to treatment-provider standards, including "adequate" staffing ratios.

The cost to the State of Alabama of instituting even such minimum-level standards of care as those specified by Judge Johnson is large and includes the expense of monitoring programs also required by the court. Today, as a result of *Wyatt* v. *Stickney*, the state of Alabama is in federal receivership (Scull 1981). Many states are quite fearful of the specification, in response to similar cases, of similar types of standards for their hospitals. The Alabama standards were applied in Ohio in *Davis* v. *Watkins* (1974) at Lima State Hospital; the judge in this case ruled that the hospital had failed to implement satisfactorily a right-to-treatment order. The state could have

1. See Statutory and Case Law References for complete legal citations. The discussion of case law is intended for illustrative purposes only and is not meant to be legally comprehensive.

been fined for contempt of court on the basis of the failure of implementation. The double jeopardy in which state budgets are placed by *Davis* v. *Watkins* is worrisome to many state officials.

Thus far the impact of these and other cases concerning the right to treatment is only local. Application of such standards to other states depends upon the pressing of similar issues there, although a coherent theory supporting the right to treatment has been developed (Spece, 1978). The absence of national standards awaits a definitive ruling by the U.S. Supreme Court; in *O'Connor* v. *Donaldson* (1975), the Court refused to rule on the right to treatment and ruled only on the narrower question of the right to liberty for a nondangerous mental patient.

The Right to Refuse Treatment

The Donaldson case also touches on the right to refuse treatment; however, there was no definitive ruling on this question either. Kenneth Donaldson persistently refused medication during his 15-year stay at Chattahoochee, on the grounds that he was a Christian Scientist. His wishes were respected—he was not forcibly medicated—but he was informed on several occasions that he would not be released unless he acceded to medication (see Chaps. 3 and 9). In California, patients do not have the right, under LPS, to refuse psychoactive medication; they may be forcibly medicated by injection. The current debate on the right to refuse treatment, as yet unresolved by case law, revolves around such questions as the patient's competence to agree to treatment and the intrusiveness, harmfulness, side effects, and efficacy of the treatment.

In the contemporary mental hospital the most common form of treatment is behavior control through psychoactive medications such as thorazine, stelazine, or lithium carbonate. Patients may not wish to take these drugs because of their soporific effects and, in some cases, uncomfortable side effects. The forcible medication of patients can have the effect of increasing their sense of persecution and resistance to confinement:

> The evidence shows that after his admission to a Veteran's Administration Hospital in June 1960 [the patient] was given Chlorpromazine, an essential means of treatment for the veteran's psychiatric disorder. After 22 days of this he developed jaundice. . . . As soon as he became jaundiced, the medication was discontinued, and the jaundice rapidly disappeared. . . .
>
> Q: (FROM A DEFENSE ATTORNEY TO A PSYCHIATRIST):
>   Is it not therefore reasonable for this defendant to worry about the fact that if he is committed to a hospital and given these drugs he will again develop these consequences which might

be serious to his health? And is there not a factual basis for his statement? In other words, it is not a complete delusional idea, is that correct?

A: No. But I think that the way he said it here it is highly exaggerated.

Q: Because he used the word "murder"?

A: Yes. But also the poisoning. No hospital is trying to poison a person.

Q: Excuse me, I'm not talking about the motives of the hospital staff at all. Even if their motives were entirely benevolent, would it not be reasonable for the defendant to believe that were he hospitalized and given this medication, it would poison his system in fact?

A: Yes. [Brooks 1974, p. 341]

A woman diagnosed as manic depressive, on lithium carbonate, came into court. As soon as she took the witness stand, she lifted one of her legs onto the dais. The leg was extremely swollen. She shouted, "Look, judge, what they are doing to me in the hospital, they are poisoning me." No one told her what the aide whispered to me: "That is a side effect of lithium."

There is clear evidence that the behavior of a majority of adult patients has improved with the judicious administration of psychotropic drugs (Kaplan, Freedman, and Sadock 1980; van Praag 1978). There is also some possibility that the state mental institutions would experience increased social control problems if they were unable to tranquilize all patients involuntarily. But the central problem of the involuntary medication of involuntary patients remains an undecided one, with the patients caught between the perceived need to subdue patients in mental hospitals and the legal right to refuse invasion of bodily space.

There have recently been two influential federal court decisions granting involuntary mental patients an extensive right to refuse treatment except in emergency situations (which have been relatively narrowly defined; see *Rennie* v. *Klein,* 1978; *Rogers* v. *Okin,* 1979). An appeal in *Rogers* v. *Okin* will be heard in the near future.

The Right to Treatment in the Least Restrictive Alternative Setting

The law of California and in some other states embodies the principle of the least restrictive alternative treatment setting for the involuntary mental patient. Unlike the right to treatment, implementation of least restrictive alternative provisions is less costly per patient than more restrictive 24-hour treatment. However, in *Dixon* v. *Weinberger* (1975) a judge in Washington, D.C., ordered that the patients in St. Elizabeth's Hospital had a right to treatment in the least restrictive placement commensurate with their mental disorder. But the judge also ruled that facilities should be created if they do not exist, a ruling which could involve added fiscal burdens.

Due both to the deprivation of liberty involved in hospitalization and the per patient cost containment in alternative facilities, there is a moral obligation to provide adequate facilities for the involuntarily treated. In a recent decision (*Halderman* v. *Pennhurst State School & Hospital,* 1977), the United States Supreme Court decided—on narrow, nonconstitutional grounds of statutory interpretation—that the Federal Developmental Disabilities Act expresses a congressional preference (but *not* a requirement) that the developmentally disabled be treated in less-restrictive facilities. The decision is written in such a fashion, however, as to invite future litigation on the constitutional status of the right to treatment in the least-restrictive alternative setting. We may therefore expect further decisions about the least-restrictive alternative principle for the mentally disordered within the near future.

The Problem of Predicting Dangerousness

The ruling on the Donaldson case left unanswered the question of whether someone committed to the mental hospital as dangerous has the right to treatment or the right to refuse treatment. The Court did rule in the Donaldson case that the state does not have the right to continue to confine involuntarily a nondangerous mentally ill person who can function adequately in the community.

There is now more controversy over the use of the *parens patriae* criterion for commitment than over police power grounds. However, a continuing difficulty with dangerousness and police power justifications for involuntary civil commitment is that it is difficult to define and predict dangerousness in a manner which satisfies the precision of the law; another is that it appears to be closely related to preventive detention or preventive confinement.

Preventive detention is the confinement of someone not accused of a crime, to prevent him or her from behaving dangerously to self or others. Stone (1975, p. 4) asserts that the "law has always implicitly or explicitly maintained a system of preventive confinement," and that in the United States this system includes such devices as bail, confinement of juveniles in need of supervision, and involuntary civil commitment. Persons who are committed involuntarily under LPS as dangerous to others are in effect being confined against the harm caused by acts they have yet to commit (Dershowitz 1973).

Defining dangerousness has proved to be very difficult for legal purposes. Dangerousness has been defined very broadly, as nuisance behavior, and more narrowly, as threats and assaults. Sometimes, dangerousness is defined as danger to property, as in check forgery (Monahan 1976).

The definition of dangerousness has both practical and ethical dimensions. In the area of policymaking, reliable and valid measures of dangerousness are needed if danger to others is not to be an arbitrary and capricious standard for involuntary confinement. Yet, since dangerous behavior is a matter of social context and social definition, it is difficult even to define it, let alone scale it reliably and validly using individual characteristics as the basis for the scale. The extreme difficulty of predicting dangerousness is the basis of much of the opposition to involuntary commitment among psychiatrists and attorneys (Ennis and Litwak 1974; Morse 1978, and Chap. 4 this volume; Szasz 1961).

The narrower the definition of dangerousness, the less predictive; the broader the definition, the more predictive. At the extreme, if all nuisance behavior were defined as dangerous to others, then psychiatrists could predict with fair accuracy that the patients they see will in fact be dangerous. But most definitions which satisfy the current law are narrower, and concerned with threats, actions or a history of violence to others.

In predicting dangerousness in the narrower context, psychiatrists can make two types of error: overprediction, and underprediction. Underprediction occurs in those empirically rare cases where a psychiatrist has released a person as nondangerous and that person then engages in violent behavior. The general public may become very attentive to these "false negatives." A case in point is that of Emil Kemper, who was released from a California state hospital as no longer dangerous, and who subsequently committed murder. Psychiatrists and judges are understandably wary of such cases with their attendant widespread and hostile publicity. Therefore, psychiatrists tend to err on the side of overprediction: predicting that persons will be dangerous when, after release, they do not threaten or harm others. Monahan (1976, pp. 16–22) discusses 14 empirical studies of released patients labeled "dangerous" and concludes that violence is grossly overpredicted. Whatever the measure employed, between 54% and 99% of those predicted to be dangerous were not found to be dangerous when followed up after release (Monahan 1976, pp. 20–21).

Mandatory Judicial Review in California

The problems of defining and predicting dangerousness, of the deprivation of liberty in preventive confinement, and of the right to treatment and to refuse treatment are all ones which must be dealt with eventually by the California mental health law system as they must be in all other states. But California's system has an immediate and pressing problem with a recent ruling concerned with mandatory judicial review.

In 1979, U.S. District Judge Warren J. Ferguson ruled in *Doe* v. *Gallinot* (1979) that the state is obligated to provide a judicial hearing for every person involuntarily committed on a 72-hour hold for grave disability, which means a statewide total of some substantial proportion of 20,000 persons. Since Metropolitan Court hears only a small percentage of the approximately 2,800 writs filed by 14-day certification patients, the caseload impact on the court and on other similar facilities throughout the state would be staggering. If no emergency plans were made to avoid this situation by the November 1, 1980, compliance deadline, mental health system personnel asserted that implementation would be the "death" of LPS:

INTERORGANIZATIONAL MEETING; HOSPITAL ADMINISTRATOR:
   This ruling can't be adopted, it will be the death of LPS.

But death has been seen as the fate of LPS in the wake of a number of social policy and legislative changes other than mandatory judicial review; death was envisaged, also, as a consequence of Proposition 13 and other state fiscal crises:

   DA: LPS won't last long—I'll predict it will die within the year.
   RESEARCHER: Why?
   DA: Because the state doesn't want to pay for involuntary holds.

The implementation responses used by mental health system personnel to avoid a disastrous impact on Metropolitan Court were to hold routine administrative hearings and to avoid certification as "gravely disabled." Since Judge Ferguson's ruling did not specify what type of hearing was required for compliance, "administrative hearings" take place routinely as patients are admitted involuntarily on 72-hour holds; furthermore, some hospitals are no longer checking "gravely disabled" on patients' LPS admission forms.

The Impact of LPS

LPS changed both the categories of persons handled under mental health law and the processes by which they were handled (see table 2.1). One added process was the right to a writ of habeas corpus for the involuntarily committed, which did not exist prior to LPS; therefore it is only possible to describe existing practices and not possible to make pre- and post-LPS comparisons. But it is possible to make some comparisons, and assess the impact of the law, by using

Table 2.1
Pre-and Post-LPS Categories

Category	Pre-LPS	Post-LPS
Voluntary	Voluntary	Voluntary
Involuntary	Observations:	72-hour detention
	Court emergency	Court-ordered
	Brief court	evaluation
	90-day admission	14-day certification
	Civil commitment	Additional 14-day
	Health officer	certification, suicide
	application	90-day postcertification
		Additional 90-day
		certification
		Temporary
		conservatorship
		Conservatorship
Other involuntary	Sex psychopath	Mentally disordered
	commitment	sex offender
	Mentally disordered	Drug commitment
	sex offender	Youth authority
	commitment	observation
	Juvenile court	Penal code
	observation and	commitments
	commitment	Mental retardation
	Youth authority	commitment
	observation and	Other
	commitment	
	Penal code	
	commitment	
	Alcohol commitment	
	Drug addict	
	commitment	
	Other	

Source: From Lamb et al. 1981.

secondary pre- and post-LPS data on state hospital treatment and the use of less-restrictive alternatives. The length of stay at the state hospitals has been reduced drastically since LPS as intended by the statute, although the population has not been reduced as drastically. The less-restrictive alternatives principle in part has been circumvented by the use of conservatorship, and in part has been neglected by the lack of provision or target population utilization of less restrictive alternatives.

The State Hospitals

Researchers at USC Medical Center collected data on nine counties, which together represent about 72% of California's population (see Lamb et al. 1981), comparing pre- and post-LPS time periods of 1960–61 to 1977–78. The rates of admission to state hospitals fluctuated considerably during this time period. Comparing the beginning and the end of the period, the rate of voluntary admissions per 100,000 population dropped from 35.76 to 16.59; however, the rate of involuntary admissions dropped less steeply, from 90.07 to 78.09. But the different counties had different experiences. In the county served by Metropolitan Court, the involuntary admission rate rose from 27.22 in 1968–69 to 165.41 in 1977–78; the rate rose in three other counties, remained stable in one county, and dropped in two counties (Lamb et al. 1981).

Using numbers of persons admitted, Lamb et al. (1981) estimate that there were about 5,000 persons under the age of 65 civilly committed in California in 1968–69. In 1976–77, they estimate, there were 22,562 14-day certifications, and 7,789 permanent conservatorships. As these researchers summarize: "While state hospital usage has shown an overall decline . . . the major reduction has been in voluntary patients and the special categories of involuntary patients such as Penal Code Admissions, Drug and Alcohol related commitments, etc. Seventy-eight percent of State Hospital admissions are now involuntary mentally ill patients."

But there has been a decline in the length of stay as a result of LPS; in the first two years after the law went into effect, the average length of stay for involuntary patients dropped from 180 days to 15 days, and for voluntary patients from 75 to 23 days (Lamb et al. 1981). But this statistic obscures the fact that the same chronic schizophrenics are being committed, released, and recommitted; the socially marginal persons in Metropolitan Court pass through the hospitals and the court over and over again. This revolving door phenomenon is postulated by Lamb et al. (1981) as one factor in the continuingly high rates of involuntary admissions to state hospitals. The revolving door becomes apparent even to the observer at Metropolitan Court, who sees the same petitioners over and over again, in both habeas corpus and conservatorship cases, at intervals ranging from a few days to a few months.

The Uses of Conservatorship

The least restrictive alternative provision of LPS presumes the existence and utilization of such alternatives. Although community mental health centers (CHCs) and other facilities less restrictive than the state hospitals do exist, they do not reach the chronic schizo-phrenics served by the hospitals (Teknekron 1978). In California, the least-restrictive alternatives principle is circumvented by the use of conservatorship to ensure long-term commitment: "Quite obviously, given the structure of the (California) law, conservatorship is the only way that the mental health system can avoid rigid time con-straints . . . it was inevitable that all the stresses for prolonging con-finement would be directed at that one escape hatch" (Stone 1975, p. 64; see also Wexler 1974, p. 671).

In support of Stone's and Wexler's argument, Morris (1978, p. 214) provides statistical evidence for the conclusion that the con-servatorship provision has been used as an "escape hatch" to pro-long the confinement of the mentally disordered. This prolonged confinement is accomplished in two ways: filing temporary con-servatorships and then dropping them (Lamb et al. 1981), and re-labeling those who came in on 72-hour holds as "dangerous" to "gravely disabled" (see Chap. 8).

This relabeling was done to avoid the pitfalls in the 90-day com-mitment for danger to others (see above) while accomplishing a longer commitment period. Morris (1978, p. 214) notes that in California as a whole in 1972–73 36,133 persons were detained on 72-hour holds, but only 18 were detained on 90-day certifications as imminently dangerous. In that same year 3,296 were processed through the conservatorship route as "gravely disabled."[2]

As I did, Morris (1978) began his study of conservatorships with the assumption that conservatees would, in the main, be elderly persons; both of us found that this was not the case. I was not able to obtain the ages of the 60 conservatees whom I observed, but no more than a quarter appeared to be over 60. Morris (1978, p. 229) found that of the 63 conservatorship cases he observed in San Diego, about a third were under 26 years old, just over half were under 36, and less than a quarter of the cases were over 60. If the grave disability label is being used on persons first labeled dangerous to others, then this finding is less surprising, since it is the young who are, in general, found to be dangerous. The following cases illustrate con-servatorships where the stress was on dangerousness and on grave disability, respectively; these cases also well illustrate the problem of social marginality:

PSYCHIATRIST: Yes, I examined him on September 22 at State Hos-pital.

2. Since the Ferguson ruling on mandatory review of grave disability 72-hour holds, grave disability has decreased dramatically, at least in some hospitals, as a 72-hour admitting label.

COUNTY COUNSEL: And what is his history?

P: From his file, he was violent at his home. He made threats at his parents. He was angry and uncooperative. Over a period of several months he improved sufficiently with medication. He received permission to make home visits.

PD: Objection [basis inaudible].

CC: I'll rephrase the question. When was the patient admitted?

P: On February of 1978.

CC: And why was he admitted?

P: He was violent towards his parents at home.

CC: And is there any other history prior to September 1978?

P: None that appears relevant.

CC: What form did this take?

P: Prior to talking with Mr. S. I spent time looking over the records. He was assaultive and combative. With medication he improved. Subsequent to the home visits he deteriorated. He became angry and assaultive to the staff. On the 17th he became assaultive. When asked why he said it was because "those people are the ones keeping me at the hospital." He didn't feel there was anything wrong with him. He has been hearing voices of ghosts who had been saying "sad and bad" things to him.

CC: Did he have an objective?

P: He wanted to leave and take an apartment by himself. He is receiving $296 from Social Security.

CC: Is he suffering from a mental disorder?

P: Yes, I think so.

CC: And what is your diagnosis?

P: Schizophrenia, paranoid type. He has a persistent anger and hostility, blaming other people for his delusional ideas. He suffers from hallucinations.

CC: Is he taking medications?

P: Yes, thorazine 200 mg. four times a day. This is quite a heavy dosage. He has taken medication in the past but appears to stop taking it. I think it's very important that he keep taking his medication.

CC: Would he take his medication voluntarily?

P: I believe he would not.

CC: Why is that?

P: His refusal to recognize his illness. And his saying things like "I'm Jesus Christ," all delusional ideas.

CC: Is he gravely disabled?

P: Yes, I think he is.

CC: On what basis?

P: On the basis of his acting out.

CC: By "acting out" you mean violent?

P: Yes.

CC: Is the grave disability related to a mental disorder?

P: Yes, these ideas he has.

CC: Can he provide for his food, clothing and shelter?

P: No.

CC: Why is that?

P: Again, the acting out, this would block his desires.

PSYCHIATRIST: This is a 30 year old white male known as "Moo." He has been begging for a living. He was picked up by the police. This man indicates that he has been mute since he was 10 years old. The family began to wander around the Western States. He communicates marginally by writing. For the past 10 years he's been begging, occasionally getting a job washing dishes . . . chronic undifferentiated schizophrenia characterized by a lack of ability to speak without a physical disorder. Not being able to speak sets him apart.

COUNTY COUNSEL: In your opinion, is he gravely disabled?

P: Yes.

CC: Does he have the ability to provide food, clothing and shelter?

P: Man brought in in a state of dishevelment . . . clothes smelled of feces and urine. He was very sparse [*sic*], not well nourished. That was his total plan—to go on welfare and get something to eat.

PUBLIC DEFENDER: Is he able to provide food and shelter on a marginal basis?

P: On his word he's able to do it by begging and dishwashing for five years. . . .

PD: Your diagnosis is schizophrenia undifferentiated on the fact that he doesn't talk?

P: Pretty much so because he doesn't talk but because he's satisfied with the animal-like way in which he lives.

In both of these cases, the petitioners were labeled as mentally disordered and gravely disabled and assigned to a permanent public conservator.

The conservatorship cases from which these excerpts were taken took longer than many: 20 and six minutes, respectively. Both Morris (1978) and I were surprised at the brevity of many of the conservatorship proceedings. I had expected that, since conservatorship was the longest form of involuntary confinement legally possible, there would be greater care taken and greater time spent in hearing cases than in Department 1. This did not seem to be the case. Ironically, Morris (1978, p. 232) found that the commitment hearings he observed were shorter than the 4.7-minute hearings (cited by Bardach 1972, pp. 101–2, as 4.1) prior to LPS; the statistic which had prompted legislative interest in involuntary civil commitment in the first place.

Summary and Discussion

Mental health legislation in California and in other states has undergone considerable change in the last several decades against a background of considerable continuity. Middle-class values continue to underlie LPS standards, and the involuntarily committed continue to be the socially marginal. The drift of legal changes has been toward more attention to involuntary patients' substantive and due process rights, and more legal intervention into what was previously a purely psychiatric procedure. The development of psychoactive drugs in the 1950s facilitated the statutory provision for treatment in a less-restrictive alternative setting; in theory, many patients can be adequately controlled in their behavior if they receive and take medication through outpatient clinics.

Another set of changes has to do with state mental hospital utilization. Patients stay in state mental hospitals for much shorter periods of time than before, and, in California at least, proportionately far more patients are involuntary than prior to LPS. The financial tribulations of the State of California which were one element in the passage of LPS have continued to take their toll on community mental health services, and chronic schizophrenics rarely receive treatment through these services.

The legal theory behind involuntary commitment has also shifted somewhat, from the need for care and treatment/grave disability or similar *parens patriae* provisions to the criterion of danger to others. However, the practical difficulty of predicting dangerousness has resulted in a de facto continuity in the law: redefinition of those labeled "dangerous to others" as "gravely disabled" later in the process. Thus, long-term commitment based on the need for care and treatment, the standard overturned by LPS, has been restored through the use of conservatorships.

The persistence of trends within an appearance of change attests to the power of interest groups in maintaining the status quo and the dominance of the material over the ideal. Those employed in the mental health law system have a financial and ideological interest in the continuation of their systems. Those who exercise the police power and social control functions of the state have a political interest in the continuation of institutionalization. And the clientele, the people on the social margins, have nowhere else to go.

But are the people of the court of last resort just socially marginal, like other types of deviants, to be controlled only for the same reasons as other dangerous or useless populations, or is there a difference? In the next chapter, I examine some of the evidence and make my case for the reality of mental illness—for its individual reality as well as its socially determined nature.

3 Perspectives on Mental Illness

Labeling theory involves presuppositions concerning who is to be selected for mental hospitalization, the power relations between labelers and labelees, and the nature of mental illness. As indicated in the first chapter, those persons heard as petitioners in Metropolitan Court are socially marginal: persons with few resources and little power. To the extent that labeling theory describes and predicts a population to be found in social control institutions, it is supported by the marginality of those persons confined in, and seeking their release from, the state hospitals.

The power relations between labelers and labelees are unbalanced in Metropolitan Court and throughout the mental health law system, just as they are in any official deviance-processing network. To the extent that the labeling perspective defines a population, it defines it accurately in this instance. However, the labeling model of power relations also includes the theory of secondary deviation and an assumption of determinism.

The theory of secondary deviation is deterministic in that the self-identity of the labeled deviant is transformed by various activities on the part of the labeler. The labeled person is more or less helpless either to engage in a contrary self-definition, or to coerce or manipulate the labeler. The deterministic logic of labeling theory dovetails nicely with the view of the mad as propelled by forces beyond their control; a view which contrasts with the legal presupposition of a rational, in-control actor. However, evidence from the behavior of mental patients indicates that they indeed may be capable both of rationally assessing their fate and of manipulating

44

their captors, as well as of insulating their self-identities against the charge of mental illness.

Labeling Theory and the Medical Model[1]

Labeling theory and the medical model make different ontological assumptions about the nature of madness. For labeling theorists, madness is not real; what *is* real is audiences' response to and labeling of certain actors and behaviors as "mad." For those who utilize the medical model of madness, insanity is a condition, either somatic (physiological) or psychological, which may be genetic or chemical (or neither), causal or predisposing, and discovered or undiscovered. Following the tradition of Freud, madness is viewed by psychoanalysts as a condition in which earlier repression of emotions precipitates later mad behavior. Following the tradition of the humoral theorists of the Middle Ages, the somaticists view madness as some type of physical condition which results in mad behavior.

There are empirical case examples of somatic madness. Both syphilis and senile dementia often involve brain changes which precipitate bizarre behavior. Similarly, there are empirical case examples of the attachment of madness labels to apparently normal people (see below). The movement to limit involuntary civil commitment in the United States in the nineteenth century was in part provoked by the publication of such cases as that of Josiah Oakes (Fox 1978). In his sixties, Josiah Oakes took up with a young woman in her twenties; his children feared he might squander the profits of his wharf business, so they had him involuntarily hospitalized to protect their financial interests. A similar empirical case cannot be stated for psychoanalysis, since psychic repression cannot be operationalized and measured like brain changes or hospitalization procedures. In principle, mental illnesses other than those which change the brain could have undiscovered physical causes.

In part because neither theories of psychic repression nor somatic theories have been adequately tested, there is great difficulty in assessing the validity of the medical model as an explanation for crazy behavior. It is much easier to demonstrate the process of labeling than it is to document the presence of an invisible condition. But I want to make the argument for a mixed model of madness, including an X factor above and beyond the process of labeling.

1. The discussion of labeling theory and the medical model, as well as the other approaches to mental illness covered in this chapter, is not comprehensive, nor, in an interdisciplinary endeavor, can it be so.

Even Scheff (1966), one of the first and still one of the most influential social scientists to apply labeling theory to mental illness, did not intend his work to be used as it has been since—as a complete annihilation of psychiatric theory. He wanted simply to draw attention to a neglected feature of madness—its social construction. Scheff asserted that the behaviors labeled as mad may arise from both sociologically defined contingencies and psychoanalytically defined pathology (Scheff 1966, p. 34). He added that his intention in the construction of a societal reaction model was a comparative one, warranting the abstracted exaggeration of an ideal type: "Just as the individual systems (psychiatric) models under-stress social processes, the model presented here probably exaggerates their importance. . . . One road of progress in science is the intentional formulation of mutually incompatible models, each incomplete, and each explicating only a portion of the area under investigation" (pp. 25–27).

The Labeling Perspective on Mental Illness

According to labeling theory, the label "deviant" is affixed to certain persons who violate the expectations of others. Scheff (1966) maintains that people are labeled as mentally ill when their deviance cannot be explained as criminal or justified in some other way: "The diverse kinds of rule-breaking for which society provides no explicit label and which, therefore, sometimes lead to the labeling of the violator as mentally ill, will be considered to be technically residual rule-breaking" (p. 34).

But only some persons who engage in residually deviant behavior are labeled as mentally ill; the societal reaction to residual deviance may be either denial or labeling. Most residual deviance is denied; observers overlook or rationalize the behavior in question (Scheff 1966; Warren and Mesinger 1980). Those who are selected for labeling are most often the socially marginal: the homeless, the elderly, the poor, welfare recipients, and the lower class (Scheff 1966; Segal et al. 1977; for a contrary view, see Gove 1975).

The most persuasive sociological evidence for the significance of the labeling process comes from studies documenting the labeling of normals as mad; these studies illustrate the significance of context and authority in the labeling process. There is even persuasive evidence that professionals and experts are willing to affix madness labels upon normals. In an experiment to determine such willingness, Temerlin (1968) had a sound-recorded interview made with a professional actor, who was instructed to portray a mentally healthy and productive scientist who had read a book about psychotherapy and wanted to talk about it. He portrayed himself as someone with a happy childhood past and warm current relationships, happy and effective in his work, secure and happily married (Temerlin 1968, p. 47).

For the experiment, psychiatrists, clinical psychologists, and graduate students in clinical psychology were told just before they heard the interview that a professional person of high prestige thought that the man was "very interesting" because he "looked neurotic but actually was quite psychotic" (Temerlin 1968, p. 47). The three sets of professionals heard the interview under the following conditions: (1) no suggestion; (2) a suggestion that the man was mentally healthy; and (3) no suggestion, and in a nonclinical setting, with the man defined as undergoing a new type of personnel interview. The fourth (control) group was a mock sanity hearing using lay persons from a jury pool.

Of the experimental group, 15 of the 25 psychiatrists defined the man as psychotic, 10 defined him as neurotic or suffering from a character disorder; no psychiatrist rated him as normal. The comparable figures for psychologists and graduate students were: 7, 15, and 3; 5, 35, and 5 (Temerlin 1968, p. 50). In the sanity hearing condition, all 12 jurors found the man mentally healthy; in the "employment interview," 17 of the professionals judged him to be normal, and seven as neurotic. With no suggestion, 12 professionals defined the man as mentally healthy, and nine as neurotic. None of the control groups saw the man as psychotic (Temerlin 1968, p. 50).

The importance of the audience in the labeling process, and of the context in which labeler and labelee interact, is also clear in Rosenhan's famous study "On Being Sane in Insane Places" (1973). In Rosenhan's experiment, he asked eight sane people to attempt to gain admission to 12 different mental hospitals by saying that they heard voices repeating words such as "hollow," "empty," and "thud," but faking no other psychiatric symptoms and giving true answers to all other admissions questions. All were admitted to a mental hospital as mentally ill, seven with the diagnosis of schizophrenia. Once admitted, the pseudopatients dropped the faking of auditory hallucinations as well and behaved quite normally on the wards. But the length of time they remained hospitalized ranged from seven to 52 days, with an average of 19 days; all were discharged with a diagnosis of "schizophrenia in remission."

During their hospital stays, only fellow patients, never staff, recognized the pseudopatients as sane. Even normal activities were defined by staff as symptoms of mental illness. The chart of one pseudopatient who consistently took notes included the remark "patient engages in writing behavior." One patient, pacing the long corridors of the hospital out of boredom, was asked by a staff member if he was "nervous." During their stays, the patients were given a total of 2,100 psychoactive pills, including Elavil, Stelazine, Compazine, and Thorazine (Rosenhan 1973, p. 68).

In a response to this experiment, another hospital asserted that such a set of errors could not occur at *their* hospital and accepted the following challenge. Staff were told that one or more pseudopatients would seek admission to their hospital during the next three months and that they should rate, on a scale of 1–10, each patient's likelihood of being a pseudopatient. One hundred ninety-three admittees were rated in this manner, with a score of 1–2 indicating high confidence that the patient was a pseudopatient; 41 pseudopatients were identified by at least one staff member, and 19 were suspected by at least two. In fact, no pseudopatients were sent to the hospital during this time period.

The findings of the Temerlin and Rosenhan experiments are interesting not only for what they say about the readiness of persons to label normals as "mad" but also for what they say about the variables which affect such readiness. Professional training, setting, and the influence of others' opinions all seem to exert an influence on audiences who label. My colleagues and myself have suggested in other studies that the motives for audiences to label others as mad, or deny madness even in the face of extremely bizarre behavior, is an interesting and somewhat overlooked problem for sociological research (Warren and Johnson 1972; Warren and Messinger 1980).

The Medical Model of Madness

As indicated, there are two major variations of the medical model of madness: the somatic or physical, and the psychoanalytic. Both focus on mental illness as an illness, or at least as a condition, which exists independently of the labeling process. Based on Freudian theory, contemporary psychoanalytic explanation asserts that psychiatric symptoms arise from the repression of conflicts between biogenetic drives and emotions—such as sex and aggression—and culture. Contemporary somaticists have argued that schizophrenia is in part genetically caused (Conrad and Schneider 1980, p. 55).

Some of the somatic studies involve a search for causation. Others rely on the fact that certain physical interventions—brain surgery such as lobotomy, insulin shock therapy, electric shock therapy, and psychoactive drugs—produce changes in patients' behavior which differ from the changes produced by these procedures in "normals." The argument then is that these physiological interventions are reacting upon as yet unknown chemical or other physiological conditions which cause madness.

Whether somatic or psychoanalytic, the cause of conduct disturbances in the medical model are seen as "inside" the individual rather than in the environment in the form of audience reaction (for the labeling theorists) or stressful socioeconomic conditions (for structural theorists). Scheff (1966, p. 11) refers to the medical model of mental illness as an "individual systems" model, which he contrasts with the sociological societal reaction model; for psychiatrists, he argues, the "external situation in which the individual is involved is seen only as an almost limitless source of triggers for a fully developed neurotic conflict within the individual" (p. 11).

Ontological Critiques of Mental Illness Models

There are a number of criticisms of both the medical model and the labeling model as ontological explanations—as explanations of the essential nature of madness. The critique of the medical model is rooted in the difficulty of demonstrating the existence of a condition which bypasses human will and rationality to produce uncontrollable behavior. This argument is well detailed by Morse in the next chapter.

The major criticism of labeling theory is that it omits consideration of the dimensions of madness—such as denial—not adequately considered by studies such as those by Temerlin and Rosenhan. Gove (1972) argues that "most of the available evidence . . . indicates that the societal reaction explanation of mental illness is incorrect. Hospitalization occurs, at least in most cases, because the individual has a serious psychotic disorder. Persons are not readily funneled into a mental hospital even if they act in a bizarre and troublesome manner; on the contrary, mental illness is denied by all concerned until the situation becomes untenable."

Critics of both models turn to anthropological and cross-cultural studies for evidence of the existence of mental illness independent of cultural definitions and audience response. In the 1940s and 1950s, the position taken by Benedict (1959) was the most common one among anthropologists: that psychotic, catatonic, and other Western "abnormals" may be regarded as normal in other cultures. They cited as evidence the trances entered into by mystical leaders they referred to as shamans.

Current anthropological thinking, however, is less labeling oriented. In an empirically based argument, Murphy (1976, p. 1019) maintains that "in widely different cultural and environmental situations sanity appears to be distinguishable from insanity by cues that are very similar to those used in the Western world." Her studies of Eskimo and Yoruba definitions of shamanism and madness led her to conclude that both cultures distinguish between shamans and the mentally ill and that the distinction rests upon the perceived appropriateness or inappropriateness of the behavior involved:

> When a shaman undertakes a curing rite he becomes possessed by the spirit of an animal; he "deludes" himself, so to speak, into believing that he is an animal. . . . Compare this to the case . . . of a Baffin Island Eskimo who believed that a fox had entered her body. This was not associated with shamanizing but was a continuous belief. . . . This woman was thought to be crazy but the shamaness not. One Eskimo summarized the distinction this way: "When the shaman is healing he is out of his mind, but *he is not crazy.*" [P. 1022]

Murphy adds that "the inability to control" bizarre behavior is, in all cultures, "what is meant by a mind out of order" (p. 1022).

The Observer and Ontological Explanations

In the Rosenhan and Temerlin experiments, it was clear that observers of behavior differed in their readiness to attach madness labels to others and that one dimension of this readiness was professional socialization. In studying or writing about mental illness, the scholar constructs a model which is created in part by observation of the data (both the mentally ill and the work of other scholars) and in part from the observer's biography both within and outside the professional sphere.

My own view of mental illness has been shaped by my exposure to labeling theory in graduate school, by my experience in Metropolitan Court and other mental illness/law settings, and by observing the psychotic breakdown of a colleague. When I first entered Metropolitan Court, I took labeling theory for granted as received wisdom. The very first case I encountered by chance confirmed all my presuppositions:

> The case (see also Chap. 2) was a black male, indeterminate age, perhaps early middle age. He did not say a word throughout the habeas corpus hearing. The evidence came from a police report, which stated that he had been standing on a street corner in a (wealthy white suburban area) at 4 A.M. when police stopped to question him. He said to them that he was trying to hail a taxi and was angry when none would stop. He also got angry and hostile to the police for questioning him. The judge said, "Is that all there is on the police report, standing on a street corner trying to hail a taxi, and getting angry at the police?" That *was* all. The judge released the man, expressing anger at his commitment.

This case fit all the presuppositions of labeling theory. The man labeled mentally ill was black and looked poor. He was alone in court, without friends or family. The police had singled him out for attention as a black person in a white neighborhood. Officials had not even developed a convincing legal-psychiatric account to legitimate the 72-hour hold.

But later experiences in Metropolitan Court drastically revised my assessment of labeling theory (for the reverse process, see the discussion of psychiatrist Braginsky's "conversion" from the psychiatric model in the Appendix on Methods). Within the next few days, I had witnessed the most extreme case of delusion I was to see in all my years at Metropolitan Court:

> PSYCHIATRIST: This man calls himself James Bond. . . . he is a
> chronic paranoid schizophrenic. . . .
> "JAMES BOND": I changed my name with a federal judge, I would
> go home to get $10,000 for my family, my brother is hiding out
> under the name of James Bond, I have $30,000 in the bank, I
> have no income since I left the Secret Service, I would live with
> my family, I speak Russian, German, English, French, Gypsy,
> and Egyptian. Ten thousand years ago I studied true Egyptian
> and it had no alphabet, I was living in Monte Carlo, I was
> going to find out where the Green Hornet died, I met the man
> who called himself Cato and was going to kill the president and
> I heard the whole conversation, I am also a disabled veteran, I
> volunteered my services, I have a son eight years old by my
> first wife, I have a little girl called Marilyn Monroe, I am here
> by order of the King of the Gypsies, I am an ambassador, I am
> recognized under James Bond 007, it is none of your business
> whose head I will have on a platter, we are all going to be killed
> by the Mafia. If you give me 24 hours I have some secret docu-
> ments from Herbert Hoover. I also have a telegram, let me
> show my lawyer, I am registered as an ambassador for all the
> gypsies, I have been tried by other doctors and found sane.
> JUDGE: I order you to remain at the hospital for the rest of your
> treatment.
> "JAMES BOND": You are going to eat my words some day, excuse
> me your Honor.

Observing James Bond and others like him but less deluded, I became more sympathetic to the idea that one trigger for the labeling process, in the case of mental illness, was some kind of condition. In the context of a sociology of knowledge, I had already realized that the labeling perspective functioned for sociologists as a sort of scholarly counter to the psychiatric medical model. Part of the reason I had adopted it was that it was sociological, and I was a sociologist. Part of the reason I later rejected it as a complete explanation was that, in Metropolitan Court, it just simply came to seem counterintuitive.

Most of the cases seen at Metropolitan Court are not as clearly definable as either the labeled black man or the delusional James Bond. Many accounts heard on the witness stand have elements of ambiguity, amenable to categorization either as instances of labeling or as instances of response to internal pressures:

An angry-looking black female around 30 years old was called to the stand. Dr. Bartlett testified that she was a paranoid schizophrenic, on the grounds that "she refuses to communicate with or acknowledge the presence of the doctor." She had been committed on an earlier 72-hour hold three weeks ago as a paranoid schizophrenic, again in part because she was suspicious and refused to speak to the psychiatrists. The circumstances of the case, more or less similar to the police report and the woman's testimony, were as follows: her car had stalled in the middle of the road. She left it there and went into a store to call friends and get help. Meanwhile, the police were investigating her stalled car. The woman used her last dime to make the call to friends, who refused to come and help her. She picked up some greeting cards and threw them on the floor because, she said, she was very angry.

Here her story and the police's diverged. The police said that she threw the cards out of the store as they came in to investigate the circumstances of the car. She said she threw the cards on the floor. The police said they then took her to State Hospital on a 72-hour hold. She said they drove her around for two hours and asked her if she would give them a "blow job" before they took her to State.

The meanings of her behavior were also differently interpreted by herself and by the police. After the police were called to the store, they asked her if there was anyone she could call to take her home. She said "no" because she was still angry with her friends, but the police found the friends' phone number on her and called them. When the friends arrived, she refused to go with them. The police interpreted this refusal as a sign of mental illness. She saw it as an angry reaction to circumstances.

The judge decided that her behavior was a sign of bad temper rather than paranoid schizophrenia and released her, saying, "There does not seem to be anything wrong with this woman other than a very bad temper."

Both an ideal typical labeling theory and an ideal typical medical model could serve as explanations for this episode. In the medical model, the woman is paranoid schizophrenic; her behavior was triggered by something (either chemical or psychic) inside her in response to external stimuli. In the labeling perspective, the behavior could be seen as triggered by frustrating circumstances in the environment which brought about residually deviant behavior and the attention of authorities.

But the explanation could also be multifaceted, interweaving both labeling and medical contingencies. The woman was perhaps frustrated by external circumstances, such as the store and her friends, and at the same time she lacked the ability to cope with stress because of a prior history of neurotic or psychotic disturbance. The doctor may have labeled her paranoid because she refused to speak with him and this piqued him, but he also labeled her because he had seen her at State Hospital several times before.

In my view, shaped by exposure to the mentally ill as well as to labeling theory, mental illness has aspects of a condition and of the outcome of a series of labeling practices which respond both to the condition and to socioeconomic relationships. The black woman in the case quoted above, whom I encountered several times afterward in the court and in the wards of one state hospital, seemed to me to have something wrong with her, something which defied classification beyond the vague and unscientific X factor.

On the other hand, my research in several psychiatric wards underlined the validity of the labeling explanation; the adolescents, most of whom did not seem mentally ill, were defined and treated as mentally ill for purposes of state and parental social control (see Chap. 9). The degree of pathology a person must exhibit to be labeled and treated as mentally ill—from none to extreme—varies with the social purposes and costs of that control, which are socioeconomically and historically determined. Today, in California, there is perhaps more interest in hospitalizing adolescents than in taking care of the socially marginal and useless.

The Law, Mental Illness, and Human Rationality

The problem with the intersection of law and mental illness, as Morse elaborates in Chapter 4, is that the legal model of human behavior depends on underlying notions of human rationality, free will, competence, and responsibility. For the law to apply to an individual, that individual must be seen as rational, able to form intentions, competent to carry out actions related to those intentions, and thereby responsible for both intentions and actions. The labeling theory of mental illness is deterministic and focuses on the audience, bypassing the question of individual rationality. The medical model presupposes a human actor whose rationality is impaired, who is incompetent, whose will is deformed by incompetence, and who is thus not responsible for his or her behavior.

In the next chapter Morse makes the case for refusing to assume, under the law, that those labeled mentally ill are irrational, impaired, incompetent, or presumptively not responsible. There is some evidence from studies of mental patients that they have a degree of control over their fate, that they are capable of developing rational motivations for action, and of intending and carrying out those actions quite competently. In the context of labeling theory, there is some indication that those labeled mentally ill can manipulate audience reactions to them to obtain a desired outcome (Braginsky, Braginsky, and Ring 1969; see also Warren and Johnson 1972).

But I do not want to argue that the mentally ill are completely rational because that is counterintuitive to my experience with them. In addition, there seems to be no need to postulate complete rationality or complete irrationality, nor opposite poles of will, competence, or responsibility. Morse, in the next chapter, implies that people either do or do not want to become mental patients; if they say they do not, they should not be committed involuntarily. Zusman, in Chapter 5, takes the opposite stance: that people who are at risk of becoming mental patients are incapable of deciding if they want to or not and thus lack will and reason. I found that many patients in Metropolitan Court were ambivalent about their hospitalization; even though they had filed writs of habeas corpus seeking release, some of them withdrew these writs before their cases came up, and others acted in ways that seemed counterproductive to being released. Their ambivalence was rooted both in a sense of personal stress and in a social context that provides no support for dependency (see Chap. 9). The work of Braginsky et al. (1969) and Goffman (1961) support, in different ways, the idea of the mentally ill as partially rational and competent.

Secondary Adjustments in the Mental Hospital

Goffman (1961) accepts initially the labeling theorists' view of the helpless, labeled mental patient, to the point at which the patient is denuded of identity and possessions upon entry to the hospital. Goffman (1961) asserts that such stripping ceremonies signal to new inmates that they are no longer possessed of adult self-determination, autonomy, or freedom of action. Within the official structure of the hospital, Goffman's patients are virtual nonbeings, without power, and liable to identity transformation.

However, Goffman's patients have some impact on their fate within the mental hospital. Their impact is *not* on the system or the labelers—staff or psychiatrists—but on their place in the everyday subculture of patients. Goffman's patients have no power to manipulate the staff's labeling activities, but they have "secondary" power to manipulate their own and other patients' lives within the institution: "Secondary adjustments represent ways in which the individual stands apart from the role and the self that were taken for granted for him by the institution" (1961, p. 189).

Secondary adjustments such as obtaining or providing forbidden goods or services provide a means for the patient to reinstitute a sense of autonomy and self-determination. Goffman's patient is *both* competent and incompetent: trapped within the labeling nexus of staff and manipulative of the small sphere of action available in the "underlife" of the institution.

Manipulation of Labelers in the Mental Hospital

In a study of chronic schizophrenics in mental hospitals, Braginsky et al. (1969) developed a model of the mental patient as manipulating the staff of the institutions. They found that the patients engaged in what might be called primary adjustment to hospital life. Braginsky et al. comment that

> in a certain sense an individual *chooses* his career as a mental patient; it is not thrust upon him as a consequence of his somehow becoming "mentally ill." But in just what sense does the individual "choose" his career? In our view, having and maintaining the status of a mental patient is the outcome of *purposive* behavior. Furthermore, given the life circumstances of most of the persons who become and remain residents of mental hospitals, their doing so evinces a realistic appraisal of their available alternatives; it is, in short, a rational, goal-directed behavior. This does not guarantee that the individual appreciates what he is up to. It is equally obvious that the residents described in this book frequently must have been consciously manipulative; many of our findings would be inexplicable without making such an assumption. All we are claiming here is that it is not necessary to suppose that the choice to become a mental patient always reflects a state of conscious volition. [1969, p. 172]

Braginsky et al.'s patient is a chronic schizophrenic from a lower-class background whose life in the hospital is more pleasurable to him or her than life on the outside. Such a patient is consciously or unconsciously manipulative of symptoms, and therefore of the labelers, in order to remain within the hospital. Scheff (1966, pp. 64–68) notes that patients, as well as staff, learn these symptoms as part of their socialization.

The desire of patients to remain in mental hospitals is an empirical question. Those who commit themselves voluntarily and remain voluntarily seem to come closest to a clear definition of willingness to remain. So do those who resist the efforts of staff to discern improvement in them or to facilitate their discharge (Braginsky et al. 1969). But patients who appear in court on habeas corpus petitions have voluntarily filed such symbols of a desire to be discharged and thus present a more complicated set of motivations. An additional set of questions revolve around the existence of motives other than release seeking which operate to bring patients into court.

Patient Use of Court Hearings

A number of the students whom I took to the mental health court asked me how it was possible that the patients did not seem to mind getting up on the stand and displaying their social marginality and delusions. I replied that the socially marginal, unlike the middle class, were used to being handled by officialdom, and sometimes publicly so. For some, the appearance in court was perhaps a shameful experience, made necessary by a strong desire for release. But for other patients, the writ hearing was an opportunity for a display of self, not necessarily related to outcome or release.

Some patients filed writs just to get a day away from the hospital. One filed writs so that he could stand outside the courtroom and watch the trains go by, since he was a train buff (this was told to me both by the patient himself and by his psychiatrist). Still others, rather than losing their sense of autonomy and dignity by appearing in court, found it enhanced by having a public forum from which to display their favorite ideas and interpretations of the world. It is not everyday that a mental patient, or a socially marginal person, can capture the attention of a room full of high-status and educated persons who, for the moment, must listen.

Of those involuntarily committed to mental hospitals in the county, only about 10%–15% file for release. An interesting question for research is to determine those factors which inhibit filing writs: a desire to stay in the hospital, or an inability to make those moves and contacts which would result in the filing of a writ. The availability of writ filing mechanisms does indeed make a difference; writ filings are indeed higher—and go further into the legal process—in state hospitals which facilitate patient-court communication, and lower in those VA and private hospitals which are notorious for blocking communication.

Patient Ambivalence about Hospitalization

Many of those patients who file writs for motives other than self-display appear, during their hearings, ambivalent about wanting to leave the hospital. Depending upon the hospital, a certain proportion of persons withdraw their writs before the court appearance (see table 3.1). Part of the difference between state hospital prior withdrawal on the one hand, and private and Veterans Administration (VA) hospital withdrawal on the other, is due to different degrees of pressure on the patient to withdraw the writ by type of hospital. But in all locations this and other indices of mind changing is probably in part due to ambivalence:

> Today I rode with the MHC to a private hospital where a patient had phoned in his wish to file a writ. We got there and the patient found us, as he shuffled through the corridor to sit with us at a table in the hall. He talked in an almost inaudible whisper. When the mental health counselor asked him repeatedly what he wanted to do and if he wanted to get out, he mumbled, "No, I think I'll stay here for a while till I get on my feet."

Observing patients in court, it is clear that they are almost all capable of observing courtroom etiquette, which they have learned perhaps from TV or from prior appearances. Even the most disoriented and delusional, such as James Bond, can take the oath, say "Your Honor," and raise the right hand. In addition to this general knowledge of appropriate demeanor, the patients have been coached on what to say and do for this specific judge by fellow patients, defense attorneys, and sympathetic aides. I observed many times in court, for example, that patients, when asked for their address, gave it very slowly and deliberately, "Sev-en-ty nine fif-ty first street, Ap-art-ment 6"; they also seemed preternaturally aware of bus routes to everywhere. When I commented on these observations, aides and others told me:

> We tell them that knowing their address is a measure of reality orientation that the judge and the psychiatrists use. We also tell them to be sure to be prepared to give the bus routes and fares to their address if they don't have anyone to pick them up.

Public defenders and others would warn the patients to testify that they were willing to take prescribed psychoactive drugs, since the judge attached particular importance to medication taking as a sign of "doing well." The judge put highly delusional patients in a "Catch-22" position. He thought that patients should be put on the stand to speak for themselves; therefore the public defenders would get their clients to testify if at all possible. If the client was too delusional to testify, or did not do so for some other reason, the judge felt he had reasonable grounds for assuming that the patient was indeed severely mentally disordered.

Table 3.1
LPS Writ Data, Metropolitan County (Compiled by Psychiatric Section, County District Attorney)

Type of Hospital (April 1978)	Writs Issued	Withdrawn by Patient	Change to Voluntary Status	Patient Escape	Discharged by Hospital	Stipulate to Release	Granted (No Show by Hospital)	Granted after Court Hearing	Denied after Court Hearing	Writs Taken to Hearing	% Hearing Writs Denied
Public hospitals:											
State	145 (100)	17 (11.7)	3 (2.1)	1 (0.7)	12 (8.3)	42 (29.0)		14 (9.7)	56 (38.6)	70 (48.3)	(80)
County	30 (100)	6 (20.0)	6 (20.0)		4 (13.3)		1 (3.3)	6 (20.0)	7 (23.3)	13 (43.3)	(53.8)
Veterans Administration hospitals:											
West VA	7 (100)		3 (42.9)				1 (14.3)		3 (42.9)	3 (42.9)	100
South VA	1 (100)							1 (100)		1 (100)	(0)

	n								
North VA	3 (100)	1 (33.3)		1 (33.3)				1 (33.3)	1 (33.3) (100)
Private hospitals:									
Sea View	19 (100)	3 (15.8)	5 (26.3)	5 (26.3)	2 (10.5)	1 (5.3)	3 (15.8)	4 (21.1)	(75)
Portals	12 (100)	1 (8.3)	3 (25.0)	6 (50.0)			1 (8.3)	1 (8.3)	(100)
City View	3 (100)	2 (66.7)		1 (33.3)		1 (8.3)		1 (33.3)	(0)
Ben Zion	3 (100)	1 (33.3)		1 (33.3)	2 (66.7)		2 (66.7)		(0)
St. Ann's	9 (100)	1 (11.1)	3 (33.3)	1 (11.1)	1 (11.1)	2 (22.2)	1 (11.1)	3 (33.3)	(66.7)
Michaelson	4 (100)	2 (50.0)			1 (25.0)	1 (25.0)	1 (25.0)		(66.7)
Montrose	12 (100)	2 (16.7)	2 (16.7)	1 (8.3)	1 (8.3)	2 (16.7)	4 (33.3)	6 (50.0)	(100)
Valley	4 (100)	1 (25.0)	1 (25.0)	1 (8.3)			1 (25.0)	1 (25.0)	(66.7)

Note: Numbers in parentheses are percentages.

Those patients who seemed unambivalent about release utilized their general and specific knowledge about courtroom procedures, displayed a good demeanor and attitude, and were either not delusional or did not display their delusions from the witness box:

> The young man on the stand had been committed as dangerous to self for a "suicide gesture." Evidence brought in by the DA and psychiatrist indicated that he was delusional and hallucinating at the time of admission, religiously preoccupied and claiming he was the son of God. The public defender's evidence was that he was drunk at the time and not mentally disordered. The defendant took the stand, responded courteously to questions, asserted that he was drunk at the time of admission, agreed that he had made a suicide gesture because of despondency over his girlfriend leaving him. He avoided catching the tails of the red herrings thrown to him by the District Attorney concerning his supposed claims that he was the new Messiah. The judge released him. After his release he smiled broadly and shook his public defender's hand as he left the courtroom.

A minority of observed patients seemed unambivalent about release both from the way they behaved during the hearing and from their reactions upon release. But other patients displayed ambivalence either through bizarre behavior during their hearing, or through reacting to release with bewilderment or despondency:

> Before the conservatorship hearing, a young man sits next to me on the bench and shows me a yellow lined pad on which he had written a dubiously literate letter to the judge pleading for his release: "I have served my country in Vietnam. And now I am loced [sic] up. I have my rights as a citizen. MY rights are to be free" [sic].

> As he enters the court, the conservatee stares at the jury, which has five black members: "I don't want to be judged by a bunch of niggers," he says loudly.

> A girl of 16 was from the local institution for neglected and abused children, where she had undertaken what the testifying psychiatrist called a "suicide gesture": scratching her wrist with a paper clip and jumping out of a first-story window. On the stand, she testified in a voice laden with depression, or drugs, or both, that if the judge released her she would not commit suicide; she no longer wished to die. The judge remanded her back to hospital. After the case, he showed me and my students a note she had scrawled and left on the witness stand while testifying: "I am going to kill myself." On the stand she insists she is no longer depressed and will not try to kill herself; at the same time, she is writing the note.

A man who was released on writ walked away from the dock and stood uncertainly by the court gate. He began sniffling and repeating, "Where shall I go?"

A man who had just been released on writ went out into the hallway and took a swing at an aide. He was immediately taken into custody by the sheriff.

Some who are released are readmitted within a few hours or days. Although the process of "institutionalism"—dependence upon the institution—has been used to explain cycles of readmission, in the case of the mental hospital part of the explanation may be ambivalence. In one case, a young woman spent several years in a cycle of admission and release. During her admission phases, she was a model and well-behaved patient, thus facilitating release. As soon as she was released, she became extremely troublesome and was reinstitutionalized; the cycle then began again. Involuntary patients who do not file writs when they know how to do so may also be expressing ambivalence; they may complain about railroading or express the desire to get out but not pursue avenues of release:

At the State Hospital, a disheveled, sleepy looking woman of about twenty sidled up to me with a conspiratorial air: "I have to get out of here. My husband put me here. He's sleeping with my sister. I'm with the FBI." Later I heard the MHC ask if she wanted to file a writ; she said, "Oh no, I might as well stay here."

The Kenneth Donaldson Case

Even among those who press their case for release insistently, signs of ambivalence may appear. One such case is that of Kenneth Donaldson (see also Chap. 2), who was released from Chattahoochee State Hospital in Florida in 1971 after 15 years of involuntary confinement. At first glance, Donaldson's case seems to be a clear example of railroading on the part of authorities and singlemindedness on the part of Donaldson. But a careful examination of his touching and well-written book *Insanity Inside Out* (1976) gives a somewhat more ambiguous picture.

Donaldson was diagnosed as a paranoid schizophrenic upon his admission to Chattahoochee; the books gives ample evidence of the paranoid schizophrenic's typical delusions that others are focusing on him in order to persecute him. Both before and after the 15-year hospitalization these thoughts persist. In 1943 he had a blackout after hearing disembodied threats in his workplace. In the early 1950s

I was still writing letters to important people.... There seemed increasing interest by strangers and by all employers in my ideas. In Los Angeles my papers were ransacked in my desk drawer and there was cigarette smoke in the room, though neither the maid nor I smoked. . . . A more baffling interference was someone's putting medicine in my food in a Lynwood restaurant. . . .

When I went to the toilet, noise would be made to taunt me. [Donaldson 1976, p. 43]

There are indications that Donaldson was somewhat paranoid and suffering from minor auditory hallucinations even after his release: "I soon had my own twelve months hammering on the ceiling and wall, blowing of a horn every time I turned on my bathroom light at night" (1976, p. 323).

But from the evidence of his book and from his psychiatric history, Donaldson was clearly not dangerous to himself or others, and he was not even very mentally disordered. Donaldson's degree of disorder, at least as it appears in retrospect, was mild (although he could have improved or deteriorated during his stay in the hospital).

Why, then, did doctors and judges insist upon his long involuntary confinement? Many times during the 15 years he was incarcerated, Donaldson came up before psychiatric boards for hearings on his sanity, and each time he was refused release into his own custody (he would have been allowed release to the custody of his family, which he refused). Some of the grounds for refusing his release come close to railroading: most particularly, continuing his commitment on the basis of his refusal to admit that he was ill, and because, as a Christian Scientist, he refused psychoactive medication. The most poignant ground for refusing his release was his "delusion" that one day he was going to write a book about his mental hospitalization.

A labeling theory approach would explain Donaldson's continued incarceration in terms of audience labeling and escalation into a mentally ill self. A medical model approach would propose that he suffered from a minor degree of paranoia. But a combined model would stress both the processes of labeling that occurred in the hospital and the existence of delusions which precipitated some of the labeling. In the context of rationality, a medical model approach would assume that Donaldson was incapable of rationally deciding about involuntary commitment, while a legal model would assume that, if mental illness was not present (he was just railroaded), then he could make a rational decision for release.

But it appears that Donaldson, just as he was both labeled and clinically paranoid, was also ambivalent. A person with enough observational power and intelligence to know just what the hospital would and would not like about his behavior, Donaldson consistently refused to take medication, admit his illness, or be released to his parents or friends:

If I gave one inch and let my daughter sign me out, I would lose the whole case against institutional psychiatry, for then the doctors could say they had cured me and let me go. [Donaldson 1976, p. 231]

[Dr.] Rich said "You're schizophrenic. I'll tell you what, Donaldson, I promise to let you go one year from now if you'll take a course of medication for six months."
    "No," I said. [P. 224]

There is no reason to doubt that Donaldson's claim that his refusal to "play along with the system" was a matter of principle. On the other hand, his refusal could also be motivated by a less conscious ambivalence about release, or a conscious or unconscious manipulation of the labelers in the desired direction.

Patients in long-term hospital situations may be so ill that they are indeed irrational, incompetent, incoherent, and incapable of expressing any will in the matter of their existence. Others may be rational enough to assess their situation and the social context and come to the conclusion that they are better off where they are, while still others preserve their rationality by engaging in autonomous activity within the hospital. Patients who come to Metropolitan Court might seem on the face of it to be the least motivated to stay in the hospital—indeed, some of them are. But there are many who, despite the filing of a writ of habeas corpus or insistence upon a conservatorship hearing, are ambivalent about their hospitalization. Some of these ambivalent patients blow their cases by actions which seem irrational but *which may be quite rational in the context of their ambivalence.*

Labeling and the Identity of the Mentally Ill

One consequence of labeling persons as mentally ill and consigning them to mental hospitals is that they may become more dependent, get used to institutional provision of their needs, and promote a cycle of institutionalism. At the same time, the stigma of mental hospitalization and mental illness can close off conventional options such as employment and family residence. Even critics of labeling theory grudgingly concede the likelihood of institutionalism in long-term hospitalization and the existence of some stigmatization for those labeled mentally ill (Gove 1975, pp. 57–67). But the question of the transformation of self-identity as a result of labeling by external audiences is more problematic.

The theory of secondary deviation, as indicated, proposes that the process of audience typing and the closure of conventional role options leads to self-identification as deviant. The hospitalized mental

patient would be expected to be extremely vulnerable to this transformation because of the pervasiveness of the typing. As the work of
Temerlin, Goffman, and Rosenhan underline, the hospitalized patient
is liable to have his or her every act classified as a symptom of mental
illness. Scheff (1966) summarizes the labeling perpsective on the self
diagnosed as schizophrenic:

> PATIENT: "We schizophrenics say and do a lot of stuff that is un-
> important and then we mix important things in with all this
> to see if the doctor cares enough to see them and feel them."
> ... Note that the patient has applied to herself a deviant
> label ("We schizophrenics") and that her behavior fits Lemert's
> definition of secondary deviation ... a stable role performance
> may arise when the actor's role imagery locks in with the
> type of "deference" which he regularly receives. [P. 62]

One of the most instructive sources of information on the purported
transformation of the self of mental patients is ex-patients' own accounts of the way they have perceived themselves.

Ex-Patients and Self-Perceptions

An interesting contrast can be made between the self-identification
of Donaldson, discussed above, and of Mark Vonnegut (1975). Vonnegut was hospitalized several times, for brief periods, for schizophrenia. By contrast, Donaldson was hospitalized for 15 years. During his lengthy confinement, Donaldson refused to accede to psychiatric labels and consistently denied that he was mentally ill; he
still insists, as indicated above, that he is not paranoid and that
person or persons unknown pay attention to, annoy, or harass him.
Vonnegut, on the other hand, views his schizophrenia as real, as a
condition—even as genetically caused—and as the trigger for a
nightmare of hallucinations he has experienced several times and
attempts to avoid experiencing again:

> Most diseases can be separated from one's self, and seen as
> foreign intruding entities. Schizophrenia is very poorly behaved
> in this respect. Colds, ulcers, flu and cancer are things we get.
> Schizophrenic is something we are. It affects the things we most
> identify with as making us what we are.
>   If this weren't problem enough, schiz [*sic*] comes on slow and
> comes on fast, stays a minute or days or years, can be heaven one
> moment, hell the next, enhance abilities and destroy them, back
> and forth several times a day and always weaving itself in-
> extricably into what we call ourselves. It can transform only a
> small corner of our lives or turn the whole show upside down,
> always giving few if any clues as to when it left or what was us
> and what was schiz. [Vonnegut 1975, p. ix]

What were the differences between Donaldson and Vonnegut? In the context of labeling theory, Donaldson seems far more vulnerable to the process and impact of labeling than Vonnegut; indeed, he was structurally more vulnerable to the process. He is from a blue-collar family; he is neither well off nor highly educated, structurally ill-prepared to withstand the definitions of more powerful others. He was isolated from his family during most of his confinement, and he had few conventional options to return to. He was subject to definition as a mentally ill person for 15 years within a total institution. Yet he did not see himself as ill.

Vonnegut, on the other hand, was a "hippie, son of a counterculture hero, B.A. in religion" (p. ix), with strong family ties, a background of wealth and privilege, continuing conventional options, and only a few months' sojourn in the mental hospital. But he came to, and still does, define himself as ill. In fact, his view of schizophrenia is that it is *more* of an illness than physical illness. Vonnegut speaks with fear and watchfulness, in his autobiography, of potential triggers for his symptoms.

The difference between Donaldson's and Vonnegut's experiences and self-identification can be more powerfully explained within the medical model rather than the labeling perspective. Vonnegut was simply far more ill than Donaldson, far more schizophrenic. Vonnegut's own experience with his condition led him to his self-definition with cogency and urgency. In contrast, Donaldson's mild illness—in Vonnegut's words, "transforming only a small corner" of his life—was not alienating enough to convince him that his audiences were correct. Donaldson's own experiences of substantial rationality and control even within the confines of a mental hospital were important aspects of his self-definition as normal.

It might be theoretically useful to separate the processes of labeling from the transformation of self-identity, at least for mental illness. I would argue that the presence, type, and degree of mental illness is the most powerful predictor of the assumption of a mentally ill identity. On the other hand, given the same level of mental illness, the deviant's resources vis-à-vis the labelers become a powerful predictor of the vulnerability to labeling and treatment as mentally ill.

But ex-patients' identities can be affected by the labels of significant others as well as the labels of social control agents. In the Bay Area Studies interviews of 17 schizophrenic ex-patients and their husbands (and other relatives), both the women and their husbands were interviewed at various intervals to determine their perceptions of the wives' mental illness. Because the interviews were repeated, we were also able to examine the impact of factors such as mood and situation on self-definitions from these data (Warren and Messinger 1980).

The women's perceptions of whether they were mentally ill or well, getting better or worse, varied with their sense of feeling well or not well at that particular time, and, interestingly, whether or not they were performing household tasks adequately (Warren and Messinger 1980). Their sense of self has been called by Messinger "fragile"; it varies with moods and situations. Sometimes, the situation included other's current or past labeling activities. More often, since these housewives were alone much of the time, their self-conceptualizations were derived from self-monitoring and self-observation. What the hospital experience had precipitated was not an automatic self-label but an acute awareness of, and anxiety about, self.

Only a few of the Bay Area ex-patient women were, over time, convinced that they were completely well and only a few that they were ill. One woman who seemed to be among the least severely schizophrenic believed that she was not mentally ill and had been railroaded into the hospital. Another woman who was severely disturbed defined her illness as a physical one, caused by such factors as menopause and a bad back. Another severely disturbed woman was the only one of the 17 who consistently viewed herself as mad and longed to be returned to the hospital. The majority were not sure whether they were well or ill, getting better or worse; they felt fragile, dubious, and variable about their selves.

At the same time, the husbands of most of the 17 women insisted in their interviews, and to their wives, that the women were not mentally ill. Put simply, these husband audiences denied mental illness. Their denial appears to be connected with their appreciation of the wives' functions as housewives and child-care specialists; whatever the source, it remains the case that, while the *audiences* massively denied mental illness, the *ex-patients* varied in their self-conceptions from a parallel denial to a sense of fragility or to a sense of illness. Not only do officials' labels within the mental hospital not determine a self-identity as mentally ill, other audiences' denial of a previously applied label does not determine a self-identity as mentally healthy.

It seems important, conceptually, to distinguish between types of deviance in applying labeling theory; mental illness, if it has aspects of a condition, may be different in this respect than other forms of deviance. It also seems important to distinguish between types of audience who react to deviance and thereby exert a potential influence on identity. Yet another dimension of identity transformation is the voluntary or involuntary affiliation with the audience doing the typing.

English studies of adults put in prisons or hospitals have confirmed the ability of identity to withstand audience labeling (Musgrove 1977). Although it would be, as indicated, an error to generalize findings from other areas to mental illness (or from England to America), Musgrove's summary of these studies is an interesting source of ideas about the self: "The case studies bring seriously into question the importance of significant others in personal change, and they make abundantly clear the importance of the historical self" (p. 221).

The historical self is an important concept for understanding the reactions of ex-patients to hospitalization; most of the Bay Area women, for example, relied both on their historical (prehospital) and patient selves to construct a sense of self in the present. So did Donaldson. But if the mental disorder is severe, as in the case of Vonnegut, that sense of historical self may be forgotten, made fearful, confused, and cognitively reinterpreted.

Musgrove distinguishes between voluntary and involuntary institutionalization and affiliation in adult life and the difference this dimension makes for identity change or continuity: "In the five groups which had voluntarily embraced a new life, change was a moral quest for one's real and authentic self. In the two groups which experienced involuntary change, holding firm to one's historic self had a similar moral purpose" (p. 224).

Using Musgrove's logic, it could be hypothesized that voluntary hospitalization would produce more change in the sense of self than involuntary; indeed, the attempts of mental hospitals to get patients to recognize their illness as a first step toward cure make sense in Musgrove's model. We would then expect the less severely disordered, like Donaldson, to hold fast to the historic self—and to do so with a sense of moral courage—and the more severely disordered, whose historic self has been fragmented, to undergo identity transformation. Confusion and ambivalence about wellness or illness would be expected for middle levels of mental disorder.

A Medical and Labeling Model of Mental Disorder

My experience at Metropolitan Court and in other parts of the mental health system has led me to a reexamination of previously taken-for-granted notions about mental illness. I want to argue for a model of mental illness that takes into account both the labeling process, with its implications of power relations and the structure of social resources, and the X factor of madness upon which the medical model is premised. I understand madness as:

1. an outcome of interactions between labeler and labelee;
2. in which sociohistorically formed categories are used to type

and process those labeled as mad, bringing power relations into the process at the level of frameworks for understanding the world;

3. having features of internal stress on the part of the labelee related to a subjective sense of loss of control, and situational, interactional, and relational factors;

4. in which power and control is negotiable and negotiated, and dependent upon the resources which can be marshaled by labeler and labelee, and on their purposes at hand;

5. in which the labelee may, consciously or unconsciously, either desire or resist the label or the process of hospitalization, or be ambivalent;

6. in which the transformation of identity of the mental patient is a possible but not necessary outcome of labeling and is dependent upon both the historical self and the subjective degree of disorder and distress;

7. in which the transformation of life-style to dependency on the institutional could be a product either of passive institutionalism or of rational decision making.

In viewing mental illness as the intersection between others' labeling and a condition, interpreted by the mentally ill self, I also take a stand on the legal and medical models of human action—and one with which I am less comfortable. The medical model is premised on a view of human conduct as shaped by internal forces of which the actor may or may not be aware; the labeling model is premised on a view of human conduct as shaped by external forces of which the actor is a pawn. Neither view gives much credence to the legal model of rationality, free will, competence, blame, and responsibility.

To define mental illness as at the intersection of labeling and the medical model is to take it outside the frame of legal rationality, even despite the attribution of considerable manipulative rationality to patients. This frame removal is what Morse argues for in the next chapter and what Zusman argues against in Chapter 5. I find the model of free-willed, responsible human action more resonant with my preferences than either the labeling or the medical model. But in the area of mental illness, I have found that I must abandon my preferences.

In the next two chapters, Morse, a lawyer and psychologist, argues for abolition of involuntary civil commitment, and Zusman, a psychiatrist, argues for its retention. Thus Part I concludes the nonmaterial dimensions of decision making—which include the law and perspectives on mental illness with the policy debate based on the categories of legal and mental illness.

4 A Preference for Liberty
The Case against Involuntary Commitment of the Mentally Disordered

Stephen J. Morse, J.D., Ph.D.

*I*n the last two decades there have been changes of immense magnitude in the laws pertaining to involuntary commitment of mental patients to hospitals (Developments 1974). In the 1960s, involuntary mental hospitalization and treatment were decisions made almost entirely within the discretion of mental health professionals. Although in theory commitment had to be accomplished in conformity with statutory requirements, effective substantive and procedural restraints on families and mental health professionals who sought involuntary commitment were virtually nonexistent. Moreover, the degree of power and discretion vested in mental health professionals was not considered problematic—it seemed fitting to allow medical personnel to make what were viewed as essentially medical decisions.

By the mid-1960s, however, the picture changed radically. Lawyers interested in civil rights turned their attention to involuntary hospitalization at the same time that various conceptual and political

Stephen J. Morse is professor of law, University of Southern California Law Center, and professor of psychiatry and the behavioral sciences, University of Southern California School of Medicine (A.B. 1966, Tufts University; J.D. 1970, Ph.D. [Psychology and Social Relations] 1973, Harvard University).

This chapter is based on a paper presented in June 1981 at the 6th International Symposium on Law and Psychiatry held under the auspices of the Institute of Law, Psychiatry and Public Policy of the University of Virginia School of Law and School of Medicine. In modified form, it was published in the *California Law Review* (1982), and it will be published in the author's forthcoming book, *The Jurisprudence of Craziness* (Oxford University Press). The author wishes to thank John Monahan, David Rosenhan, and Serena Stier for providing perceptive and helpful, if not always assenting, comments on earlier drafts; and his research assistants, Joan Mussoff, Jan Harris, Peg Casey, and Maureen Lee, for their help.

critiques of psychiatry (Laing 1967; Szasz 1961, 1963), especially institutional psychiatry, gathered momentum. In addition, the theory of community mental health and the wide usage of psychotropic drugs appeared to render long-term involuntary hospitalization less advised and less necessary. The legal watersheds, in my opinion, were California's Lanterman-Petris-Short Act (LPS), which went into effect in 1969, and the 1972 Wisconsin federal district court decision, *Lessard* v. *Schmidt,* both of which limited the state's power to commit persons involuntarily. Following LPS vast majority of the states legislatively reformed commitment laws (e.g., Mass., 1970; N.C., 1973), again limiting state power. After *Lessard,* numerous cases found state commitment laws unconstitutional and applied stringent substantive and procedural due process protections to the involuntary commitment process (e.g., *Lynch* v. *Baxley,* 1974). Most recently, as courts have faced a "new generation" of issues concerning rights of mental patients, there has been an expansion of the right of involuntary patients to refuse treatment (*Rogers* v. *Okin,* 1979, 1980; *Rennie* v. *Klein,* 1978, 1981; but see *A.E. & R.R.* v. *Mitchell,* 1980). The balance between individual liberty and autonomy on the one hand, and the state's paternalistic right to confine and treat persons involuntarily on the other, has clearly shifted to a preference for liberty.

The "legalization" of commitment laws and practices has occasioned an enormous and all too often dismaying debate which has been marred by charges and countercharges that are overblown and unfair. Involuntary commitment and the actors in the system are portrayed in quite polar terms as good or evil. Proponents of legalization are accused of lack of compassion and of not understanding clinical realities. Many mental health professionals are outraged by what they view as wrong-headed legal intrusions on their right properly to practice their professions. They believe that, on balance, patients have been harmed by legalization, and they have described the outcome using phrases such as patients "dying with their rights on" (Treffert 1977), or as patients having "the right to rot" (Appelbaum and Gutheil 1980). These professionals concede that there have been abuses in commitment practices and hospital conditions in the past, but they believe that legalization is an unwise remedy and that it certainly has gone too far. Conversely, proponents of medical authority are in turn indicted for being unconcerned with liberty and dignity and for acting in bad faith. Well-meaning mental health professionals are labeled jailers or worse.

To buttress their positions, advocates find or hypothesize apparently clear cases that seem to make difficult issues easily resolvable. Such cases arouse sympathy or anger, but they do not stimulate sensible discussion. It is relatively simple to find or construct "easy" cases, but doing so is an injustice to the enormous social, moral, and legal complexity of the question of involuntary hospitalization. Comparatively few actual cases are so extreme that most reasonable persons would agree that involuntary hospitalization was or was not warranted.[1] Furthermore, society would not create a complex and expensive system of involuntary commitment to deal with the few cases of extreme craziness and disability that undeniably might seem to warrant the need for involuntary hospitalization. Nor would society abolish such a system to avoid a few clear cases of "railroading" normal persons into hospitals. All those concerned with the involuntary commitment debate should recognize that most proponents of commitment are not unconcerned with the liberty of those affected and that most proponents of legalization or abolition of commitment are not lacking in compassion or concern for citizens who are disordered and apparently unable to cope successfully in our society. Name calling should cease, and advocates should no longer use unrepresentative cases to support their positions, for such evidence produces both poor social science and unsound bases for sensible public policy. What should be clear is that there is no ideal solution to the personal, family, and social problems associated with mental disorder. Maintaining *or* abolishing (or severely limiting) involuntary commitment will create costs and benefits for disordered persons and society at large. What is needed is reasonable and realistic analysis of the likely outcomes of various approaches to the problem of involuntary hospitalization.

The purpose of this chapter is to offer a reasonable policy argument—not a constitutional argument—in favor of abolishing or severely limiting involuntary commitment of the mentally disordered.[2] It must be acknowledged at the outset, however, that some clearly avoidable harm will come to individuals and to society if the positions taken were adopted as social policy. It must also be acknowledged that a reasonable and coherent case can probably be

1. This is especially true, I believe, if the necessity for hospitalization is considered in a context where decent alternative treatment programs are available.

2. Discussion will focus on abolition in order to set forth the views most starkly. It should be understood, however, that the arguments may also be used to support extensive limitations on involuntary commitment. Constitutional arguments are not presented. A coherent argument that involuntary commitment is unconstitutional can be constructed, but it is clearly unpersuasive and probably incorrect. Because the basis of the argument is not grounded in constitutional law, it should be understood that the meaning of terms like "liberty" and "fundamental rights" as used herein is not coextensive with their meaning as declared by the Supreme Court. Nevertheless, even if involuntary commitment is constitutional, I believe its existence is a gravely erroneous social policy. Finally, the case presented applies only to adults. I believe the case against committing minors is even stronger, but the issues are sufficiently different to require separate consideration.

made for maintaining involuntary commitment and for extending the authority of mental health professionals within the system. Nevertheless, I conclude that *on balance* our society, the mentally disordered, and even mental health professionals, will be better off without involuntary commitment. At a time when many argue that legalization has gone too far, this chapter suggests that it has not gone far enough. To support these conclusions, this chapter will consider systematically the assumptions, evidence, and arguments concerning involuntary hospitalization. Although I hope to persuade by this effort—or at least to help shift the burden of persuasion to the proponents of involuntary hospitalization—I will be satisfied if this chapter convinces readers that a reasonable and compassionate argument can be made for abolition of involuntary commitment and if it helps place the commitment debate on a more realistic and reasoned basis.

The Argument against Involuntary Commitment

Involuntary commitment is an extraordinary exercise of the police power and paternalism of the state. Although liberty is constantly infringed in various ways by state action—prevention detention through certain bail practices is but one example—the deprivation of liberty authorized by involuntary commitment laws is among the most serious restrictions on individual freedom the state may impose. Moreover, it may be imposed on the basis of predictions, without the prior occurrence of legally relevant behavior such as dangerous acts. Typically, there must be exceptionally weighty interests justifying such an exceptional exercise of state power. It must therefore be asked, in light of our national preference for liberty, whether a system of involuntary commitment, whereby some mentally disordered citizens may be deprived of their liberty according to wide substantive standards and relatively lax procedures, can be justified? It is argued that it cannot be.

The lesser preference for liberty in the civil commitment system is supposedly justified because its primary purposes are the care and treatment of sick persons who allegedly lack mental competence and/or a normal degree of ability to control their behavior, which leads them to harm themselves and others. Comparison to the criminal justice system will be illuminating here. Criminals are considered blameworthy and thus are held properly to deserve punishment. Crazy persons are considered sick and thus in need of care and treatment. The criminal justice system incarcerates primarily for the good of society; the civil commitment system allegedly incarcerates primarily for the supposed good of the individual committed. Because the civil commitment system aims to do good for the sick recipients of its ministrations, its lesser standards and procedures for the deprivation of liberty are allegedly warranted (*Addington* v. *Texas,* 1979; *Parham* v. *J.R.*, 1979; Livermore et al. 1968). It would be inhumane, it is argued, to prevent needy persons from receiving services because of unnecessarily precise and stringent substantive and procedural requirements for involuntary hospitalization. Even if involuntary hospitalization is often a poor remedy, it is argued, on grounds of humanity and social safety and comfort it is necessary.

The objections to involuntary civil commitment are both theoretical and practical. First, it is difficult or impossible to support, with theory or data, the differential treatment of mentally disordered persons that allows them, but not normal persons, to be involuntarily committed.[3] Second, the system is unlikely to identify accurately those persons who should arguably be committed; consequently, large numbers of persons who are not properly committable will be unjustly and needlessly deprived of their liberty. Third, it is unlikely that the states will be able to provide the quality of care and treatment for those committed that is absolutely necessary to justify the enormous deprivation of liberty caused by commitment. Finally,

3. Since this chapter, like the whole book, deals with persons who allegedly suffer from a mental disorder, it will be useful for purposes of clarity to describe how mental disorder is defined and used in this chapter. It is impossible to provide a noncontroversial generic definition of mental disorder. The American Psychiatric Association admits as much in its currently operative and authoritative *Diagnostic and Statistical Manual of Mental Disorders (Third Edition) - DSM-III* (1980), but then provides the following "conceptual" influences on the decision to categorize a "condition" as a mental disorder in DSM-III:

"In DSM-III each of the mental disordes is conceptualized as a clinically significant behavioral or psychological syndrome or a pattern that occurs in an individual and that is typically associated with either a painful symptom (distress) or impairment in one or more important areas of functioning (disability). In addition, there is an inference that there is a behavioral, psychological, or biological dysfunction, and that the disturbance is not only in the relationship between the individual and society. (When the disturbance is *limited* to a conflict between an individual and society, this may represent social deviance, which may or may not be commendable, but is not by itself a mental disorder.)

"In DSM-III there is no assumption that each mental disorder is a discrete entity with sharp boundaries (discontinuity) between it and other mental disorders, as well as between it and No Mental Disorder" (1980, p. 6).

I have argued previously that the categories of mental disorders all describe behaviors that are considered crazy, meaning inexplicably irrational, weird, wild, nonsensical, or the like. The severity of mental disorder, according to this view, is simply a reflection of the degree of craziness exhibited by the actor. I prefer the term "crazy" because it is more descriptive and carries fewer connotations about disease processes that beg important questions about self-control (the full argument is presented in Morse [1978, pp. 543–60]. In this chapter the terms "mental disorder" and "craziness" as described in this footnote will be used interchangeably. Of course, the chapter is concerned primarily with those crazy persons who are hospitalized involuntarily, and it should be recognized that these persons are usually those considered severely crazy or mentally disordered.

most, and probably all, of the alleged benefits of involuntary hospitalization can be provided by less-intrusive alternatives that are equally efficacious but produce much less deprivation of liberty. Let us consider these objections in order.

Mentally Disordered Persons Should Not Be Legally Distinguishable from Normal Persons

The primary and overriding theoretical reason for allowing involuntary commitment of only the mentally disordered is the belief that their legally relevant behavior is the inexorable product of uncontrollable disorder (Developments 1974), whereas the legally relevant behavior of normal persons is the product of free choice. Because it is believed that much of the behavior of mentally disordered persons is the product of their disorder, it is presumed that disordered persons are not factually, morally, and legally responsible for their behavior (Chodoff 1976; Parsons 1970; Siegler and Osmond 1973). It is believed, for example, that a normal dangerous person is capable of choosing not to violate the law and of repentance if the law is violated. Furthermore, he or she can be deterred by the sanctions of the criminal law (LaFave and Scott 1972). Thus, to preserve that person's autonomy and dignity, the dangerous normal person cannot be incarcerated until he or she offends the criminal law, even if the person's future dangerousness is highly predictable (In re *Williams*, 1958). But if a mentally disordered person only appears dangerous or simply utters threats, he or she can be committed because it is believed the individual will ultimately have little or no choice in deciding whether or not to act violently. The disordered person allegedly lacks understanding or behavioral control and therefore cannot change his or her mind or be deterred (Model Penal Code §4.01, 1955). Consequently, it does not violate the disordered person's dignity or autonomy to hospitalize him or her preventatively, even in the absence of strong predictive evidence of future dangerousness (see Chap. 2).

The belief that disordered persons in general particularly lack competence or behavioral control is a strongly ingrained social dogma that underlies the special legal treatment accorded mentally disordered persons (Goldstein 1967). But what is the basis for this belief? A major distinguishing aspect of most behavior labeled serious mental disorder is that it is irrationally inexplicable; it is crazy behavior that makes little or no sense to others (Fingarette 1976; Fingarette and Hasse 1979; Moore 1975). When a person behaves in such a way, there is a tendency to believe that the person is out of control (Rabkin 1972; Sarbin and Mancuso 1970) (see Chap. 3). After all, who, in his or her right mind, would choose to act crazily? If we simply cannot make sense of the behavior of another, then we believe there is something wrong with the person, a state believed to be beyond an actor's control in most cases (Morse 1978). For example, if a patient tells us that he will not take his medicine because the doctor is a hostile agent trying to poison the patient, we are likely to believe the patient is mentally disordered—the reason for the drug refusal is delusional, after all—and that this treatment refusal is incompetent because it is the product of the delusion and not of the patient's free, rational choice.

But the assertion that the irrationality or other behavior of mentally disordered persons is compelled, in contrast to the freely chosen behavior of normal persons, is a belief that rests on commonsense intuitions and not on scientific evidence (Morse 1978). Indeed, whether a person has sufficient behavioral control or sufficient competence to be held morally and legally responsible and autonomous, and thus not subject to involuntary commitment, is fundamentally a moral, social, and legal question—not a scientific one (Morse 1978). Social and behavioral scientists commonly provide information about the pressures affecting an actor's freedom of choice, but the law must determine for itself when the actor is no longer to be treated as autonomous and competent (Hardisty 1973; Morse 1976, 1978; Suarez 1967; Szasz 1957).

In fact, empirical evidence bearing on the question of the control disordered persons have—and empirical evidence cannot definitively prove or disprove that anyone has or lacks free will (Mackie 1977)—would seem to indicate that mentally disordered persons have a great deal of control over their crazy behavior and legally relevant behavior related to it; indeed, often they may have as much control over their behavior as normal persons do (Morse 1978). Even in apparently easy cases where it seems clear that the legally relevant behavior is the product of mental disorder—for example, the delusional person who refuses needed medication or attacks the doctor because he or she believes the doctor is a hostile agent—we cannot be sure that the person was incapable, as opposed to *unwilling*, to behave rationally or to control him or herself. All that is certain is that the person did not behave rationally compared to dominant social standards.

For comparison, imagine the case of a habitually hot-tempered person who takes offense at something his or her doctor says and threatens to harm the doctor. Is this person more in control than the delusional person? Or, consider the case of a severely ill cardiac patient who refuses to modify dietary, exercise, or smoking habits because the person prefers his or her habitually unhealthy life-style. The person's behavior can disrupt the well-being of the family, help drive up health care and insurance costs, and, if the result is an untimely death, might impoverish the family. Is this person more rational or in control than the delusional person, and, if so, in what sense? Of course, we all "understand" the behavior of the hot-tempered person or the cardiac patient, but the inexplicably irrational behavior of the delusional person makes no sense whatsoever. Still, there is no conclusive means to prove that any of these persons has greater or lesser capacity for control or rationality than the other. Despite this, civil commitment is possible only for the delusional person; the hot-tempered person may be detained only *after* striking or attempting to strike the doctor, and the cardiac patient cannot be forced to enter a hospital or to change his or her life-style.

Because there is little support for the proposition that the mentally disordered in particular lack the general ability to control their behavior compared to normal persons, I submit that there is little reason for the state to authorize the involuntary civil commitment of only mentally disordered persons. I am not suggesting, of course, that all mentally disordered persons are capable of reasonable rationality and self-control; such a claim would be unrealistic. Nevertheless, the capability for rationality and self-control is distributed along a continuum, and most disordered persons meet the low threshold in these capacities necessary for freedom from involuntary state intrusion in a society that highly values liberty. Moreover, many people not considered mentally disordered repetitively behave in ways that are most harmful to themselves and society. Although such behavior is attributed to character or weakness or some other cause not based on mental disorder, the intuition is that this behavior also is out of control. Yet, although the capacity for control of disordered persons is in general indistinguishable from that capacity in normal persons, only those labeled mentally disordered can be massively deprived of their liberty by involuntary hospitalization. The language and conceptual apparatus of the disorder or disease concept is the primary support for this distinction, but in fact the labels are conclusions about alleged lack of control, not proof of it. A system of involuntary commitment for only disordered persons cannot be justified on the basis of the alleged lack of free choice of disordered persons. They should not be treated differently to their disadvantage in terms of their freedom from confinement and freedom to live their lives as they choose.[4]

A second possible reason that only crazy persons may be com-

4. And, as we shall see presently, involuntary commitment of only the mentally disordered is not sensible on utilitarian grounds either. Little benefit accrues to society or to the committed individual from a system that applies only to the mentally disordered. The costs are too great and the benefits are too few to justify a commitment system that is mainly theoretically based on only an intuitive hunch.

mitted is the belief that they are especially dangerous (Cocozza and Steadman 1976; Sarbin and Mancuso 1970). If so, society might be justified in instituting special measures that would make it particularly easy to intervene in the lives of crazy persons for either their own good or the good of society. But this argument may be disposed of relatively easily. Mental disorder is both an over- and under-inclusive predictor of dangerousness; most crazy persons are not dangerous and many normal persons are (Rappeport 1967).

At one point it was believed that mentally disordered persons were especially prone to violence, but later empirical studies tended to support the opposite conclusion, which in turn became the accepted wisdom for many years (Brill and Malzberg 1962; Monahan and Splane 1980; Rappeport 1967) (see Chap. 2). In the last few years, however, a series of studies has tended to show that ex-mental hospital patients have higher arrest rates (not conviction rates) than nonpatients (Rabkin 1979). Such findings have led some to conclude that mentally disordered persons may be especially dangerous. But close analysis of the data reveals that prior criminality rather than mental status is the variable that accounts for the recently increased arrest rates among mental patients—patients now tend to have higher previous arrest rates than formerly (Steadman et al. 1978b; but see, also, Sosowsky 1980). In sum, mental patients are not especially dangerous, and, if they are slightly more dangerous than nonpatients, it is not a consequence of their mental disorders (Morse 1978). Therefore, social safety is a primary goal of involuntary hospitalization, it will not be served by singling out the mentally disordered. As a class they are not especially dangerous, and, in terms of absolute numbers, they account for much less violence than normal persons do.

A third reason given for allowing commitment of only the mentally disordered is the view that such persons are especially incompetent, that is, incapable of deciding rationally what is in their own best interests (Developments 1974; Morse 1978; Stone 1975). The concept of incompetence is difficult to analyze, but it is clear that it refers to an *inability* to decide rationally or to manage one's life, rather than to the fact that the individual in question makes decisions that might be considered irrational or based upon seemingly irrational reasons. The legal system focuses on the decision-making process rather than decisional outcomes in order to protect liberty and autonomy (*Colyar v. Third Judicial District Court*, 1979; Livermore et al. 1968):[5] so long as

5. Of course, process and outcome cannot always be so neatly separated. Process only becomes significant, typically, in cases where an outcome or series of outcomes seems unduly irrational. Moreover it will often be assumed that the process must have been irrational if an irrational decision is reached, even though an individual may be able to provide an apparently rational explanation for the behavior.

one is capable of rational decision making and managing, the person will be left free to make irrational decisions or to mismanage his or her life (and to suffer the consequences) (Morse 1978). If, however, the person is not so capable, overriding the actor's judgment and substituting the judgment of the state appears justified. Of course, a person who consistently demonstrates bad judgment or gives apparently irrational reasons for his or her decisions is often assessed as being *incapable* of exercising sound judgment, at least in particular areas of his or her life. Nevertheless, it is generally believed that, unless the person is crazy, he or she is probably capable of deciding rationally, even if most of the evidence is to the contrary (see e.g., *Commonwealth* v. *Mutina*, 1975).

Are the mentally disordered particularly incompetent? The question is crucial because involuntary commitment substitutes the state's judgment about the necessity for hospitalization (and often for treatment as well) for the judgment of the individual. Commitment at least implies the judgment that the person cannot cope or make decisions in his or her own best interest (Allen et al. 1966). There is, however, little empirical or theoretical justification for the belief that the mentally disordered as a class are especially incapable of managing their lives or deciding for themselves what is in their own best interests (*Rogers* v. *Okin*, 1979). Available empirical evidence demonstrates that the mentally disordered as a class are probably not more incompetent than normal persons as a class (e.g., Buttiglieri et al. 1969; Howard 1975; Tolor et al. 1976). Indeed, there is no necessary relationship between mental disorder and legal incompetence (Morse 1978). Again, mental disorder is an over- and underinclusive indicator: many normal persons are incompetent (*Los Angeles Times* 1975), and many, if not most, mentally disordered persons are not (Brakel and Rock 1971). Consequently, the premise of the commitment system that crazy people are particularly incompetent is unsupported. Some disordered persons are clearly incompetent according to any reasonable criteria, but the social goal of reducing the consequences of incompetence is not well-served by allowing involuntary hospitalization, guardianship, or treatment of only the mentally disordered.

A final reason for allowing commitment of only mentally disordered persons is the belief that they are specially treatable (Livermore et al. 1968; but cf. Katz 1969). The mental disorders themselves and the dangerous and incompetent behaviors that allegedly ensue from mental disorder supposedly are particularly ameliorable by mental health treatment methods. Although this assertion seems reasonable, once again there is little evidence to support it (Livermore et al. 1968; cf. May 1976; Stone 1975). There is every reason to believe that normal persons who are dangerous or incompetent people are equally treatable (or untreatable). Indeed, there is good reason to believe that normality is positively correlated with likelihood of treatment success (Frank 1973; Schofield 1964). Moreover, the consequent social disabilities that are in many cases more worrisome than the mental health symptoms themselves, are far harder to treat (May 1976; White and Bennet 1981). Differential treatability is thus not a supportable rationale for allowing involuntary commitment of only the mentally disordered.

These comments on the lack of self-control, dangerousness, incompetence, and treatability of the mentally disordered, do not imply that no seriously mentally disordered person lacks self-control or is dangerous or incompetent as a result of his or her mental disorder, nor do they mean that the mentally disordered are per se untreatable. A person who is assaultive because of delusions is dangerous. And although lack of self-control and incompetence are hard to assess, in some cases a commonsense determination that a crazy person lacks self-control or is incompetent can be made. Finally, many mentally disordered persons are treatable with some likelihood of success. Both data and theory indicate, however, that the mentally disordered as a class are not particularly lacking the capability for rationality and self-control, nor are they particularly dangerous, incompetent, or treatable. There would seem to be little support for an involuntary civil commitment system which is imposed only on the mentally disordered. Involuntary commitment of only the mentally disordered will not specially protect society, nor will it protect large number of persons from themselves.[6] And, large numbers of citizens will lose their liberty based on a premise that robs them of dignity (Morse 1978).

At the very least, the analysis offered in this section should suggest that if involuntary commitment of only the mentally disordered can be justified at all, it should be limited to cases of persons who, first, are so clearly crazy that all reasonable persons would agree that their capability for self-control or rationality fails to pass even the lowest of

6. One answer is that perhaps normals, too, should be involuntarily committed if they behave in the legally relevant ways that now in part support involuntary hospitalization. This answer is consistent with the cases I have suggested. But instituting a broad preventive detention scheme applicable to all citizens would constitute a vast shift in the relative power of the state versus the individual, and it would be an utterly extraordinary infringement on liberty in our society. Nor is such a scheme consistent with historical, constitutional and social values (see Dershowitz 1973; but see also *Hirabayashi* v. *United States*, 1943; and *Korematsu* v. *United States*, 1944; both Japanese relocation cases).

legal thresholds;[7] second, are so dangerous or incompetent, as demonstrated by objective acts, that preventive confinement is clearly and absolutely necessary to prevent grave harm; and, third, are clearly and only treatable on an inpatient basis. Only in such cases can singling out the mentally disordered be reasonably justified on theoretical and utilitarian grounds.[8]

The Involuntary Commitment System Will Produce Unacceptable Numbers of Improper Commitments

Proponents of commitment often concede that the commitment net swept too widely in the past, ensnaring many persons who did not need to be committed. But, they argue, there are persons for whom involuntary commitment is truly appropriate, and therefore commitment should be properly limited rather than abolished (Chodoff 1976). Then the excesses of the past will be avoided, the system will operate fairly, and the small amount of liberty sacrificed will be justified by the benefits flowing to society and those committed. This argument has plausibility and appeal if one accepts, as many do, that the mentally disordered are different enough to warrant a commitment system applicable only to them and that proper limitation of involuntary commitment is possible. This section challenges the latter assumption and argues that it is highly unlikely that the involuntary commitment system will operate so as to commit only properly

7. It should be clear that a diagnosis of mental disorder would not be helpful in assessing this criterion. The question would be whether the person's thoughts, feelings, and actions are so crazy that the assumption about lack of capacity for rationality or self-control is clearly reasonable (Morse 1978).

8. There are, of course, also nondisordered people who meet these three criteria, but here I am accepting, *arguendo*, the threshold reasonableness of distinguishing disordered from nondisordered persons. It may be objected at this point that the argument is reasonable when applied to all persons who may be labelled mentally disordered according to the criteria of *DSM-III* (APA 1980); after all, many of the categories refer to behavior that is hardly very crazy according to anyone's definition. But the persons who are involuntarily hospitalized are typically very crazy indeed, and it appears that the capacity for self-control is far removed from that of the average noncrazy or mildly crazy citizen. It is admittedly difficult to make any sense of severely crazy behavior in a large number of instances, and it is hard to believe that very crazy persons have any control over such craziness and its further behavioral consequences. Yet it is clear, for instance, that delusional people do not always act on their delusions, and in most ways very crazy people act just like normal persons. Moreover, many seemingly normal persons seem fixed in irrational and repetitive behavior patterns that are destructive of their health, happiness, and welfare. Even if such normal persons can give reasons for their self-destructive behavior that make some sense, it is hard to believe that these reasons are not rationalizations or that these persons would continue so to act if they could help it. In sum, the argument that the mentally disordered do not specially lack self-control is less intuitively persuasive when it is applied to very crazy persons, but this does not vitiate its conceptual and empirical underpinnings. In any case, if the argument fails when applied to the subclass of severely crazy persons, then the law should only apply to them. Of course, present civil commitment statutes are not so limited.

committable persons. Indeed, unjustifiably high overcommitment will necessarily result from the existence of any commitment system that applies only to the mentally disordered.

One factor likely to lead to the overutilization of involuntary commitment is the use of commitment as a mechanism for the control of "overflow" deviance. As a social control system, involuntary commitment provides a solution to the problems caused by troublesome, annoying, scary, and weird persons (Miller 1976; Rachlin et al. 1975; see, also, Lamb et al. 1981) (see Chap. 7). Even if such people are not particularly harmful to themselves or others, they often disrupt—frequently severely—their families, friends, colleagues, and the public. In short, they tend to cause interpersonal problems and to make those around them feel profoundly uncomfortable. The criminal justice system may be unable to control this type of deviance, because in many instances the deviant behavior may not constitute crimes (Monahan, Caldeira, and Friedlander 1979; Warren 1979; but cf. Dickey 1980). Still, severity of social disruption and nuisance cannot be denied. Involuntary commitment thus satisfies a perceived need to have an alternative system to deal with this type of conduct. Nevertheless, family and interpersonal problems and the perceived discomfort of others are not sufficient reasons in a free and pluralistic society to deprive people involuntarily of their liberty: the right of people not to be bothered is important, but it is far less weighty than the right of the bothersome person to be free (*O'Connor* v. *Donaldson*, 1975).

Limited involuntary commitment laws seek to avoid undue incarceration, but the social pressure to incarcerate troublesome, crazy deviants is so powerful that such laws are likely to be misapplied (Hiday 1977; Hiday and Markell 1980; Lipsitt and Lelos 1981; *Psychiatric News* 1977; Stier and Stoebe 1979; Warren 1977). People who do not fit the commitment criteria will be held to do so, and the system will continue improperly to sweep into hospitals persons who are capable of living freely without significant danger to themselves or others. Civil commitment is such a simple, although unfair, answer to interpersonal, family, and comparatively mild social problems that it is certain to be overused (Miller 1976). It simply will not do to say that we must have commitment for such cases because society will insist on it. To date, few of the "horribles" predicted by opponents of enhanced rights for the disordered have occurred as a result of greater freedom for the disordered. Society has and can manage to tolerate crazy behavior without resort to incarceration.

Another factor that increases the likelihood of improper overcommitment is the difficulty attending proper conceptualization and diagnosis of mental disorder. There is much disagreement among mental health professionals about how to define and categorize mental disorders (American Psychiatric Association [APA] 1980; Dershowitz 1974; Ennis and Litwack 1974). Further, there are those who go so far as to claim that mental disorder does not exist, that a medical model of deviant behavior is misguided and perhaps dangerous (Szasz 1974; see also Sarbin and Mancuso 1980). A common theme in many of the criticisms is that it is far too easy to declare any deviant behavior to be the symptom of a disorder and thus to bring it within the ambit of the commitment system (Morse 1978; Schwitzgebel 1978b). The debate about the medical model and the proper conceptualization of crazy behavior has been intense for at least two decades, and it shows little sign of abating (Sarbin and Mancuso 1980; Wing 1978). At present, a medical/biological view seems to have regained its ascendency within the psychiatric profession (*Los Angeles Times* 1980). Nonetheless, the conceptual and scientific problems attending the medical model cannot be gainsaid by possible discoveries of biological causes for some disordered behaviors or by the apparently clear success of some somatic treatments, most notably chemotherapies, in reducing crazy behaviors in significant numbers of patients (Morse 1978). The controversy concerning the medical model will not disappear, and, indeed, it will probably reappear with renewed intensity with the almost inevitable failure of the new psychiatric biology to fulfill the lofty hopes it has engendered. And so long as the debate is unresolved, the group with the power to define disorders will retain the ability to overinclude deviant behaviors as mental disorders.[9]

Even if one accepts the validity of the medical model as a reasonable working model, a related but seemingly decreasing problem is that of diagnostic reliability. Prior to the promulgation of *DSM-III*,[10] it was fair to claim on the basis of the research evidence that the reliability of diagnoses of mental disorders, including those considered the most severe, measured by independent rater agreement, often failed to rise over 50% (Spitzer and Fleiss 1974). This was the

9. The classic historical instance was the debate centered in the American Psychiatric Association over whether homosexual behavior per se was a mental disorder. In response to intense lobbying by gay rights groups and sympathetic elements within the APA, the organization held a referendum to decide whether homosexuality was a mental disorder. By the technique of a vote, behavior that was formerly viewed as a disorder was relabeled normal. The history of this extraordinary event is chronicled in Bayer (1981).

10. *DSM-III* is the abbreviation for the American Psychiatric Association's newly promulgated *Diagnostic and Statistical Manual of Mental Disorders*, 3d ed. (1980). *DSM-III* replaced its predecessor, *DSM-II* (1968), which had been much criticized because its diagnostic entities lacked reliability and validity. The diagnostic categories of *DSM-III* are based to some degree on research data rather than solely on clinical supposition and consensus, and they are far more operationalized than those of its predecessor.

case even when the study used clinicians from a major psychiatric research center and precise research diagnostic criteria (Helzer et al. 1977). But, unlike the categories of *DSM-II*, those of *DSM-III* are relatively precisely defined and include specific inclusion and exclusion criteria. Consequently and unsurprisingly, the initial field trials of *DSM-III* have demonstrated far higher reliability than most previous studies. For example, in the second stage of the *DSM-III* field trials, the reliability coefficients (kappa) for schizophrenia, major affective disorders, and organic brain syndrome—the disorders that are diagnosed in the major proportion of hospitalized patients—were .81, .80, and .76, respectively (APA 1980). Accordingly, there is perhaps reason for optimism about the possibility of achieving reasonable accuracy on the threshold involuntary commitment criterion, the presence of mental disorders (Roth 1979; Stone 1975).

Even if very high reliability can be achieved under controlled research conditions, however, can such reliability be matched by diagnosticians with less interest in diagnosis in the tumult of everyday practice? Although it is reasonable to be optimistic about the reliability of *DSM-III*, caution is warranted until the results of general use and further careful research studies are available (Ziskin 1981).[11] In any case, the diagnostic criteria of *DSM-III* are still sufficiently vague

11. Despite the initial favorable findings on the reliability of *DSM-III*, caution is nonetheless warranted before it can be ultimately concluded either that *DSM-III* diagnoses are highly reliable (or that such higher reliability will partially solve the overcommitment problem). There are questions one may raise about the field trials. The experimenter diagnosticians in the field trials were completely self-selected; only 365 psychiatrists responded to advertisements that reached the whole membership of the American Psychiatric Association. It may therefore be surmised that the volunteers were more interested in diagnostic accuracy than the average practitioner and correspondingly unusually careful in their diagnostic work during the field trials. Moreover, although the methodological instructions to the numerous diagnosticians were filled with instructions and admonitions to avoid biased case selection and to maintain rater independence, there was apparently no direct supervision by the project staff over the groups carrying out the trials, and, in any case, the cases were not randomly selected. Although there is no clear evidence of systematic bias in the case selection, the process was "catch as catch can." Furthermore, the enormous increase in reliability over the Helzer et al. (1977) study seems difficult to explain because the Helzer study used explicit research criteria and, presumably, motivated diagnosticians from a major research center. The American Psychiatric Association is to be commended for trying to test *DSM-III* fairly, but one may appropriately wonder if the reliability figures would have been so high if all the field trials used random cases and were carefully controlled and supervised. Moreover, although the diagnostic entities of *DSM-III* may be more reliable than their predecessors, there is considerably more reason to question whether the new entities are valid. A psychiatric disorder is said to be valid if it is distinguishable from other disorders not only by its facial criteria but also by its course, family patterns, pathophysiology, specific treatment response, and the like (Feighner et al. 1972). (For the vast majority of psychiatric disorders, there are no conclusive anatomical or chemical signs to validate the presence of a disorder.) To date, in my view and the view of others, substantial research evidence for the validity of most *DSM-III* categories is lacking (Letters to the Editor 1979; Overall and Hollister 1979; Ziskin 1981).

to allow a diagnostician with biases toward treatment or hospitalization to fit a large number of persons into the most serious disorder categories. For example, persons diagnosed as schizophrenic according to *DSM-III* may behave quite differently depending on the subtype of the disorder exhibited and range along a very wide continuum of craziness. *DSM-III* notes that persons with the same diagnosis may behave differently in important ways, such as, one may surmise, the degree of craziness or social disability evidenced (APA 1980, p. 6). Thus, even if high diagnostic reliability is theoretically possible under *DSM-III*, this possibility will not effectively prevent overcommitment, because even *DSM-III* diagnoses do not map precisely the degree of craziness necessary properly to support involuntary commitment. Many persons who legitimately may be given a severe diagnosis and who may be committed on that basis will nevertheless not be sufficiently crazy to warrant involuntary hospitalization.

A final related point is that, even if mental disorder may be diagnosed accurately, the law has rarely defined mental illness or disorder for legal purpose (Lelos 1978). Will all conditions called "mental disorder" support involuntary commitment (if the behavioral component is also met), or should only severe mental disorder be sufficient? In only severe disorder is sufficient for legal commitment purposes, how is "severity" defined and who should decide which disorders fit the category of "severe" (see Stier and Stoebe 1979; Stone 1975)?[12]

12. There are undeniably serious problems with a "medical model" of disordered behavior, with diagnostic reliability in psychiatry, and with the legal definition of mental disorder, but these problems need not unduly undermine the proper workability of a commitment system. To the extent the law continues to rely on mental health categories to answer legal questions, such as who should be committed involuntarily, then the law remains at the mercy of the vagaries, unreliability, and internecine disputes of mental health science. Once freed from such reliance, however, the law's identification of the mentally disordered becomes less problematic. I submit that for involuntary commitment purposes the law is seeking to identify those persons who seem so severely disturbed, so crazy, that the intuition about the lack of behavioral control appears justified. Even if there are conceptual problems with the concept "mental disorder," there are certainly some people who behave so inexplicably irrationally, so crazily, that society is perhaps warranted in believing that something is "wrong" with such persons. Identification of these persons, rather than being a scientific matter, requires a social, moral, and legal assessment that these people are fit subjects for preventive detention because they behave in an inexplicably irrational manner betokening lack of fundamental autonomy. If the legal identification of mental disorder were placed on this commonsense, social basis, fewer "incorrect" legal decisions would result, and the liberty of citizens would not depend on the particular diagnostic theories and skills of the testifying mental health professionals (Morse 1978). This solution would not be a panacea, however. Judges and juries might still differ widely about who is sufficiently crazy, and overcommitment could still result. But at least the system would be asking the proper questions, and over time I believe a relatively clear legal standard of severe disorders would develop. Further, the fact finder would be more inclined properly to focus on the actor's behavior rather than on diagnostic labels.

A third basis for the claim that the commitment criteria will be overapplied is that the behavioral component standards are too vague or require predictions that are beyond the present capability of mental health professionals or anyone else. Standards such as "dangerousness" or "need for hospitalization" have no generally agreed-upon meaning among lay persons or professionals (Menzies, Webster, and Butler 1981; Simon and Cockerham 1977; Warren 1979). Of course, there is likely to be a great deal of agreement about extreme cases among lay persons and professionals alike (Simon and Cockerham 1977), but such cases are unusual. Thus, it may be claimed, each witness, lay or professional, and each fact finder injects his or her own private meaning into the criteria, rendering the system essentially lawless.

It would be possible to ameliorate such vagueness by rewriting the criteria to allow commitment only if rather specific behavioral criteria were met (*Stamus* v. *Leonhardt,* 1976). For instance, the dangerousness criterion might be written and interpreted to mean only substantial physical danger—for example, death or serious bodily harm to oneself or others as evidenced by a recent (e.g., within the past seven days) act or attempt (see, generally, Hiday and Markell 1980). Such a standard is not terribly vague, or at least not more so than many substantive criminal law criteria (see Schwitzgebel 1978a), but a few observations are in order. In a free society, preventive detention should be authorized only for serious harms, if at all. Additionally, persons whose dangerousness is evidenced by acts or attempts can be removed from society by the criminal justice system. Thus, if dangerousness is evidenced only by a threat, the question of the predictability of real harm, discussed in detail below, is raised (Groethe 1977; Stier and Stoebe 1979; Stone 1975). Finally, there is the fundamental question of whether it is the proper role of the state to intervene massively in the life of an individual to prevent the person from doing harm to himself or herself. Thus, philosophical and political objections to paternalistic commitment are not resolved by operationalizing the criteria. Although less vague criteria simply insure that the system will operate more fairly, the system's foundation remains unsound.

Commitment laws almost always authorize preventive detention and thus generally require predictions of future behavior. For example, commitment criteria often require that the person is "likely" (Iowa Code §229.1, 1979) to be a danger to self or others. On occasion no qualifying phrase referring to probability will be found, and a person may be committed if he or she is simply "dangerous to others" (Schwitzgebel 1978a). There are two related problems with these criteria: first, it is rarely if ever clear what specific probability of the requisite harms is required; and, second, only poor predictive ability exists.

The former difficulty could be remedied by more precise statutory specification of the probability required. What probability of harm (and which harms are required) is surely a political, legal, and constitutional question. In a free society, however, it seems clear that for preventive detention there should be a high probability of the occurrence of the harm (*O'Connor* v. *Donaldson,* 1975). But how high is sufficient? If the standard of "likely" or similar standards are interpreted to mean 51% probability, this will mean that persons may be incarcerated when there is just slightly more than a 50-50 chance that they will actually cause the specified harms. Assuming that the probability data are accurate, it is therefore possible that just under half the people committed do not pose the requisite danger in fact. This number of wrongly committed "false positives" is completely unjustified in a society that values liberty. Although I, as one member of society, cannot specify the "correct" and constitutional probability required for preventive detention, most informed persons would probably agree that it should be much higher, say, in excess of 75%–80%. But even then, it should be noted, one person in five will be unnecessarily committed. It might be argued that the probability and the degree of harm required should be inversely related: the greater the harm predicted, the lower the probability of its occurrence that is required (Monahan and Wexler 1978; cf. Genego et al. 1975). But if such an inverse sliding scale were permissible, the probability of harm required for even great harms should still be quite high.

Whether or not the predictive criteria are defined more clearly, there is little evidence that even a moderately high probability of future legally relevant behavior, especially in the long term, can be predicted by anyone with substantial accuracy except in clear cases (Cocozza and Steadman 1976; Diamond 1974; Monahan 1978). As always, most cases will not be clear, and many false predictions will ensue. Indeed, studies of the prediction of violence to others demonstrate that an accuracy rate of 30%–40% is unusually high (Monahan 1976, 1981). For predictions of suicide, an accuracy rate of about 20% appears to be the upper limit of present predictive skill (Mackinnon and Farberow 1976). Of course, if the probability of harm required for commitment is lowered enough, fewer improper commitments will ensue. But most persons would probably agree that preventive detention should not be authorized on the basis of a small probability of harm. The answer to the "prediction problem" is not to lower the probability required.

The prediction problem is particularly acute in the involuntary commitment context, because the increasing adoption of dangerousness criteria increases the necessity for relying on predictions to make commitment decisions, and mental health professionals tend to err in the direction of overpredicting rather than underpredicting legally relevant behavior (McGarry and Schwitzgebel 1978; Shah 1978; Steadman, in press; Wenk et al. 1972). Stated another way, the percentage of false positives is almost always likely to be greater than the percentage of false negatives (Monahan 1981). This will occur even if society adopts libertarian, strict commitment standards (Steadman, in press). For many reasons, professionals are more likely to believe incorrectly that harm will occur or involuntary treatment in a closed institution is necessary than to believe incorrectly the opposite (Dershowitz 1968; cf. Scheff 1963). Lack of predictive accuracy leads far more often to incorrect commitment than to incorrect release. The improper incarceration of a vast number of hapless citizens who safely could, and properly should, remain at liberty is the unfortunate result in the context of the increased use of predictions.[13]

Inaccurate predictions create a powerful object to involuntary commitment because a society with a strong preference for liberty should seek to minimize incorrect involuntary commitments, even at the risk of increasing the number of "incorrect" rejections of commitment (but cf. *Addington* v. *Texas,* 1979). The analogue to the criminal justice system, of course, is the belief that it is far better to acquit the guilty than to convict the innocent. As Mr. Justice Harlan wrote in In re *Winship* (1970), "In a criminal case . . . we do not view the social disutility of convicting an innocent man as equivalent to the disutility of acquitting someone who is guilty." Until predictive

13. A possible caveat to the negative assessment of predictive accuracy is necessary when considering predictions of short-term behavior based on immediately past behavior. John Monahan has suggested that predictive accuracy in such situations is likely to be quite good and therefore should not vitiate the propriety of short-term emergency commitment (Monahan 1978). This suggestion is plausible and sensible, but to date there is almost no research on the question, and one study that might seem to support it was insufficiently controlled (Rofman et al. 1980). Nevertheless, I suspect Prof. Monahan may be correct. But even if so, strong inroads in the case against involuntary commitment are not made. First, if the emergency situation involves harm to others,the behavior will properly invoke the criminal justice system which I and others (Stone 1975) believe is the most appropriate system to deal with such behavior. The other major type of emergency situation where predictions may be reasonably accurate will be cases of acute, active and clear suicidal actions. If short-term emergency commitment is allowed in response to such cases, this would create only a very limited and limitable possibility of involuntary commitment. These cases will also meet the three clear criteria for ever justifying commitment. In any event, most predictions leading to commitment are not made in such clear cases. Finally, Prof. Monahan's suggestion does not apply to release decisions.

accuracy becomes immeasurably greater, the involuntary civil commitment system will result in unacceptably disproportionate numbers of unjust commitments.

A final reason that overcommitment is inevitable is the procedural laxity that apparently characterizes commitment proceedings nearly everywhere, including those jurisdictions where the law requires rather stringent protections. Hearings tend to be perfunctory, rarely applying fully the procedural protections required (Morse 1978). A reasonably complete exploration of the factual basis for commitment or the possibility of less restrictive placements is not made. Appeals are infrequent, thus leaving judges relatively free to apply substantive criteria too loosely and to fail to insist on the requisite procedural safeguards. Most important, the lawyers who represent the allegedly mentally disordered often fail to act in a fully adversary manner, even when trained to do so (Poythress 1978). Finally, although the intermediate standard or proof that the Constitution requires (*Addington* v. *Texas*, 1979) is stricter than the civil preponderance standard, it creates a much higher risk of error and wrongful commitment than if the criminal, "reasonable doubt" standard were required.[14]

It is sometimes argued by those who are aware of the overcommitment danger that the problem is not serious. Even if some persons are wrongly committed because they are not significantly dangerous to themselves or others, it is contended, these persons probably are mentally disordered and will therefore benefit from a regime of hospital care and treatment.[15] This argument fails, however, for at least two reasons. First, society has decided that provision of treatment does not outweigh liberty interests in those cases that do not meet the statutory criteria for commitment. Wrongful commitment is unjustified, abusive, and stigmatizing even if treatment is provided (*O'Connor* v. *Donaldson*, 1975). Second, as we shall argue in great detail in the next section, state mental hospitals are unlikely to provide quality care and treatment, even to those who arguably need it the most.

14. Many cases have required the reasonable doubt standard, e.g., *Lessard* v. *Schmidt* (1972), *Estate of Roulet* (1979), *Supt. of Worcester State Hospital* v. *Hagberg* (1978). Critics of the reasonable doubt standard have claimed that the standard is so high that it would be impossible to commit anyone. But such criticism confuses the probability of harm required to commit with the burden of persuasion necessary to prove that probability (Monahan and Wexler 1978), and it is contradicted by the experience of jurisdictions where the reasonable doubt standard applies (Zander 1976).

15. A good fact situation on which this type of argument might be based is presented by In re *Hatley* (1977). Hatley was evidently clearly disordered, but the dangerous behavior proven was merely careless backing up of her automobile. On appeal, Hatley was released. This case is also a good example of the use of involuntary hospitalization to extrude a difficult and perhaps disruptive family member.

It is sometimes argued that professional review and the support of family and friends are effective buffers against erroneous commitment. This argument was made by the United States Supreme Court in *Addington* v. *Texas,* in support of its holding that, in order to avoid erroneous commitments, the Constitution requires an intermediate standard of proof higher than the civil standard of "a preponderance of the evidence," but it does not require the criminal, "beyond a reasonable doubt standard." This line of reasoning is stunningly mistaken, however. Truly adequate professional review or care is a rarity in the public hospital system (and in some private hospitals), and, as much research demonstrates, commitment often occurs in cases where there are not concerned families or friends or where families reject the person (see Chap. 7). Moreover, where families and friends exist, they are usually only too glad to have the bothersome person removed from circulation. The checks on erroneous commitment suggested by the Supreme Court simply do not exist to a substantial degree.

The Court observed further in *Addington* that a debilitatedly disordered person already suffers from stigma and diminished liberty by reason of the disorder. Therefore, the Court naively concluded, it is not better for an ill person to be freed than for a normal person to be committed.[16] In a word, erroneous commitment is serious, but it is not a grave social error. But can the Court possibly believe that hospitalization increases liberty or decreases stigma for severely disordered people? If so, they are quite wrong; our public hospitals (and many private hospitals) rarely cure, nor do they decrease stigma. A severely disordered person is stigmatized to some degree and has restricted life choices in the community; but involuntary hospitalization is a further extraordinary restriction on liberty that should be avoided at all costs, and, in many cases, an increase in stigma also results. Until a person is hospitalized involuntarily, there is no authoritative public labeling and recording that the person is mentally sick. Hospitalization is an unfortunate outcome for almost any citizen, and it is egregiously harmful for those who do not meet the statutory criteria for commitment. The Court's argument is astonishing; only by overlooking the reality of the social circumstances of those committed, the vast overcommitment that now occurs, the quality of the public hospitals (and many private hospitals), and the consequences of hospitalization, can it be so cavalier about wrongful commitment and about the balance of state and individual interests.

16. The Court therefore refused to draw the analogy between the criminal justice system—where it is better to acquit the guilty than convict the innocent—and the involuntary commitment system.

In sum, for a variety of reasons—the desire to control deviance, difficulties in the proper definition and diagnosis of mental disorder, the vagueness of commitment standards, difficulties in accurately predicting future behavior, and procedural laxity—the involuntary civil commitment system will produce unacceptably high numbers of improper commitments and thus will continue to function as an unjust system. This will be true even in those jurisdictions which have reformed their commitment statutes in an attempt to limit their application only to those persons who allegedly truly require involuntary hospitalization.

The claim that a high likelihood of overcommitment is inevitable is supported by empirical studies of the application of reformed commitment statutes (Hiday 1977; Lipsitt and Lelos 1981; Stier and Stoebe 1979; Warren 1977). Careful studies demonstrate that as many as half the persons committed in a jurisdiction do not meet the jurisdiction's statutory criteria for commitment (Lelos 1978). We must therefore note in conclusion that there is little support for claims that civil commitment can be reasonably limited. At best, as suggested above, one can try to develop precisely defined standards that would be satisfied only by rare, clear cases. If such standards were accompanied by rigorous, adversary procedures, reasonable limitations on wrongful commitment might result. Such standards and procedural behavior do not seem likely to be instituted, however, and as we have seen, statutory reform does not seem to make much difference.

Is a system that improperly incarcerates a substantial percentage of its inmates—perhaps as many as half or more—supportable in our society? It is clear that if the standards and procedures of the criminal justice system led to a 50% erroneous conviction rate, the system would be blatantly unconstitutional (see In re *Winship*, 1970; *Patterson* v. *New York*, 1977). Until recently, the justifiability of the involuntary commitment system has been accepted without much question, and the burden of demonstrating its inequities has been firmly on the opponents of involuntary hospitalization. The burden of persuasion in the commitment debate should now shift to the proponents of the system to demonstrate that commitment can be appropriately limited. If they cannot do so, our duty to protect the liberty of all persons must lead us to forgo commitment in those few cases where many persons might agree that it is warranted. Unless the system can be demonstrably reformed, too little benefit will be provided at the expense of far too much deprivation of liberty.

The States Will Not Provide Adequate Care and Treatment to Involuntarily Committed Persons

To buttress the acceptability of involuntary commitment and the wisdom of its wide standards and relatively lenient procedures, a crucial argument advanced is the contention that proper care and treatment will be provided to persons in need of such intervention. Indeed, the involuntary commitment system is distinguishable from the criminal justice system and justifiable in large part because commitment allegedly has and achieves benign, therapeutic aims (*Addington* v. *Texas,* 1979). If involuntary civil commitment can ever be justified, this claim is surely an indispensable and obligatory part of the justification. Accordingly, it must be asked whether the promise of adequate care and treatment is likely to be fulfilled or is even capable of being fulfilled given present knowledge and attitudes toward mentally disordered persons, and given the levels of present and probable future expenditures for their care.

It is generally agreed that most mental health treatments, especially those useful for severely disordered persons, ameliorate symptoms rather than cure allegedly underlying illnesses (Committee on Research 1979; Scheff 1976), and all treatments are unsuccessful and sometimes harmful in a substantial percentage of cases (Jeste and Wyatt 1981; Klawans et al. 1980). Furthermore, reducing symptoms rarely causes major improvement in the broad range of social disabilities that led to involuntary commitment (May 1976). Indeed, treatments of severely disordered people, for whom involuntary commitment is allegedly most necessary, have a low likelihood of success compared to treatments of less disordered individuals. For this reason and because mental disorder is often *not* causally linked to legally relevant behavior, successful treatment of mental disorder does not guarantee the diminution of the legally relevant behaviors such as dangerousness or incompetence that are also required for commitment (Morse 1978; Rosenblatt and Mayer 1974). For the most part, our public (and many private) hospitals treat their patients almost entirely by removing disordered persons from their supposedly stressful environments, by prescribing psychotropic medication with more or less indifferent care (see, e.g., Kaufman 1979; Mason, Nerviano, and DeBerger 1977), and by providing a purportedly therapeutic milieu.

There are simply not sufficient funds to provide any substantial fraction of patients with the type of services that would yield the optimum chance of improving both symptoms and general psychosocial disabilities. Even providing maximally beneficial chemotherapy requires expert and substantial staffing that is beyond the resources of most public hospitals. More general therapeutic services to remedy psychosocial disabilities are highly labor intensive (see, e.g., Paul and Lentz 1977) and would require funding that is literally unimaginable at present. And without social rehabilitation, it is highly likely that patients will simply revolve back into the system once more, again to be rendered less symptomatic by chemotherapy, but still lacking the skills to make a successful adjustment in the community. Moreover, many hospitals are not able to provide minimally adequate custodial care. Even in "advanced" states that supposedly maintain the best hospitals and provide the best services, the public is constantly shocked by the revelations of the inadequate and sometimes inhumane care and treatment that too often characterize public mental hospitals (see, e.g., *Los Angeles Times* 1976). It is well to remember that the gruesome conditions in Alabama hospitals exposed in the *Wyatt* cases were occurring in the 1970s, not the 1870s, and even today inhumane and antitherapeutic conditions continue (*Flakes* v. *Percy*, 1981).

The inadequate conditions of public mental hospitals have been a feature of state mental health care for over a century (Kaufman 1979; Talbott 1978). Many of the psychiatrists are poorly qualified, especially those who are foreign trained, if "qualified" at all; physical conditions and staffing are inadequate; and satisfactory treatment is a myth (Bower 1981; Torrey and Taylor 1973; see *New York State Assn. for Retarded Children Inc.* v. *Rockefeller*, 1973). Conditions in the hospital are often depersonalizing, dehumanizing, and unpleasant (Cockerham 1981). Periodic exposes and calls for reform have not yet led to acceptable improvement, although courts have shown a willingness to supervise public mental hospitals when the level of care provided drops beneath a minimally humane level of decency (*Halderman* v. *Pennhurst State School & Hospital*, 1977; *Wyatt* v. *Stickney*, 1972. Still, there is no evidence that legislatures will be willing to allocate the money necessary to insure optimum care and treatment (Chambers 1978). Indeed, states faced with right-to-treatment decrees that force them to expend far grater resources on their patients have responded by "dumping" the patients into the community (Brown and Bremer 1978) instead of treating them with the degree of care and expertise dictated by decency and medical ethics. This is not to say that there have not been improvements in state hospital care—obviously there have been. It is simply to underscore the reality of inadequate care and treatment nearly everywhere. Arguments that what is available is better than nothing are unacceptable. People who are locked up because they are sick must be treated properly. If they are not, let us admit that the major goals of involuntary hospitalization are preventive detention and warehousing, and let us analyze the system on that basis.

Finally, most mental health treatments are still in a relatively rudimentary state, although definitely improving, and no major breakthrough is in sight. Even if the level of efficacy increases sharply in light of new discoveries, it is doubtful that the new treatments will be cheap and easy to administer. As we have seen, even adequate chemotherapy, a relatively cheap and easily administered modality, is beyond the current capability of most public hospitals. And if new treatments are efficacious but costly, in the light of past history is there any reason to believe that legislatures will vote the funds necessary to provide these treatments at a level consonant with reasonable psychiatric and psychological skill?

An appealing answer to the appalling state of affairs in our public hospitals is this: If commitment is limited to the few, extreme cases of severe disorder where it seems warranted, then treatment resources will not be spread thin, and those committed involuntarily may be cared for adequately and treated. If the states do not reduce their funding of hospitals in response to a decrease in the patient population (an extraordinarily unlikely event), services to individual patients could certainly improve. But even the costs of full treatment plans would be enormous, and it is doubtful that states would be willing to spend that much money, especially for so few patients. It must be admitted, however, that adequate custodial care and medication could be provided if the present funding levels were maintained and there were many fewer patients. Nonetheless, such treatment is unlikely to alleviate general psychosocial disabilities, and minimally adequate care is hardly a reasonable substitute for liberty. And, as argued above, it is highly unlikely that commitment would be limited to only a few polar cases; if it is not so limited, adequate care and treatment is problematic at best. Moreover, even if the best treatment resources now available were offered, many patients would not improve.

Until and unless, (1) legislatures show a greater willingness to allocate money to public mental patients, (2) truly qualified mental health professionals demonstrate a willingness to enter the public hospital system in great numbers, and (3) mental health treatments improve greatly, I believe that the benign and therapeutic aims of the involuntary commitment system will remain an unattained myth that in part results in the massive deprivation of liberty. The inadequate funding of hospital *and* community mental health services is an indication of both social distaste for the mentally disordered and a lack of social commitment to humane treatment. Both society at large and the mental health professions are to be blamed for this scandalous state of affairs. To maintain that involuntary commitment is ultimately beneficial to the vast majority of incarcerated patients is to propagate a myth. The short-term reduction of symptoms, although sometimes useful, is simply not adequate treatment. It is not claimed that involuntary hospitalization is never beneficial or that involuntarily hospitalized patients uniformly hold negative views of their hospitalization experience—such a claim is contradicted by reasonable evidence (see, e.g., Gove and Fain 1977; Weinstein 1979; *but see* Essex et al. 1980; and Weinstein's reply 1980). Nevertheless, involuntary hospitalization as currently practiced will not alleviate chronic disorders and social disabilities that will otherwise lead to a lifelong series of commitments, nor will it restore its inmates to lives of productive happiness.

Sweeping disordered persons involuntarily into hospitals on the ground that real help is available helps society avoid confronting the hard social questions caused by disordered behavior. If the true goal of commitment is to remove disturbing members from the community and to offer them only minimal custodial care (and often much less), then let us be honest about this and argue the merits of commitment on that basis.

Hospitalization Is Not Necessary for the Efficacious Treatment of the Vast Majority of Involuntarily Committed Patients

Almost all mental health treatments now available can be provided as efficaciously and usually more cheaply in less restrictive community settings than in closed hospitals (Bachrach 1976; Becker and Schulberg 1976; Dickey et al. 1981; Murphy and Dantel 1976; Sharfstein and Nafziger 1976; Weisbrod, Test, and Stein 1980; but cf. Borus 1981; Braun et al. 1981; Sheridan and Teplin 1981). Starting at the lowest end of the "treatment" spectrum, custodial care can be provided easily in the community in decent board-and-care type facilities. Indeed, many persons who would reject hospitalization in large, impersonal institutions might willingly accept residence in small, reasonable community homes. There is little reason why the prescription of medication or the provision of convulsive, psychological, and social therapies also cannot be accomplished on an outpatient basis. Research evidence supports the view that hospitalization, especially long-term hospitalization, is rarely necessary and is often antitherapeutic (Stuart 1970; Test and Stein 1978).[17] Many disordered

---

17. Persons who are too disabled to look after themselves minimally and to offer an opinion on hospitalization may be treated as nonprotesting and hospitalized for their own safety and care. And some hospitals should exist for those who voluntarily want inpatient services and who understand the costs and benefits of such services compared to the alternatives.

persons would probably be quite willing to accept good outpatient treatments, nursing visits, or other reasonable interventions if they were offered and explained by caring and careful professionals who behaved respectfully toward the disordered. This might be especially true if the prospective patient or service recipient were sure that seeking help for mental disorder or its consequences would not lead to incarceration.

It has been suggested that hospitalization is necessary because neither courts nor lawyers have the ability to discover and coordinate the less-restrictive community services that admittedly would be efficacious if they were utilized. Although there is a present lack of resource information and coordination, one cannot imagine a weaker argument in favor of the necessity of depriving a person of liberty. The difficulty in gathering information about community treatment resources and coordinating a treatment plan is significantly outweighed by the individual's interest in avoiding unnecessary involuntary commitment. Judges, mental health advocates, and allied social service staff plainly will have to educate themselves and learn to create sensible community treatment alternatives.

Some courts have held that the use of the least restrictive alternative is constitutionally compelled in the treatment process (Chambers 1978; *Lessard* v. *Schmidt*, 1972), and some legislatures, including Congress, have utilized the same doctrine as a matter of social policy (Developmentally Disabled Assistance and Bill of Rights Act 1976). This doctrine is based upon the sound assumption that, if the primary purpose of commitment is to treat people and not simply to remove them from the community, hospitalization is almost never justified. And in those cases where it may appear justified, creative use of community resources is likely to be as efficacious, cheaper, and far less restrictive of the disordered person's liberty than involuntary hospitalization. In other words, if the necessary services were seriously pursued, most persons now committable do not need to be committed even if they met the statutory criteria.

Of course, society can fail, as it does now, to provide services to people at liberty in the community as much as it fails to provide them to incarcerated patients. The condition of many "de-institutionalized" ex-patients in the community is a national disgrace (see Chap. 9). Moreover, the relatively rudimentary knowledge of mental health science is as true in the community as it is in the hospital. But if society is willing to expend the resources and to make the human commitment to caring for and treating people who may need and want such services, these services can be provided as efficaciously and more cheaply in the freedom of the community.[18] The involuntary commitment system hardly seems justified by the tiny fraction of cases that perhaps can be treated best in a hospital, especially in light of the justifiable pessimism about hospital conditions and treatment and the likelihood of overcommitment.

The Benefits of Abolition

The benefits of abolition or severe limitation of involuntary commitment will be an increase in liberty that is not outweighed by the increased harms, a reduction in the role confusion and onerous tasks of mental health professionals, the enhancement of treatment, and the freeing of wasted resources. This section will consider these benefits in order.

The Extension of Liberty

The major benefit of abolition will be an increase in liberty in our society. People who are not demonstrably dangerous will not be preventively detainable, nor will the state be able to substitute its judgments for those of its citizens. But even if a commitment system could be devised that accurately identified very crazy and clearly dangerous people and limited commitments to those who could be treated successfully only in a hospital—a proposition that I have argued is almost certainly impossible—I would still oppose involuntary commitment. Most important, as a matter of values, I prefer a system that maximizes liberty. Preventive detention is simply insupportable because it is a vast deprivation of liberty that is not outweighed by needs for public protection. The model of the criminal law is worthy of emulating; persons should not be incarcerated, no matter how dangerous they are, until they violate the criminal law (LaFave and Scott 1972). And, so long as a person is capable of expressing a preference about hospitalization and treatment, the state should not substitute its judgment for that preference. Nonprotest-

18. If society made the commitment to provide reasonable care to its disordered persons in the community, mental health care might become more expensive than it is at present. The greater expense would probably not be created by the high costs per patient of community treatment compared to hospitalization. Rather, the increase would be the result of providing adequate treatment to vastly greater numbers of persons. I assume that, if fine services were freely available in the community, there would be great demand for such services. Nevertheless, the cost per patient of community services is probably cheaper than the cost of hospitalization. Finally, a resultant increase in the use of services because they are reasonable and available is hardly a reason to cut off such services to needy people.

ing persons could be hospitalized and treated until they indicated they no longer desired such services. But commitment to human dignity and liberty requires that we let persons decide for themselves about issues as important as psychiatric hospitalization and treatment, even if the reasons that they give seem crazy or unsupportable (Morse 1978).

One argument against the increase in liberty is that a false dichotomy has been set forth: liberty and humane benefit to crazy persons are not incompatible goals. But, while they can be made less incompatible by stringently limiting involuntary commitment, the incompatibility is fundamental and cannot be eradicated so long as involuntary incarceration in a hospital is allowable for some persons. The argument that freedom is illusory for crazy persons because they are "possessed" and controlled by their illnesses or because they lead lives of degradation and misery cannot be proven to proves too much. The argument that the mentally disordered are not autonomous is little more than an intuitive hunch. My view is that even the craziest person has substantial control over his or her behavior, and, more important, an inalienable right to liberty that is indistinguishable from that of more "normal" citizens. Moreover, a greater number of persons who are not crazy lead lives of degradation and misery that allegedly render the notion of liberty irrelevant, but we do not deprive them of their freedom because of their right to liberty. To claim that we care about the "effective" liberty of crazy people but also to ignore its lack in "normals" simply exposes the hypocrisy of the involuntary commitment system.

Of course, there are cases of disordered persons that seem to cry out for intervention: the delusional person who seems on the verge of a violent outburst or who appears to be destroying the fabric of his or her family; or the terribly disorganized person whose life is apparently in jeopardy because the person seems unable to cope with minimal food, shelter, clothing, or medical needs; or the person in the throes of a manic episode who appears to be jeopardizing a career or reputation; or, perhaps most compellingly, the person on the verge of suicide who appears clearly to be making a mistake in judgment about his or her own helplessness and the hopelessness of his or her life situation. Proponents of commitment point to such cases and claim, in the name of decency and humanity, that society must intervene (Chodoff 1976). My answer, in the name of liberty and dignity, is that society must not intervene. Of course, useful voluntary services should be offered in such cases, and we should attempt to persuade needy citizens to make use of them. Moreover, as noted, nonprotesting persons may be treated.[19] But we do not preventively detain the most dangerous normal offenders, and we do not override even the most horrendous decisions of normal persons that endanger their lives and often the welfare of their families (consider again the example of the heart attack victim who continues to overeat, over-work, and smoke). Because of a commitment to liberty, our society has always been "willing" to allow much preventable harm. There is simply no supportable reason to authorize greater deprivation of liberty for those who are termed mentally disordered. Of course, abolition will allow some harm that could be prevented if commitment were maintained, but this would be even more true if normal persons were committable.

Another counterargument to the position that liberty will be increased by abolition stems from the observation that some objecting patients are in fact ambivalent about their hospitalization (see Chap. 9). On the basis of this observation, one might argue that some of the protesters are not being wrongly committed because they "really" want to go into hospital. Stated another way, the commitment system is simply helping large numbers of persons to obtain hospitalization without having to admit to themselves that they desire it. Although ambivalence surely exists, this argument in entirely unpersuasive.

How can the relative strengths of the conflicting desires be measured and compared? How do we know what a person "really" wants to do? There is no way at present to answer these questions, and therefore a sensible legal system must develop reasonable decision rules that use workable and reasonably objective criteria. The most reasonable and workable solution is to accept the overtly articulated desire of the person, even if other behavior gives some indication of

19. By a nonprotesting person, I mean a person so disabled that he or she is unable to respond coherently or to respond at all to an offer of services. In such cases, emergency services can of course be provided, but a guardianship should be sought to look after the person's longer-term needs. At any time, however, that the person recovers sufficiently to express a preference about hospitalization and treatment, that preference should be respected and the guardianship should terminate. It may be objected that this system will not work because some persons might manage to pull themselves together for a brief moment and express a preference for treatment to cease, and then lapse back into incoherence. The system will be inefficient and useless in such cases. In a polar case, this objection would be valid, but, again, most cases are not polar, and difficulties can be surmounted if a rule of reasonableness is applied. Most patients will not move in and out of incoherence so rapidly, and, if they do, treatment clearly should not cease. On the other hand, the wish of a patient who is recompensating with reasonable stability should be respected. If the patient asks when coherent to be left alone even when incoherent, this request should be respected too. Again, reasonably offered good treatments are less likely to be refused. Of course, the system will not be perfect, but it does strike a balance between liberty and paternalism that errs, properly I believe, on the side of liberty.

ambivalence. Assessing unconscious motives is problematic in itself (Morse 1982) and basing decisions on such motives is simply an invitation to subjective and widely discretionary decision making. In the criminal law, to use an analogous example, a person who consciously intentionally shoots at and misses another will be guilty of attempted murder even though alienists of the unconscious may try to show that the person did not "really" intend to kill because of unconscious conflict. This is surely the correct result (Moore 1980), unless we are to make a mockery of notions of criminal responsibility and the relevance of mental state explanations to moral, practical, and legal judgments. And so it should be in the commitment system. If a person "really" wishes to enter the hospital, let that person sign in voluntarily. If reasonable and respectfully offered community treatments are available, ambivalence about accepting care should be reduced substantially although admittedly it probably cannot be eliminated entirely. But if the person consciously protests, that decision must be respected although there is evidence of ambivalence. Liberty, dignity, and principled decision making require this.[20]

Another counterargument against the increase in liberty produced by abolition is based on the consequences of the deinstitutionalization movement. Large numbers of ex-patients have been forced to live in our inner cities, untreated and uncared for, in conditions of misery and degradation (Arnhoff 1975; Brown and Bremer 1978; Scull 1981) (see Chap. 9). Under these conditions, it is observed, theoretical arguments about liberty bear the same relation to reality as do unicorns. It is said that such persons lack "effective" liberty. Although the scandalous and appalling results of deinstitutionalization are undeniable, the conclusion often drawn— that involuntary hospitalization is necessary—is a breathtaking non sequitur.

Some crazy persons (and noncrazy persons) are apparently incapable of avoiding lives of misery and degradation without some form of intervention by others. It is outrageous that our society has followed a sensible de-institutionalization policy with the malevolent neglect of truly needy ex-patients. If chronically disabled persons truly lack "effective" liberty, as is so often claimed, the answer is not involuntary incarceration which sweeps in too many people and provides too little to those who are incarcerated (especially to those who are the most disabled). Hospitalization for chronically and se-

20. There will be some model cases where the person objects to hospitalization but his or her behavior appears to be a clear cry for hospitalization. But such cases will be few, and even they will be open to other interpretations. Again, moreover, one does not construct a system that will operate largely wrongfully because there may be a few cases for which the system is theoretically appropriate.

verely disabled persons simply serves as a means for avoiding facing the reality of the misery and problems of such persons. As argued above, the solution is to provide the resources in the community to insure decent food, clothing, shelter, and treatment services for those who need them. One should not compare the all-too-questionable benefits of hospitalization to complete or near-complete neglect in the community. The only fair comparison is to community living and treatment where society meets its moral obligations rather than cynically avoiding them. Hospitals are not necessary for adequate care and treatment, but the expenditure of money and the provision of humane care are. Even the most disabled crazy people have a right to liberty, and to the extent that "effective" liberty can be provided at all, it can be provided in the community under conditions that minimize constraints on freedom. Involuntary hospitalization only allows us to ignore the problems, not to alleviate them significantly.

A final and admittedly problematic counterpoint to the liberty argument concerns the relationship of the involuntary commitment system to the criminal justice system. Both are deviance control systems that often deal with the same behavior. For instance, an assault, a petty theft, or vagrancy may be seen as a misdemeanor, a symptom of mental disorder, or both. Depending on a number of factors, a policeman, for example, might decide either to arrest the person or to take the person to a hospital. Many persons believe, with much cause, that if criminal conduct is a consequence of mental disorder and not too serious, it is unwise policy to use the criminal justice system to respond to the behavior. It is argued that the criminal justice system is an inefficient and cruel institution in which to place persons who are not really responsible for their acts and who need treatment, not punishment. If involuntary commitment is abolished, the argument concludes, large numbers of crazy persons will be improperly forced into the criminal justice system: as a consequence, the supposed liberty benefits provided by abolition of involuntary commitment will be undermined and the mentally disordered will be subjected to cruel conditions.

The first answer to this counterargument is to note that it entirely begs the question of criminal responsibility. It assumes that the miscreant could not have been responsible because he or she was mentally disordered. But, as I have argued above and at length elsewhere (Morse 1976, 1978), it is fair to hold nearly all persons, including crazy persons, responsible for their behavior. I cannot recreate the argument to defend that assertion here, but if it is correct, then ab initio there is no reason not to use the criminal law to control criminal deviance. People can be both mad and bad. And to the extent they are bad, they deserve to be punished. (Perhaps, too, treating people as responsible encourages them to take responsibility for themselves.) Further, the counterclaims, first, that the criminal sanction including jail terms cannot deter disordered persons because their crime is a product of disorder, and, second, that hospitalization will more effectively reduce criminal recidivism among the mentally disordered, are simply unproven assertions.

The goal of providing treatment to disordered persons who commit crimes should not preclude use of the criminal justice system. If treatment, such as drugs or psychotherapy, is required, it can be provided in jails; hospitals provide very little that is necessarily unique to them. Although it is unlikely that jails will provide treatment services equal to those available in hospitals, it is equally unlikely that many petty, disordered criminals will spend much time in jail. In any event, the treatment services available in jails are often inexcusably poor and should be vastly improved. To the extent that the criminalization problem is created by putting mentally disordered persons in inhumane jails for minor crimes such as vagrancy, perhaps the solution is to abolish such crimes and to improve the jails, and not to maintain hospitals so that jail can be avoided as a response to such arguably unnecessary crimes. Of course, vagrancy and like crimes may be maintained on the books, but reform in one area cannot always await reforms in other areas. To require thorough reform of all the intertwined parts of a system before allowing reform of any one part is effectively to prevent any reform at all.

In sum, if involuntary commitment is abolished there may well be an increase in the criminal justice processing of relatively mild deviance, and increased numbers of crazy persons may spend some time in unpleasant and often terrible jails (Dickey 1980; Urmer 1973). But if crazy persons are almost always responsible for their behavior, and, if incarceration in a jail is ever justified, there is no reason why they should not go to jail. This outcome is in fact more respectful of the dignity and autonomy of crazy persons than assuming they are nonresponsible and must be "fixed." Jails and locked hospitals are both massive intrusions on liberty. If the argument against jails is that they are bad places, as they surely are for noncrazy and crazy inmates alike, they should be cleaned up. Using unjustified hospitalization—which is itself incarceration and which offers little if any of its promised benefits—to avoid jails is not a sensible solution to the problems of criminal justice; it only allows us to avoid those problems.

The actual account of harm likely to flow from abolition is small (Test and Stein 1980), and the promised workability and benefits of the involuntary commitment system are illusory. If involuntary commitment is maintained to "save" the very few, enormous amounts of liberty will be unjustifiably deprived without sufficient corresponding benefits. Society is willing to allow some preventable harms in order to increase the liberty of all citizens. If involuntary commitment is abolished, the climate of freedom in our society will increase; no longer will the mentally disordered be specially subject to unnecessary restraints on their rights to physical liberty, freedom of speech, freedom of association, and other fundamental rights of citizens in a free society.

Benefits to Mental Health Professionals

Mental health professionals would benefit enormously from the abolition of involuntary commitment. First, abolition would clearly reduce the role confusion and waste of resources engendered by professionals acting as both healers and incarcerating social control agents. Second, if the involuntary aspects of mental health practice were prohibited, the tensions, discomforts, and resource waste created by legal regulation of mental health practice would be vastly reduced.

There would seem to be little reason for mental health professionals to assume the role of agents of social control. If involuntary commitment and treatment were abolished, mental health professionals would still be faced with more voluntary patients than they could treat adequately, and the era of legalization that has been a source of so much tension and discomfort to mental health professionals would end. It may reasonably be estimated that roughly 5 million persons in our society suffer from severe mental disorders and could benefit from treatment (Talbott 1981; Task Panel 1978). Of these 5 million, somewhat over 2 million are chronically and severely disabled (Talbott 1981). If all "pedigreed" mental health professionals (psychiatrists, psychologists, psychiatric social workers, psychiatric nurses) ignored all other client populations and treated only severely disordered persons, there would still be far too few professionals and other resources to provide even moderately good treatment to all the members of this group. Thus, large numbers of the most severely disordered persons—not to mention all others— would not be treated adequately. Moreover, I think it is reasonable to assume that, within the group of severely disordered persons, the subgroup of those who would be willing to consent to services is still larger than could reasonably be treated optimally given current mental health resources. One must ask, therefore, why mental health professionals want to confine and treat some severely disordered persons involuntarily—that is, persons who do not want services— when there are insufficient professionals and resources to treat adequately those severely disordered persons who *do want* services and when behaving directly as social control agents is antithetical to their professional desires and training?

A first answer often given is that there are dangerous people who need to be confined for the protection of others. But if so, why not turn this task over to the criminal justice system as Stone (1975) and Roth (1979), for example, have suggested? Social control of truly dangerous people should be left to the institutions expert at dealing with such problems—the police and the criminal justice system (Stone 1975). Another response is that, if society did not intervene involuntarily, some disordered persons who are dangerous to themselves would be abandoned to preventable suffering and degradation (and perhaps even death). This is perhaps true, but, in the context of severely limited resources, time spent treating involuntary patients is time spent *not* treating patients who want services and who will face equally preventable harm. If only a limited amount of suffering, degradation, and other harms can be prevented, why not help only those who want help? Not only would the maximum amount of care and prevention still be offered, but, as we shall see, all the ancillary costs created by the involuntary system would be avoided.

Healing is a goal that is and should be distinct from social control. The former is benign and seeks to help needy individuals. The latter in punitive in fact and seeks to protect society at the individual's expense. The business of mental health professionals should be to give care, comfort, and treatment to disordered, disabled persons who seek their help. When mental health professionals are asked to decide who should be locked up or to ensure that those who are locked up remain incarcerated, they are asked to perform functions for which they lack the training and the desire. They are trained to treat patients, not to house inmates. If healing proceeds on a voluntary basis and separate from social control functions, it will avoid a conflict of interests for patients and professionals alike.

Mental health professionals often complain with considerable justification about the legalization of public mental health practice (Stone, in press). They believe it intrudes unduly on professional prerogatives and makes the provision of adequate mental health care almost impossible. The critics of legalization fail to recognize three important points, however. First, legal reform was in part a response to undoubted medical and legal abuses, and there is little reason to believe such abuses would not recur if the fetters of legalization were removed. Second, in our society, legal regulation of a system that leads to such an extensive deprivation of liberty and stigmatization in unavoidable. Legalization clearly intrudes on mental health practice, but it is absolutely necessary to protect the rights of patients who may be incarcerated and treated involuntarily. Third and most important, proponents of involuntary hospitalization fail to recognize that, if the involuntary aspects of mental health practice were abolished, most of the intrusive fetters of legalization would also be abolished. Court hearings and other legal second guessings about decisions to hospitalize and treat a person are necessary only if these decisions are made against the will of the patient. If psychiatric services were voluntary, their regulation, like regulation of most medical practice, could be left to internal professional review and suits for malpractice. If patients do not like a hospital, mental health professional, or treatment, they can refuse the treatment or seek help elsewhere; there will be many patients to replace them. If involuntary hospitalization and treatment were not available, mental health professionals could devote their full time to doing what they are trained for and desire to do—caring for and treating suffering persons who want help. This is why they entered psychology or psychiatry as a profession. Mental health professionals would then be practicing as they always hoped they would, and they would not be forced into the unpleasant role of coercive control agents with interests opposed to those of the patient.

In addition to removing the shackles of legal regulation, abolition would also largely remove mental health professionals from the role of courtroom experts, a role ill-suited to their training and societal needs. Civil commitment hearings generally require expert testimony from mental health professionals who are often given the de facto power to decide the ultimate legal issue of whether a person should be involuntarily incarcerated in a mental hospital (Cohen 1966; Fein and Miller 1972). Of course, such professionals are not legal, moral, or social experts, and thus they are being asked to decide questions beyond their competence. Although these problems can be largely prevented by asking experts the right questions and by not allowing them to testify on ultimate legal issues, expert testimony and the examinations upon which it is based require the expenditure of much professional time that would be better spent on the provision of therapeutic services (Shwed 1978; Slovenko 1977). When a psychiatrist or psychologist from an understaffed state hospital must spend a morning in court, many hours' worth of treatment expertise is being wasted to the detriment of needy patients and with little consequent benefit to society or the persons involuntarily committed. This problem cannot be remedied by abbreviating commitment hearings. If much mental health professional time is not being used in commitment hearings, the fact finder is not being provided with the competent and complete information necessary for a full and fair hearing.

Abolition of involuntary commitment would thus seem to be in the self-interest of mental health professionals. Not only would they be able to practice without the shackles of the legal system, but they would be able to spend their time using their talents in the most productive way—helping patients who want to be helped.

The Enhancement of Treatment

As a matter of well-grounded speculation, it is reasonable to expect that treatment in general will be enhanced if it is offered voluntarily. This point seems to be recognized generally as evidenced by the clear preference nationwide for voluntary services (Wexler 1974). If the treating professional is entirely the patient's agent and is not perceived also as an agent of the state, the therapeutic alliance and the ameliorative influence of the therapist's authority will surely be strengthened. If treatments are offered in a respectful and caring fashion and the benefits and costs are explained clearly and patiently to the disordered person, one can expect much less resistance to treatment and the optimum chance for therapeutic gain. This type of behavior will consume substantial therapist time, but it is merely the preferred traditional, voluntary, and contractual mode of treatment initiation. And instituting such a voluntary scheme would not limit the work of mental health professionals. There are sufficient numbers of disordered persons who want or would accept help if it were properly offered to keep all therapists occupied full time. There would be no waste of therapeutic resources.

Cost Savings

A final benefit of abolition will be the freeing of the resources now spent on unnecessary hospitalization, custodial care, and the legal apparatus necessary to insure the minimal fairness of the system. We have already noted that custodial hospitalization is terribly expensive and wasteful and that most needed mental health treatment and services can be provided effectively and cheaply on an outpatient basis (Chambers 1978; Weisbrod et al., 1980). The influx of funds resulting from abolition of involuntary commitment, if legislatures were willing to reallocate them for community mental health needs, could be used to enhance community services to reach a greater number of needy citizens at a higher level of quality.

It may be contended that de-institutionalization will not be cheaper if it is accomplished properly because community treatments are also expensive and there might be greater utilization of such resources. Mental health treatment is undeniably expensive, but per patient it is almost certainly cheaper overall in the community than when involuntary hospitalization is employed. And, if increased utilization is the result of offering quality treatment in the community on a voluntary basis, it is unthinkable to use such an increase as a basis for decreasing community services and increasing involuntary hospitalization.

Involuntary commitment provides very few persons with few benefits at great cost. Abolition would make possible the treatment, under conditions of freedom, of greater numbers with greater benefit.

Summary Discussion: Legalization and the Future of Involuntary Commitment

For the past two decades, lawyers and others interested in liberty and humane treatment for mentally disordered persons have litigated and lobbied ceaselessly to restrict the criteria for involuntary commitment, to promote de-institutionalization and other alternatives to involuntary incarceration, to increase the procedural protections accorded to those in danger of commitment, and to expand the civil liberties of patients and ex-patients. The result has been a cascade of litigation and legislation that has "legalized" the commitment process and has nearly uniformly furthered the described goals of the patients' rights advocates (Schwitzgebel 1978a). In response, the favored objections to legalization are that needy persons are not receiving necessary care and treatment and that the law and legal advocates are intruding improperly and harmfully into what are allegedly medical and mental health matters. That legalization has done some good and that patients should have rights (at least in theory) nearly all will admit (Kahle and Sales 1980), but, it is countered, the process has nonetheless gone too far (Brakel 1981).

The argument that legalization has gone too far or has caused more problems than it has solved is entirely incorrect. Before the interventions of the patients' advocates, patients had almost no rights in practice, and most commitments involved little more than warehousing under often brutal conditions. One must constantly remember that the right to treatment and the right to habilitation suits which exposed the utterly shocking and inhumane conditions in state hospitals in various states (*Halderman* v. *Pennhurst State School & Hospital*, 1977; *New York State Assn. for Retarded Children, Inc.* v. *Rockefeller*, 1973), were products of the 1970s, not the distant past. There is little if any indication that in general patients were obtaining rights or decent care and treatment prior to the legalization movement. I am not claiming that legalization has been a panacea; indeed, vast problems remain (see Arnhoff 1975; Dickey 1980; Stier and Stoebe 1979; Warren 1977). Nor am I denying that untrained and overzealous advocates may have overstepped their bounds and disrupted programs in some instances (Brakel 1981).[21] But even now patients are overcommitted, and the conditions of confinement and the treatment they receive are often only a tiny fraction of what they really require.

Legalization has not gone too far—it has not gone far enough. Society and the mental health professions have not been willing on their own initiative to provide sufficient services to its needy, mentally disordered citizens. The continued legalization of the involuntary commitment system would be unnecessary if society cared for its chronically disabled citizens and if the mental health professions were willing to put their houses in order. But neither of these conditions obtains, and it is the duty of legalization proponents to seek to limit current involuntary commitment, to make it more humane, and ultimately, one hopes, to contribute to its abolition.

Many will argue in response to the argument in favor of abolition (or restriction) that abolition will not abolish mental disorder and the social and familial problems it causes. Moreover, it is predicted that many disordered persons will live in the community, as they do now, in a state of misery and degradation. The first point cannot be gainsaid: mental disorder—whether it is conceptualized as disease or deviant conduct or whatever—and its consequences will continue, and it is true that the conditions under which many disordered persons now live in the community are repulsive and a moral disgrace to our society. These are problems that need attending to, and there are persons who need care. But, as argued throughout this chapter, the answer is not to maintain involuntary hospitalization. The involuntary commitment system, as now constituted, does not alleviate substantially the ills of the disordered; rather, it only partially removes disordered persons and their problems from the consciousness and conscience of our society at an enormous cost in liberty. If there is any solution, however partial, it is to provide the resources to insure that decent food, shelter, clothing, and treatment are provided vol-

---

21. It should be pointed out, however, that some disruption is the inevitable product of a system that exists in tension between liberty and paternalism and that allows advocates to help patients. Disruption could be minimized, however, by various procedural innovations. For instance, if the conditions of confinement, including the provision of involuntary treatment, were adjudicated and ordered at the initial commitment hearing, conflict within the hospital might be lessened and would arise mainly if there was a substantial deterioration in the patient's condition, or if the hospital failed to provide the requisite rights and care to the patient. Of course, most disruption of this sort would be eliminated if all psychiatric treatment was voluntary.

untarily *in the community* in the least restrictive manner to those who need them.

The legalization movement is forcing society and the mental health professions to come to terms with what it is willing to do for and to its most disordered citizens. Do we mean to treat and cure people, or do we mean to cast them out and warehouse them? The movement has been successful because it has exposed the unfulfilled claims and promises and the cant of the involuntary commitment movement. Indeed, it appears to me that setbacks to legalization occur in precisely those cases (such as *Addington*) where a court or legislature succumbs to the unjustified and incompletely analyzed assertions of those favoring involuntary commitment. Much of the argument in favor of commitment is predicated on a vision of mental health care in state hospitals that can only be described as mythical. If judges or legislators envision relatively pleasant hospitals with reasonably sufficient and trained staff who form caring relationships with most patients and who deliver quality treatments offering treatable patients a reasonable possibility of cure, it is then relatively easy to reject legalization. Although an involuntary commitment system may seen reasonable in theory, the history is clear that the system does not and cannot work in practice. Legalization has been and continues to be a success for just this reason.

I fear that the seductive superficial reasonableness of the arguments in favor of commitment will prevent its abolition in the near future. But to accept the false vision of the need for and quality of care provided by involuntary commitment will be once again to ignore hypocritically the true plight of the mentally disordered. If society never faces the reality, there will be cycles of greater and lesser civil rights for patients, but the substandard quality of care in public and many private mental hospitals will remain constant (Lamb 1979). Moreover, as the success of legalization continues, I also fear that society will be unwilling to pay the price in terms of caring, tolerance, and material outlay that are necessary and that further inroads on patients' rights may occur. Nevertheless, proponents of abolition should strive to terminate or at least severely restrict involuntary incarceration of disordered persons and to encourage the provision of adequate care in the community.

If care and treatment services are voluntary and reasonably provided to disordered persons in the community and if social control is left primarily to the criminal justice system, freedom will be vastly enhanced without an inevitable reduction in efficacious service. Hospitals will still exist because some needy people will desire to enter a hospital and perhaps some can be treated best or only in such an environment. The vast majority of citizens, however, will be able to obtain needed service in an atmosphere of dignity-enhancing freedom, and professionals will be freed to devote their full time to the tasks for which they are truly trained—the diagnosis and treatment of mental disorder. Of course, if involuntary incarceration in a hospital is not available, disordered citizens on occasions may seriously endanger themselves or others; no social intervention, no matter how beneficial, is entirely cost free. But our social climate of liberty will be immeasurably increased; persons will be treated as dignified and autonomous human beings. I believe abolition of involuntary confinement and all its ramifications are well worth the costs that are likely to result.

5 The Need for Intervention
The Reasons for State Control of the Mentally Disordered

Jack Zusman, M.D.

*T*he need for a mechanism of state control[1] over the lives of severely mentally disordered persons has been a constant though unpleasant aspect of organized society. This need has been recognized for centuries; a variety of psychiatric and judicial procedures has developed in response (Alexander and Selesnick 1966; Deutsch 1949). But as life in modern industrial society has become more complicated and individuals have become more interdependent, the need has become greater. Paradoxically, with the increased need for assistance to and control over those who have been rendered dangerous or helpless by mental disorder, the questioning of the existence of this need and the attacks upon the mechanisms by which the need is met have also become greater.

Some aspects of these attacks have indeed been justifiable. In some states, particularly in years past, the law has permitted involuntary hospitalization of any person found by a physician or a judge (depending upon state law) to be no more than in need of treatment for a mental disorder (Brakel and Rock 1971; Stone 1975). In many cases, such as that of Kenneth Donaldson (see Chaps. 3 and 9), this involuntary hospitalization has continued for years without any review of

1. By state control, I refer to civil commitment or involuntary hospitalization, guardianship or conservatorship, involuntary treatment, and a variety of less common means by which mentally disordered persons are officially compelled to obey the decision of others. By mentally disordered, I refer to persons who are mentally ill, alcoholic, mentally retarded, or suffer from other conditions which lead to loss of intellectual ability or self-control. I do not mean to imply that there are no distinctions among these conditions but, for the purposes of this brief discussion, I will treat them as if they were alike. Furthermore, I do not mean to imply that state control is appropriate for all persons who suffer from these conditions. Only a small number of the total group fits into the category of needing control.

whether the patient had recovered, was being helped, or might not be better off without hospitalization (Rock, Jacobson, and Janopaul 1968; *O'Connor* v. *Donaldson*, 1975; *Wyatt* v. *Stickney*, 1972). In most states, treatment efforts were almost nonexistent in the large public hospitals to which involuntary patients were usually sent for treatment (Deutsch 1971). Judges, attorneys, legislators, administrators, and physicians all supported and participated in this farcical system, and patients' rights as citizens, let alone as patients, were never considered. In retrospect, it seems strange that it could have happened. Then, it seems even stranger when one recognizes it is still happening (*Los Angeles Times* 1979; Staats, 1976).

Some have used the appalling past condition of public mental hospitals to argue that state control over the mentally disordered is never justified (Leifer 1969; Szasz 1963). Perhaps appealing in part to the emotional reaction produced by the contrast between the needs of the mentally ill and the shameful way in which society responded to these needs, such persons have argued for the abolition of involuntary psychiatric treatment, or even for the abolition of all psychiatric treatment. But the wrong which has been done in the past does not change the fact of present and future need. There are some adults who are mentally unable to fend for themselves. If some person or agency does not step in, these individuals will be severely harmed and in some cases will harm others.

No doubt that with good educational systems, strong community support networks, and tolerance and goodwill by all citizens, the number of such disordered persons can be reduced below what it has been in the past. Nevertheless, it is impossible to conceive of a world in which there is no one who lacks the mental capacity to care responsibly for himself and others and also lacks the capacity to recognize his deficits. If such a world cannot exist, the only practical questions then are, How many such disabled persons are there? How do we accurately recognize them? And what mechanism do we wish to use to help both them and us avoid injury?

It is important to emphasize that such persons are not any less human than the rest of us, that is, they should not be treated with any less respect. However, their condition requires that they lose some of their human rights—particularly those rights relating to self determination. Just as children below the age of judgment are human but unable to determine independently of their parents or guardians what the courses of their lives will be, some mentally disordered persons must also be governed by others. No matter how much we may dislike facing the facts, the facts are that some adults are unable to perceive the world accurately, other adults are unable to predict the consequences of their actions, and still others are unable to communicate their desires. Some persons suffer from all of these dis-abilities. Such persons cannot survive in the world without help, including direct control. Often the disabled person is not able to understand or decide the issues relating to accepting help. In other cases, the person is apparently able to understand but does not ap-preciate the possible consequences of refusing help. Such persons must have outside direction over their lives if they are to survive. For many of them, freedom from control means suffering or death—a fate which they cannot comprehend, much less rationally choose.

This is not to imply that, even if state control is limited to a small group of the mentally ill, there will not be occasional mistakes and injustices. No system which is used to screen masses of people can ever perform perfectly. Some persons who should not be subject to state control will be screened in, and some persons who should be subject to state control will be screened out. Some of these errors undoubtedly will lead to serious injury of innocent persons—loss of freedom on the one hand, and loss of life on the other.

But before discarding a system because of its errors, one must consider how significant the errors are in comparison to the results of an alternative system or no system at all.

In the remainder of this chapter I will explain the bases of these statements and show why I consider some of the objections com-monly raised to state control of the mentally disordered, such as those raised by Morse in the previous chapter, to be insufficient.

A Matter of Values

Though I believe that both logic and experience support the con-tinued existence of state control, I believe also that in the final analysis the decision must be based on values not facts. This recog-nition of the centrality of values is particularly important because many of the statements which both proponents and opponents of state control use to support their positions (including myself) are of a sort which ordinarily are expected to be based on an examination of data and a weighing of facts. Unfortunately, for the most part in this case, the data are lacking. Necessary systematic studies are yet to be done, and discussion must rely on no more than estimates and anec-dotes based on personal (and therefore probably unrepresentative) experience. But for every presumed instance of a life saved by invol-untary hospitalization which proponents describe, opponents have no difficulty countering with a life destroyed by years of unjust in-carceration. Neither side knows how typical such instances are nor how distorted they have become in the telling. Indeed, this danger of unrepresentativeness may particularly apply to some of the famous patient subjects of the landmark lawsuits.

The Problem of Data

If hospitalization were a medication to be prescribed for the mentally ill by physicians, its use undoubtedly would not be permitted by the federal government because it is so poorly tested both as to negative and positive effects. To be sure, our experience with it goes back hundreds of years, but our knowledge of it goes barely deeper than personal opinion. Thus data gathering and unbiased analyses of the effects of state control are long overdue. These studies take years to design and complete, so it is sad to see they will still be lacking for some time to come, since current interest in and support for such studies are scarce. But even when the data are in and we have some idea of how often state control is helpful and how often harmful, the final weighing must still be a matter of values. Data will considerably focus the issues under consideration and will eliminate the need to rely on estimates and untested assumptions but will not make the hard decisions for us.

In part this is because studies rarely can be designed to give yes or no answers to practical problems. Thus studies of involuntary hospitalization might tell us, for example, given 100 patients of a certain degree of illness who had a certain minimum of time in hospital, that five years after onset of the illness so many were alive and so many of those were recovered. The experimental design would enable us to predict that had the same 100 patients not been hospitalized, five years later their conditions would differ in some particular way. Included in the study might be comparisons of some of the other effects of hospitalization and nonhospitalization such as costs of treatment, extent of damage and disruption to the lives of family members, disability and discomfort resulting from prolonged hospitalization.

Yet when the study or series of studies were completed, we would be left with the extremely difficult task of sensibly applying them: What do the results of a study of 100 patients of one particular type mean in relation to the illness outcome of a patient similar to but not quite the same as those studied? What about patients hospitalized in settings different (better or worse) than those in the study? What is the effect of intermittent hospitalization when the study was concerned only with continuous hospitalization? We are never sure exactly how to apply what we know from the past to what we predict for the future. We must make estimates, knowing that there will be errors.

The second and more important issue is that, even if we could know exactly what the outcome would be in a particular case, how can we weigh the positive outcome elements against the negative ones and arrive at a decision? If we could reliably predict that hospitalization would prevent some irrational act, for example, what course should we choose? Is the loss of freedom from involuntary hospitalization worth the avoidance of injury? If we know that by locking up 100 apparently dangerous mentally ill persons we could prevent 3 suicides, 5 homicides, and 10 injuries but would also incarcerate 82 persons who would not have injured anyone, should we do so? How much of an innocent person's liberty is another person's life worth? These are not technical, scientific, or medical questions. They are questions which concern us all and about which everyone ought to have a voice. The decision to trade the prevention of a particular number of suicides or homicides for a certain number of years of unnecessary incarceration ought to be made by voters and legislators trying to put into practice what they feel is right and necessary. Facts and logic can help to make this weighing more precise but cannot replace the role of values.

To the extent that such a tradeoff has already been made—as seen in the mental health laws of each of our states—it is clear that our values favor some degree of state control (Brakel and Rock 1971). Admittedly, the present laws have been written in ignorance of all the facts and in part based upon impressions—prejudices if you will. But I do not see the slightest indication that any additional facts which could conceivably come to light will change the fundamental attitudes of the public. These attitudes obviously prescribe that the state not stand by while some of the mentally disordered group destroy themselves and those around them. These values call for intervention, both to aid the helpless and to prevent disasters to others. They call for the involvement of experts and specialized institutions in the intervention system. Thus, the only useful question to consider, it seems to me, is not whether state control should continue, but what form it should take.

The Need for State Intervention

The need for state control and intervention in the lives of the mentally disordered who are helpless or dangerous is increasing. The power which each of us has to damage ourselves or those around us has been greatly magnified by the universal accessibility of modern technologies. Thus, in the past the carrying out of an irrational (or for that matter rational) homicidal impulse often required catching and physically overpowering the victim and then applying great physical force. The alternative was to use an elaborate scheme and materials, such as poison, not easily available. Suicide, too, was not very easily accomplished because instruments of destruction were not very effective nor readily available. Successful homicide or suicide usually required strength, or persistence and planning—a combination not frequently found among the mentally disordered.

These days a child can direct or control physical force far beyond that available even to the most powerful ruler of years ago. Cars, electrical and gas appliances, guns, airplanes, noxious chemicals, even the electricity which can be drawn from the wall outlet, all are more or less freely available as destructive instruments capable of being misused by the mentally disordered through error, accident, or misjudgment. Combined with easy availability is the closeness of quarters in which we reside in urban areas. We must rely upon each other's benign motivation, self-control, and carefulness to avoid damaging incidents.

At the same time as the potential for damage has increased because of the physical energy now under control of the ordinary person, the tolerance for error, accident, or misjudgment in the inanimate systems with which we live has declined. Where years ago, the confused or "absent-minded" person who prepared a cooking fire in a coal stove but forgot to light it lost no more than a delay in meal preparation, now such a person may produce a gas explosion which can destroy a neighborhood. A minor misdirection of a car on a freeway lasting no more than a fraction of a second can result in many deaths and injuries. In a completely different sphere, failure to mark the proper place on a complicated application for government benefits can lead to a response delay of many months or even the loss of thousands of desperately needed dollars. Ignorance of the availability of and eligibility requirements for a particular social welfare program can lead to failure to receive benefits which could provide otherwise unaffordable food or housing.

Where previously many mentally disabled persons would unhesitatingly and easily be cared for by family members who would do what seemed right and necessary without considering state intervention or legal issues, this arrangement has now become far more complex. At least in part because of changing living arrangements—nuclear families living in cities, rather than extended families living in rural areas—and changing values involved in the increased availability of public facilities and social welfare funding, these days the family of a mentally disordered person cannot be relied upon to care for the ailing person (Roth 1973). Impersonal, complex, expensive bureaucracies must step in instead.

Though no doubt in many ways we are better off than our ancestors, technologically and socially the world has now become a much more dangerous and complicated place. Because the person whose ability to cope with modern demands has been significantly diminished by mental disorder stands in far greater danger of injuring self or others than in years past, there exists a greater need for state control.

The Benefits versus the Harms of State Control

Yet, removing an individual's ability to determine essential aspects of his or her own life in order to place that individual's destiny formally in the hands of other persons—whether these other persons be loving relatives or impersonal civil servants—is a violation of fundamental human rights not to be undertaken lightly. Only a careful weighing of the benefits and harms resulting from stepping in to take control versus the benefits and harms from not stepping in and a determination that the good in the former case outweighs the bad in the latter will justify such a step. As already discussed, such a comparison is a subjective one and will always be a matter to debate.

The comparison of the harms and benefits of the two positions takes place on two levels: the general and the specific. The general, philosophic issue is usually examined by the legislature: can state control *ever* be preferable to personal freedom? If so, in what kinds of cases?

Our state legislatures, which are the groups with primary jurisdiction in this instance, have uniformly decided that state control should be permitted in some cases. Details vary from state to state, but the concept is everywhere approved in principle (Stone 1975, p. 47).

A second decision process occurs in regard to each individual mentally disordered candidate for state control. Here, the forum is usually the courtroom. A judge must decide, using state law as the basis, whether state control is justified for a particular individual. Expert testimony is commonly used, and increasingly the legal process is a genuine adversarial one, with arguments presented to the judge both for and against control (*Addington* v. *Texas,* 1979; *Estate of Roulet,* 1979). This is the way it should be, since no expert and no decision maker is ever in possession of all of the facts or of the ability to forecast the future with certainty. Examination of conflicting points of view ensures that the weaknesses underlying an opinion will be considered.

The Mentally Ill Are Different

Why do we need a special means of dealing with the mentally disordered? Why can we not treat them like everyone else, as responsible for their own actions, free to do as they wish and reap the benefits or take the consequences?

The answers to these questions are based on our social philosophy—a collection of shared beliefs, revered traditions, laws, and common practices—which is only partially written down and is probably best learned from observation of what we[2] do.

We believe in free will and self-control. We assume that most persons are able to make considered decisions most of the time about what course of action to take among the many usually available, and then are able to make themselves act in accordance with their decisions. To assist each of us in acting in such a way as to maximize our ability to live with each other, we promulgate rules and establish a series of rewards and punishments to back up the rules. (The origin of the rules is, of course, an unsettled issue but one we need not bother with here.) Some of the rules are laws, others are customs.

When someone violates a rule we assume that person has deliberately chosen to forgo the rewards of obedience and to take the risks of disobedience. We do not hesitate once the individual is identified to hold that person accountable. When a person achieves success, we provide rewards to that person—the other side of our belief in individual accountability.

We have great confidence in the efficacy of this arrangement and, for the most part, it seems to work extremely well. We can confidently cross the street with the green light, knowing the traffic will stop for the red light. We can hand our money over the the bank teller, knowing we will get it back whenever we ask for it. We sign contracts with each other, never doubting that, even if it turns out one party loses by the agreement, the agreement will still be in effect despite the loser's displeasure. In every case we know that the individuals involved will respond in a predictable way despite any temporary annoyance, discomfort, or loss the individuals feel. Even the losers in a transaction recognize that predictable behavior will lead in the long run to greater gain for them and for the things they care about. And the individuals are capable of controlling their behavior in accordance with their knowledge and their rational decision making.

Thus the rules of society and our confidence in their effectiveness bind us together and make us a society rather than a group of individuals.

---

2. "We" in this case refers to the people of the United States (and to the extent that citizens of other countries have similar customs, to these countries as well).

Rule Breakers

But, what about the individual who cannot understand the rules or who, despite understanding them, is incapable of exerting the self-control to follow them?[3] (These people are to be distinguished from "ordinary criminals" who presumably break rules for rational reasons—e.g., for personal financial gain or in response to realistic enmity—and who could refrain from rule breaking if it seemed in their interest to do so.) We often do not feel safe in the presence of persons in the former group because the usually effective encouragements and deterrents do not work with them. Rules, rewards, threats, physical force, even a pointed gun, may not influence the individual who is unable to judge the significance of anyone of them. Their behavior is unpredictable—at least to the average person.

Traditionally we deal with these individuals in several special ways (Parsons 1951). First, we do not hold them accountable for their actions or omissions. We feed them, clothe them, and care for them, though they do nothing to earn these resources, because we believe in helping the helpless. We do not punish them for their rule breaking because we recognize their rule breaking is not deliberate and, therefore, is not blameworthy.

Second, usually we try to remove these individuals from society or to remove their access to potentially damaging instruments and forces otherwise easily available. This is for the protection of everyone else, since we recognize that the rule-breaking individuals are ordinarily not responsible to repair any injuries which they do. Thus most such damages are borne strictly by the injured party who is as innocent as the disordered person if not more so.

Third, we try to change these individuals, to make them rule obeyers like everybody else. We recognize that the process of undergoing change—that is, treatment—may involve some discomfort or loss of freedom for them. But we believe that in the long run if they do change they will be far better off, and their investment of time and trouble will be amply repaid.

To put it another way, many of the individuals under discussion as rule breakers are mentally disordered. When we come upon someone who seems to break rules without good reason (see Murphy's discussion in Chap. 3) or who does so repeatedly and seems unaffected by rewards and punishment, we call for the psychiatrist. The psychia-

3. I do not mean to suggest that self-control is an all-or-none process—i.e., either one has it or one does not. I believe that individuals have differing degrees of ability to control themselves and that situations call for differing degrees of self-control for successful accomplishment. Nevertheless, there are some persons whose control is obviously far below that of the average individual and far below that required for navigation among life's ordinary challenges. These people we treat as if they had no self-control. For most purposes, they do not.

trist is expected to determine if a mental disorder is present and, if so, to hospitalize the person and treat the illness. One sign of recovery will be the individual's reacceptance of the rules (though not necessarily obedience to the rules, since there can be good reasons for taking the risks of violation).

State control over the mentally disordered is thus an inherent and inseparable part of the belief in free will, individual responsibility, and personal accountability, upon which the governance of the United States and much of Western civilization is built. The fact that state control of the mentally disordered is available offers an essential safety valve. It provides a logically and legally consistent way of dealing with those few individuals whose behavior cannot be understood to be a result of free will without discarding the free-will concept for the rest of us.

To force these mentally disordered persons into the free-will mold, to hold them personally accountable, to deprive them of rewards and give them the punishments which the rules prescribe for their rule-breaking behavior would be inhumane and—if much of contemporary theory is correct—ineffective. Holding such persons accountable would be inhumane because punishment would cause them great pain without changing them. Furthermore, much of the rule breaking is done unintentionally, without recognition of the effect or import of the behavior. It is as if the behavior in question were accidental.

There is an ancient, revered tradition in our jurisprudence that punishment is only for crimes which are intended. (There are a few exceptions to our adherence to this doctrine but they are rare and so technical in a legal sense they are not worth considering.) Therefore we cannot punish these individuals who are innocent in the eyes of the law (Slovenko 1973, p. 77).

In addition, as far as we currently know, many mentally ill persons would not be changed by being held accountable or being punished for their behavior. The illness interferes with their ability to learn from experience and/or to predict the consequences of their behavior.

Finally, holding all rule breakers fully accountable simply for the sake of logical consistency would be so cruel, it is inconceivable we would do it. For we not only believe in free will, we believe that people are something special and cannot be treated with absolute logic and consistency like animals or machines. The rules must bend for special circumstances. But, in bending, the rules must not give way.

Therefore, though we do not hold mentally disordered rule breakers personally accountable, we do not ignore their rule breaking, and we do not leave all the rest of us exposed to their inadvertently damaging behavior. The state control mechanism is the major means available to deal humanely and as fairly as possible with rule breakers. The mechanism makes it simple for society simultaneously to accomplish several contradictory elements: believe in individual freedom, free will, and personal accountability; excuse the serious deviations of a group of persons who seem unwittingly not to fit into everyone else's scheme of beliefs; protect all concerned from many of the effects of the deviations. To paraphrase a cliché, if such a mechanism did not exist we would have to invent one.

As has been suggested already, not all rule breaking is mental disorder. Some rule breaking is a considered effort to gain an advantage. We all know that not everyone who breaks rules is caught and punished. Some rule breakers achieve great gains by rule breaking. Therefore there are those who decide to gamble on not getting caught. Other rule breakers determine that for them the likely gains outweigh the penalties, even if they are caught. Both types of individuals, though they may be frequent rule breakers, are not in the group under discussion. These people know and accept the rules and do control themselves. They simply choose not to obey.

Rule Breaking without Gain

Not all rule breaking turns out to be to the individual's advantage or to the disadvantage of others. Sometimes no one seems to benefit and all the losses are to the individual rule breaker. Such a situation would seem to call for a laissez-faire approach, if anything does, rather than state intervention. Nevertheless our social values dictate that the state step in here too to prevent harm. We recognize—perhaps basing our view on what we know of children and their needs—that it is wasteful and cruel to allow a person to carry out a self-damaging act which the person does not knowingly intend. When such acts occur we may even hold the bystanders who did not intervene morally accountable. We clearly believe that at least to a limited extent we are our brothers' keepers.

Failure to provide adequately for one's own physical needs is rule breaking in that we expect all adults to care properly for themselves. The individual who inadvertently starves to death or freezes to death is breaking rules whose violation does not call for punishment but which, nevertheless, calls for some social action, as does giving one's assets away and getting nothing material in return.

Suicide is rule breaking and probably the epitome of acts in which almost all of the negative consequences are directed against the actor rather than the rest of us. Since so much of the harm involves only the actor, should suicidal persons be restrained? Consensus among the public and among mental health professionals clearly is that they should be restrained for several reasons (Shneidman 1971).

The primary one is that, for many suicidally intent persons, the desire is an impulsive one, not a considered one. Once the impulse or mood has passed—which may be hours or a few days later—the individual who has been restrained has changed and is then thankful for not having been permitted to make an ill-considered, irrevocable decision. Having reconsidered the potential benefits of continued life versus the losses of ceasing to live, the individual now sees life as preferable. A short-term loss of freedom seems a small cost to pay for the benefit of avoiding a terribly costly mistake.

Other suicidal persons may be so not because of impulse but because of a disorder of perception or thought resulting from mental illness. Such a person may, for example, hear voices commanding suicide or think that jumping from a tall building will not result in harm. Behavior resulting from these types of problems calls for restraint and treatment as much as any other kind of harmful behavior does. The fact that the harm is directed back at the actor only is not really relevant in that we cannot assume that the person has deliberately made a decision to carry out the act despite appreciating its consequences.

By no means are all suicidal persons mentally disordered and, therefore, appropriate subjects for this sort of restraint. The question of whether all suicidal persons, mentally disordered or not, should be briefly restrained to insure deliberation will not be discussed but is one requiring consideration. Suicide can be the result of a thoughtful decision. Having carefully considered all the possible courses open if alive, an individual might determine that none of them is attractive enough to endure whatever negative consequences may be associated. Suicide can also be a careless or impulsive act by a person who is not mentally disordered. These individuals are not subjects for state control.

Inconsistencies in Mental Health Law

There are many apparent inconsistencies in the way we deal with rule breakers. Some suicidal persons are subject to state control and involuntarily hospitalized, others are not. More generally, some rule breakers are jailed as punishment after the fact; some persons thought to be likely future rule breakers are hospitalized without having committed any overt acts. If they do engage in rule breaking they are not punished. Other persons, also thought likely to be rule breakers but not because of mental disorder, are nevertheless not restrained in advance but are severely punished afterward. How can these inconsistencies be justified? Can the fact of these inconsistencies serve to support an argument for abolition of state control over the mentally disordered?

First, it ought not to be necessary to defend one set of inconsistencies alone among the many inconsistencies in our laws and customs. We are usually content to live with all of them. Indeed, inconsistencies serve the important functions of facilitating the testing of new legal approaches, offering flexibility to take unusual circumstances into account, and providing a way of meeting contradictory but equally important social needs. If all of law were based on logic and consistency, there would be far less need for judges and juries. Once facts were ascertained, a computer could probably apply the logical principles of the law and come up with a decision. Instead, we expect circumstances, values, traditions, and individual beliefs to be weighed in the application of our laws.

Research has demonstrated that eyewitness testimony is likely to be inaccurate, yet the law accords great weight to such testimony (Loftus 1979). Well-established scientific theories indicate that the world can be described only in terms of probabilities, not certainties. Still, the courts reject probability statements and look for testimony in terms of certainties (Tribe 1971). In law, consensus and tradition seem to be more important than logic or science.

Beyond the fact, though, that inconsistency is a necessary part of law is the fact that not every rule breaker is the same nor is every breaking of the same rule. We *always* take into account the reasons behind an action in determining how to deal with the action (Slovenko 1973, p. 77). We look upon and deal with the person who does not know or cannot know the rules differently from the person who is in full control but who makes a mistake. The latter person is treated still differently from the person who breaks a rule deliberately in the hope of not getting caught. We must continue to have different means of dealing with people who break rules for different reasons.

Involuntary Treatment

Forcing an individual to take treatment is a significant step beyond restraining the individual to prevent a harmful act. While incarceration to prevent rule breaking or to render it relatively harmless is unpleasant, forcible treatment violates physical and mental integrity of the victim and changes the doctor-patient relationship radically from the one both doctors and patients expect. The doctor is no longer employed to advise the patient and carry out the treatment the patient selects. The patient cannot discharge the doctor or change the treatment. The dependency and damage to self-esteem which any serious injury or illness produces is made worse by the physician's added power over the destiny of the patient. Though state laws usually authorize both restraint and treatment simultaneously for mentally disordered rule breakers, the latter is a far stronger measure requiring separate discussion.

To begin with, let us grant for the sake of discussion at least that treatment is ordinarily effective though it has some dangers. It is employed to reduce or eliminate the effects of the mental disorder so that the individual can evaluate the consequences of rule breaking and exert self-control. Its dangers include the side effects—unwanted, deleterious physical or mental responses—it can produce which are temporarily or permanently harmful, and the fact that it may be used inappropriately, also resulting in harm.

Treatment despite the patient's objections can be justified in limited circumstances on three grounds. First, some individuals are so confused as a result of mental disorder that they cannot understand the issue of accepting or not accepting treatment. A refusal to take treatment in such a case is not meaningful—it is little more than a chance determined response (as would be an agreement in the same circumstances to go along with treatment). There is no way that extremely confused individuals can offer a meaningful opinion about anything. Some of these people do not respond when asked about treatment. Others respond but obviously do not comprehend. They are as incapable of assenting to or refusing treatment as is an infant or an unconscious person. Still others are highly ambivalent (see Chap. 3).

What then should be done? To deny the person treatment on the grounds of lack of consent means condemning at least some persons to continued illness which they do not want. At least some of these individuals would choose treatment if they could know what was going on or may even be attempting to communicate such a desire but failing to do so. Is refusal to provide treatment because of lack of consent in such circumstances any less harmful or less intrusive than treatment? The consensus seems to be no. The state therefore authorizes those measures which medical specialists familiar with the issues advise, and the state does what it seems most likely the average individual would want done under such circumstances.

Second, a number of the candidates for involuntary treatment are potentially physically violent. They are dangerous to hospital staff, other patients, and themselves. Unless measures are taken to calm them, such as administration of tranquilizing drugs, to avoid injury to others they must be treated in such a restrictive manner that their confinement is very inhumane and harmful. Specifically for some persons, the alternative to involuntary medication is to be locked alone in a cell for long periods or tied in restraining clothing while being avoided by other patients and staff.

It may be, as some have pointed out, that a portion of the violence which the treatment is intended to control results from the involuntary patients' rightful indignation at and resistance to unjust incarceration or other inappropriate treatment by staff (Ennis 1972, p. 194). Violence is then no more than self-defense, this argument goes, and would best be prevented by eliminating incarceration. But this does not make the violence any less dangerous for nearby staff and patients, nor their reactions to the violent individual any less negative. Whatever the cause, the cycle of mutually antagonistic reactions between the patient and those nearby must be broken to achieve the outcome which all desire—the release of the patient. Furthermore, without a provision for involuntary treatment of the potentially violent, most treatment settings could not operate because staff could not function properly or safely. This would lead to the loss of the whole system of state control and a diminution of freedom for all.

Third, the availability and use of involuntary treatment makes it possible to alleviate many mental disorders in involuntary patients which otherwise could drag on for years, if not for lifetimes. Such long-term mental illness is not only an unnecessary cost to the ill individual—in money not earned, pleasure not enjoyed, and abilities not developed—but also a similar unnecessary cost to those close to the individual and to all the rest of us. Though the individual may have the right to forgo treatment and thereby incur his or her own costs—for the sake of discussion, let us agree—but does the individual have the right to impose the costs on others?

The costs to others come about in several ways. Several studies of severely mentally ill persons living in the community have shown such persons can be very disruptive to the lives of their families, friends, and neighbors (Sainsbury and Grad de Alarcon 1973; Yarrow et al. 1955). Some mentally disordered persons are uncooperative in family life, loud or violent, or act in such a way as to be health hazards, nuisances, or generally unpleasant. The psychic cost to family and neighborhoods in putting up with this disruption indefinitely is great. To be sure, in principle, families can evict the disordered member and neighbors can press criminal charges, but these are not realistic options. Such actions are often seen by the people who would be required to undertake them against the mentally ill person as hostile acts against a helpless, guiltless individual.

For the rest of us, the costs are in the social welfare services we must pay for year after year for the person unnecessarily disabled by illness because of the refusal of treatment. The repeated police services, hospitalizations, disability payments, support for unwanted and uncared for children, etc., all add up to significant sums which we are taxed to pay.

The Diagnostic Problem

Central to the operation of a just, effective system of state control is the ability to discriminate between those who are proper subjects for control and those who are not. In essence, this means separating those who cannot conform (and therefore are subjects for state control before the damage occurs) from those who will not conform (and therefore are subjects for punishment after the damage). Such a process is related to but yet not the same as conventional psychiatric diagnosis.

Conventional diagnosis involves categorizing or labeling persons utilizing a standardized and abstract set of terms in relation to their symptoms and previous experiences. Diagnosis is a crucial process for treatment since selection of the treatment usually depends upon diagnosis. Diagnosis is also important for predicting the eventual outcome of the problem and for research.

However, mental incapacity and dangerousness—the two traits of particular concern here—are not directly related to diagnosis. To a large extent they cut across diagnostic categories, and the extensive studies of diagnosis and attempts to refine diagnostic abilities are not relevant.

A fundamental question is how effectively psychiatrists—or any other group—can recognize those who are proper subjects for state control. Unfortunately, the research on this subject is rather indirect and so leaves us in doubt as to the answer. Even more unfortunately, the research, for whatever it is worth, suggests that psychiatric ability to recognize dangerousness is very poor.

Dangerousness

A direct study of dangerousness would involve having psychiatrists examine a large group of people and separate them into dangerous and nondangerous. All of these individuals would then be permitted to go on their way and be checked again after some interval. At that point a comparison would be made between the prediction and the outcome. A series of such studies would not only reveal how good psychiatric prediction is right now, it would serve as the basis for improving prediction ability and for learning a good deal about the characteristics of dangerous persons.

No such studies have been done—nor are they likely to be. Just the problem of gathering a group of persons to be examined and then not interfering with those who seem to be dangerous and in need of help may be insoluble. If such a study were begun and the "dangerous" individuals were incarcerated, treated, or given special help of any sort, the study would be ruined. There would be no way to know what those persons were really like without treatment or to compare their outcomes with the nondangerous, untreated group. Any changes in the treated group could be due either to the treatment or simply the passage of time. There would be no way to tell.

As a result, students of the issue have turned to less satisfactory methods of inquiry. These usually involve locating a group of persons who have been labeled as dangerous for some legal or institutional process and then examining in retrospect what their behavior turned out to be. There are many difficulties with this (Frederick 1978).

First, the dangerous label usually has been applied by many different clinicians operating under a variety of conditions and with little guidance or control to facilitate uniformity. Second, the entire labeled group usually has been subjected to incarceration or some form of treatment after labeling. There is no way then to know how these people would have turned out without the treatment—that is, when a labeled person turned out later not to have been dangerous, was this because the labeling was wrong or because the treatment was effective? (It is important to remember that the term "treatment" is used broadly here. It might refer to no more than hospitalizing someone so that the person has few opportunities to act dangerously.)

Third, the determination of the occurrence of dangerous behavior is complex and fuzzy (Warren 1979). Retrospective studies such as those which have been done usually have to be limited to counting some official indication of dangerous behavior as an arrest or conviction. Obviously, much dangerous behavior will then go uncounted.

The fact that use of inadequate study techniques—though no doubt the best available—casts doubt on psychiatric abilities to recognize dangerousness is no more than suggestive (Ennis and Litwack 1974). It certainly does call for better studies even if the ideal studies cannot be carried out. In the interim, it seems reasonable to continue to assume some psychiatric ability rather than to discard the present system and be left with nothing.

Recognition of persons who although not dangerous are nevertheless proper candidates for state control is no more advanced than recognition of the dangerous. In fact, since the task is more complicated, success is probably further away. Yet here, too, the only reasonable course is to continue as we presently are until a better way is found. The alternative is to discontinue our present intervention approach and then wait for the damage to occur. This would obviously not be acceptable to our legislators and our citizens.

The Case for Guardianship

Special attention needs to be devoted to those whose mental disorders result not in homicidal or suicidal behavior but in failure to provide adequately for themselves or to safeguard their resources. Many of these persons suffer from illnesses which do not benefit from hospital treatment; they can reside in the community provided there is a way to manage their affairs. These are persons for whom gaurdianship is usually recommended (Massad and Sales, 1981).

Guardianship (and its close relative conservatorship, discussed in Chap. 2). involve the legal appointment of a person or agency to act on behalf of the mentally disordered person. Typically the guardian (or conservator) is given the control of the mentally disordered person. This control is taken away from the disordered person, thus leaving him or her without control over many fundamental aspects of life. The guardian is appointed by and accountable to a court rather than the individual.

An individual who suffers from a gradually increasing intellectual deficit will at some point become incapable of functioning in the accustomed and expected manner. The point at which the deterioration is serious enough to warrant protective action is hard to determine. It is probably some time before a severely damaging accident occurs. On the other hand, premature intervention can result in a severe blow to the self-esteem of the person and, itself, be sufficient to push the person past the danger point.

Furthermore, in contrast to the situation with homicidal and suicidal persons, the point at which state action is necessary and for how long it should continue is in large part determined by the characteristics of support services in the community rather than by the characteristics of the person. If we take inability to provide one's own food, clothing, or shelter, inability or ability clearly depends upon what is available in the community. For example, in one community, an individual who because of mental disorder is incapable of purchasing food or preparing meals could be maintained by a "Meals on Wheels" agency—one providing prepared, home-delivered meals. In another community, without such an agency, a mentally disordered person without relatives or friends could starve to death despite having money to buy food. Institutionalization would probably be necessary.

But why hospitalization via state control and involuntary institutionalization rather than voluntary action? Because such a person might well not be able to consent meaningfully to voluntary institutionalization, nor could another person step in to carry out necessary formal financial arrangements without obtaining legal authority to do so. As our system is set up, a court must step in to give the guardian legal power and thereby take it away from the disabled person.

The complications of having numerous options available other than state control also make this area of decision making difficult. For proper decision making, those deciding on guardianships (i.e., judges) need to know what social support agencies there are in a community. This knowledge is often not easily available. Judges, attorneys, and physicians do not have automatic access to such information, are not trained to search it out and use it, and in any case are in no position to require an agency to provide service or force the individual to accept it. Though in principle the existence of a strong network of less-restrictive social services ought to reduce the number of persons in need of state intervention, in practice connecting the individual cases with the appropriate agency may be difficult or impossible. Furthermore, neither physicians nor courts are well situated to do this. The result is state intervention, which seems clearly inappropriate to the outsider (and may indeed be inappropriate in principle) but which usually appears to be the only possible course to decision makers.

What is the justification of depriving individuals of their liberty simply because they are unable to care for themselves or safeguard their resources? Why not give them freedom to do as they please despite the risk of harm? Are they not the only ones who could suffer in any case?

The answer is that it is inhumane and dangerous to leave such persons on their own in order to protect their freedom when they are in a situation with which they cannot cope and where damage to them or their interests is almost certain. To protect their freedom to the greatest possible extent we must remove some of their freedom. Otherwise, we jeopardize all of it.

The Concept of Freedom

Moreover, freedom is a relative and vague term. For the sake of discussion, let us assume freedom means maximum opportunity to pursue available options. Exercise of one's freedom (or liberty) then has several components. First, there is having the mental capacity to conceive of wanting some action. Second is having the mental or physical capacity to be able to carry out the desired action. Third is the availability of the external resources necessary to complete the action.

State control via guardianship can diminish freedom by restricting the individual's access to resources—the guardian can refuse to provide them. But in most instances in which state control is involved, the individual's freedom has been even more severely restricted by loss of mental or physical capacity. Indeed, by providing assistance to the individual through the conservatorship or guardianship, the state can in effect increase capacity and thereby increase freedom.

For example, being hospitalized or being made legally powerless to spend one's money through state control is a diminution in freedom. On the other hand, is not a disability leading to a failure to be able to obtain sufficient food to sustain life also a diminution in freedom? Does not the process which provides the food and increases strength while it prolongs life then increase freedom?

Another example: use of freedom requires resources, basically money. Appointment of a guardian to handle a person's affairs restricts that person's freedom. But does not the individual who is entitled to funds either from the government or other persons and who is too intellectually enfeebled to know about the funds, request them, or fight for them, and therefore does not obtain the funds, lose some freedom? Does not the guardian who is given responsibility for protecting the ward's assets and successfully obtains the otherwise lost funds increase the ward's freedom?

Opponents of state control have argued that its existence jeopardizes everyone's freedom—we are all in danger of becoming victims of unjust state interference in our lives. This is true. However, we must consider the magnitude of this danger in relation to the magnitude of the danger to our freedom if we do not have some degree of state control.

The mentally ill person who refuses to take treatment can cause the types of disruption and disturbance to family and neighbors already discussed. Though perhaps no single relative or neighbor then suffers a loss of freedom to a degree as great as the incompetent person may suffer from hospitalization, the cumulative disruptive effects on many people must be given some weight. There is also another kind of negative effect upon others particularly relevant to these cases— the distress caused by seeing a beloved family member deteriorate from mental illness while having to stand by and do nothing; or, if not do nothing, attempt repeatedly to get through to the person with offers of help which are rejected. This is a cost which should not be overlooked.

It is true that each person should be allowed to make therapeutic and life-affecting decisions for him or herself. But to the extent that all of us depend upon each other for help and affect each other through our troubles, there ought to be a limit beyond which there is a right to intervene. Should, for example, adult children have to wait helplessly and watch a parent who is obviously no longer in complete possession of faculties move toward starvation or impoverishment? Should not the children be able to petition the state to step in to prevent needless suffering, perhaps death, *which even the parent may not want* but is no longer competent to avert.

To be sure, in some cases what seems to children to be a hopelessly mistaken and dangerous decision of the parent which they move in court to block may be a carefully thought-out plan based on values different from those of the children. If the children can convince a judge that they are correct, then the elderly parent will be needlessly penalized. Court cases and studies suggest this kind of thing has happened (Alexander and Lewin 1972). On the basis of such cases, it has been proposed that state control be eliminated. Again the basic point is missed: how representative are such cases and how many persons are saved from destruction by state control? Are we willing to trade the avoidance of a limited number of cases of improper restriction for the endangering of many persons whose only current method of getting assistance is through conservatorship or guardianship?

Making the Best of What Is Available

In considering state control of the mentally disordered, the point is often raised that, if better treatment facilities and supporting agencies were available in our communities, far fewer persons would have to be handled involuntarily. Many more mentally disordered persons would willingly accept voluntary treatment if more attractive facilities were available at reasonable cost. Fewer persons would be unable to care for themselves in the community if their weaknesses were strengthened by proper social services. For example, easily accessible services for financial advice, food delivery, apartment finding, door-to-door transportation, etc., all would go far in this direction. Undoubtedly, this point is correct.

Does this mean, however, that state control mechanisms should be eliminated? No—because, unfortunately, though the knowledge of how to provide all these services exists, the willingness to pay for them does not. There apparently is no community in the United States which is close to providing a range of such services, and the norm is far over in the direction of providing no such services.

Thus, faced with the daily decisions as to what to do regarding mentally disordered or incompetent persons, decision makers cannot postpone their decisions until services develop, nor can they conscientiously refuse to authorize state control on the grounds that the unavailable less-restrictive alternatives should be used.

Many officials involved with state control over the mentally disordered agree that better and more service facilities are needed and hope that such facilities will be developed. In the meantime, they would be abdicating their responsibilities both to the mentally disordered and to their communities were they not to use the available mechanisms.

Summary and Discussion

A position in favor of the involvement of the state in control of the mentally disordered does not imply a belief that all is well with the system through which control takes place. It is well established that living conditions in state mental hospitals have been abominable in the past and in some cases remain unimproved. Physicians working in these hospitals have sometimes been unable to obtain state licenses to practice medicine outside of the hospitals and, in other cases, have been untrained in psychiatry or unable to compete in the marketplace of private practice. Researchers have demonstrated that mental hospitalization per se is harmful to patients. Even the best public hospital cannot compare with some of the good private hospitals which remain beyond the financial reach of most individuals.

Numerous studies of psychiatrists' predictions of patients' dangerousness have failed to show that psychiatrists can make such predictions accurately (see Chap. 2). One study has shown that psychiatrists are not familiar with details of the laws under which they operate and which accord them so much power, implying psychiatrists are not staying even within the very wide limits which present laws place upon them (Affleck, Peszke, and Wintrob 1978). Other studies have shown that lawyers and judges carry out their responsibilities to protect patients' interests only in a perfunctory way (Hiday 1977; Scheff 1964; Warren 1977; Wenger and Fletcher 1969; Wexler 1971). Finally, though individual states show wide variations in criteria for state control and in the rates of mental hospitalization, there is no evidence that the citizens of the states where hospitalization is frequent are any better off than those of the states where hospitalization is uncommon.

Yet, acknowledgment of the weaknesses in the system and the strong tendencies among officials responsible for the system to ignore its needs should not justify discarding the framework of what may be the most effective way available of compromising the conflicting needs of all the groups involved. It is hard to conceive of any other feasible means of dealing with the small group of potentially destructive mentally disordered persons but the present one, which has the possibility of being politically acceptable and is not inhumane to the mentally disordered, to their victims, or to both. The most obvious alternative, to eliminate state control as a preventive measure and allow the mentally ill to be accountable for any law breaking or mistakes, is completely unacceptable without a massive shift in law and public opinion. Punishment of rule breaking regardless of mental state is unjust and contradictory to the very foundations of our law. Furthermore, such an alternative does not deal with the many instances where the major victim of the rule breaking is the mentally disordered person. Complete disregard of rule breaking by the mentally disordered—that is, freedom to do whatever they please without any consequences—is a politically unacceptable alternative.

The most reasonable course seems to be to pinpoint the weak areas of the present arrangement and then do what can be done to strengthen them. There is a need to undertake research to sharpen the diagnostic and predictive skills of the mental health professionals who are the front-line decision makers. Such research will help to decrease the number of errors through which state control is inappropriately applied.

In addition, increased accountability needs to be placed in the system so that decision makers are more highly motivated to avoid mistakes and institutional administrators are more concerned with upgrading the quality of institutional care. More social support and institutional-alternative services need to be developed in all communities. This will reduce the number of persons for whom state control is needed and the length of time in each case for which state control is appropriate.

Finally, legislatures should be encouraged or required to reexamine state laws in the light of current diagnostic, predictive, and treatment capabilities. Such examinations are likely to reveal large gaps between the purposes behind various legal provisions and the capabilities of mental health services to accomplish these purposes. For example, some state laws are apparently based on the assumption that most (or all) mentally disordered persons are in need of treatment and that refusal to take treatment must be an irrational act. (This is certainly not a correct assumption.) Another common assumption is that admission to a public psychiatric hospital will result in appropriate treatment. (This is often not so.) Many states require psychiatrists to certify before releasing a hospitalized individual (particularly one involved in criminal behavior) that the person is no longer dangerous. Such a law puts a terrible, improper burden on the psychiatrist to make a prediction for an indefinite period of time. It encourages keeping patients hospitalized even though no further treatment is necessary or offered.

Our present system of state control has a long history. The history is one of consistent, modest success in the face of seriously inadequate resources and increasingly severe demands. There is much in the system which still needs improvement, but the knowledge of what to do and how to do it to make the improvements is available. The social and medical needs which state control is designed to meet are as great as ever if not greater. It would be foolhardy and dangerous to abandon a time-tested approach and replace it with a completely new scheme, or with nothing, rather than try to improve what is already in place.

Part Two Decision Making in
Mental Health Court

In Part I, I developed a conceptual framework for understanding decision making in Metropolitan Court; a framework encompassing both laws and ideas about mental health law, and sociological interpretations of these. In Part II the focus shifts to material (interactional and observable, and structural) determinants of decision making in the court, which are also relevant for the discussion of social policy and social change in Chapter 9.

Labeling theory directs the analyst's attention to the actions of those labelers who implement systems of social control. In Part I the processes of rule making and identity transformation were considered as aspects of social control related to those in power. In Part II the enforcement of rules is the focus. Those who enforce the rules both add to the debates and idea systems discussed in the first part and, by their actions, translate these idea systems, with their own self-interests and role interests, into the praxis of decision making.

The courtroom is unlike most other organizations which process deviants—and unlike the backstage areas of the court—in that justice must not only be done in the law, it must be seen to be done. Therefore, rituals designed to convince the audience that routine business is justice are grafted on to the decision-making practices common to all organizations and inter-organizational networks. Decisions in the organization are described against a background of structural determinants. The inflow of the mentally ill, and the selection between them of which to retain or release, is in part a reflection of conflict and power relations in society related to social marginality, age, sex, and ethnicity.

6 The Courtroom
Ritual and Topos

*D*ecision making within the courtroom brings together a number of elements: a clientele about whom decisions must be made, a body of legal rules supposed to guide decisions, and a set of decision makers. As such, courtroom decision making is no different from decision making in other organizations. But there is one additional element that makes all courtroom decision making different: it is at least potentially public. Not only are decision makers supposed to implement legal rules upon a body of clientele, they must do it in a context of public accountability and recording. Everything said by clientele and decision makers in the courtrooms of Metropolitan Court during a case disposition is taken down and filed away for potential future reference.

Decision making within the courtroom has been the subject for close analysis by Blumberg (1967), Feeley (1979), Heumann (1977), and Eisenstein and Jacob (1977). Metropolitan Court shares many features with courtroom processing in the criminal (and juvenile) justice systems, such as public procedures, ceremonies, rituals, and routines. But it includes an additional element which makes it different: its clientele is mentally ill.

Decision making takes place at the intersection of legal theories and theories about mental illness. But both legal theories and theories about mental illness are superseded by, on the one hand, organizational practices (see Chap. 8, and Feeley 1979), and, on the other, commonsense notions about mental illness (see Scheff 1966, and the remainder of this chapter).

The new observer of Metropolitan Court is caught within and between the rituals of the court and the mysterious world of mental illness, whose afflicted seem intruders on rationality and legality.

137

The rituals of the law make Metropolitan Court seem like any other courtroom; its clients, moving in and out of this ritual world, sometimes do not. Most of the time, the intensely solid structure of the court and its expectations shape clients' action to whatever is required, as indicated in Chapter 2. But sometimes they do not, and that is when the odd contrast is experienced between the ritual world of the court and the seemingly arbitrary world of mental disorder.

In the arena of knowledge, the medical and legal models of human action are in conflict in the mental health courtroom. As indicated in Chapter 3, the law assumes that human action springs from rationality and is subject to rational scrutiny and an attribution of responsibility. But psychiatry interprets human action as springing from sources hidden from actors, and in many ways as being beyond blame or innocence.

The mental health law literature often assumes that this ideological and interpretive conflict leads to role conflict for psychiatrists and lawyers in the performance of their respective civil commitment functions. Brooks asserts that both professionals find the other professionals' interpretive schemes mysterious and complex, and that "professional value systems are different and often sharply conflicting. The interaction between psychiatrists and lawyers has not always been a happy or productive one. The lawyer stresses civil liberties and individual rights; the psychiatrist emphasizes his role in helping people without expressing particular concern for their legal 'rights'" (Brooks 1974, p. 1). But conflict in the realm of ideas is mediated by two factors: the everyday interaction of psychiatrists in Metropolitan Court (see Chap. 8), and a shared commonsense model or topos of mental illness which departs from both the medical and legal models.

The Topos of Mental Illness

Beyond the theories of mental illness described in Chapter 3 is what Santos (1977) calls a topos or commonsense model of mental illness (just as there is a topos for all types of commonly experienced phenomena):

> No matter how precisely a norm is written, nor how carefully a legal concept is defined, there is always a background of uncertainty and probability which cannot be removed by any deductive or apodictic method. The only solution is to employ the inventive art . . . of finding points of view or "common places" (*loci communes, topoi*) which being widely accepted, will help to fill the gaps, thus rendering the reasonable convincing and the conclusion acceptable. . . . These *topoi* (sing. *topos*) in their origi-

nal form, are endowed with conviction power, not with truth power. They refer to what is evident, to public policies or to *communis consensus. . . . Topoi* are based on common sense, on the "logic of the reasonable." [Santos 1977, pp. 15–16]

The topos of mental illness is part of the culture, and, as Scheff (1966) says, later psychiatric or legal models of madness merely add to, and do not cancel out, commonsense concepts. In the intersection of the law and psychiatry that occurs in mental health court, the topos becomes one basis for shared understandings and decision making.

Scheff's and Santos's concepts of the commonsense model of madness as the fundamental one even in professional work is an important tool in understanding the mental health attorney's role in commitment proceedings. The role of the psychiatrist in Metropolitan Court is clear-cut—to testify to the mental status of the involuntarily committed—although some, such as Morse, do not believe that it is valid or useful. But both the ideal and the actual dimensions of the attorney role have been the subject of considerable debate in recent years.

The Attorney Role in Mental Health Law

In the criminal court (although not in some special interest courts such as juvenile) the public defender (and the private attorney) is expected to adopt an aggressive advocate stance. In contrast, according to Hart, in the mental health court "[m]any hearings give the impression of being merely a 'rubber stamp' of the psychiatrist's decision, and not a true adversary process" (Hart 1974, p. 131). He asserts that the psychiatrist has become the "unimpeachable witness" in mental health cases (Hart 1974, p. 125), a situation which he regards as anomalous because of the traditional combativeness of attorneys. He proposes three reasons for this anomaly, related, respectively, to the legal, medical, and commonsense models of mental illness.

Mental health attorneys may be passive and nonadvocate in deference to the medical model (see also Chap. 5); or they may be passive because they feel bewildered by the medical model and be unable to cope with it in the legal setting (see also Cohen [1966] and Andalman and Chambers [1974] who concur in part with this medical-model explanation). Hart finds both explanations unsatisfying. Lawyers, he says, are willing—indeed eager—to apply their legal knowledge to any new area; furthermore, they are unlikely to defer to competing definitions of reality.

Hart concludes that the problematic role of the mental health bar can be explained in a manner related to the commonsense model of mental illness: "[A]ttorneys often agree with the psychiatrist that the person should be committed, and therefore do not offer the type of 'defense' one would expect in normal legal proceedings" (Hart 1974, p. 133). Goode (1975, p. 1542) adds that attorneys regard mentally ill persons as unable to decide what is best for themselves, and asserts that this aspect of madness is what leads to "role ambiguity" on the part of defense attorneys (see Chap. 4). In short, attorneys view their clients as crazy and therefore refrain from standing firmly in the way of their involuntary incarceration.

The Clientele as Crazy

Attorneys and other personnel at Metropolitan Court consistently referred to their clients as "sick" or "crazy," with references to the legal model or medical model appearing mainly within the court hearing, and generally as subsidiary to the commonsense model. In informal conversation, patients were designated as sick, crazy, weird, different, and hopeless. The following comments are representative of many:

RESEARCHER: What type of people come here?
PSYCHIATRIST: Crazy ones.

JUDGE: Mental illness is like a lurking shark—the surface of the waters may be calm, but it is always there waiting to come out again.

PUBLIC DEFENDER: The people we get here are weirdos, freaks, look at that! [he points at a woman in bedroom slippers and a very short, brightly colored dress].

DISTRICT ATTORNEY: Some say, "There but for the grace of God go I" when they look at the patients. I don't believe that. Not this "I."

The effect of the commonsense model in Metropolitan Court is to help mesh the roles of the participants into a neatly functioning unit. Although the medical and legal frames may appear to conflict on the surface, there is an underlying commonsense and a taken-for-granted perspective on mental illness. The practical effect of this underlying consensus is *not* a struggle for dominance of the medical or the legal personnel of the court, nor a rubberstamping of medical decisions by awed lawyers and judges, but a working consensus both on practices and interpretations that is expressed by a familiar phrase at the court: "We all work together here" (see Chap. 8).

This does not mean that the judge and the psychiatrist always agree. During the period of this research, the judge released about half the persons who came before him on writs; persons whom the psychiatrists were attempting to keep in the hospitals. But this (for California) high rate of release does not anger the psychiatrists any more than a 90% rate would necessarily imply rubber-stamping or bring about the ire of the public defender's office. The other personnel just accept philosophically the well-known beliefs and practices of this judge—that if family members are available to relieve the fiscal burden of hospitalization on the state, the patient should be released. To both judge and psychiatrist, the patient is still equally crazy. In fact, during writ hearings or debates personnel will appeal to common sense if the evidence conflicts with *their own* ideology as well as if it conflicts with "the opposition":

PSYCHIATRIST: She is a paranoid schizophrenic. . . .
JUDGE: She is just a lady with a very nasty temper.

JUDGE: I have to release this man because the law says so, the law says that he can go and kill himself after thirty one days. I can't help the law . . . I wish I could.

PSYCHIATRIST: She's back at State Hospital again for care and treatment, so they say, it's all a farce, she won't get anywhere from it, she'll go right back where she came from. We might as well leave her alone.

As Scheff (1966) indicates, "professionalized" models of mental illness are learned long after, and do not replace, the cultural topos—even in mental health law decision making.

Courtroom Ritual

Departments 1 and 2, like other courtrooms in other times and places, are places of ritual. The ritual is important at several levels: it is important in the everyday lives of the workers who participate in it, it is important in the experience of courtroom observers, and it is important as it symbolically links the activities which take place in the courtroom to the legal mandates elaborated in Chapter 2.

Following Manning (1977, pp. 304–5), I define ritual as acts of communication with a high degree of invariancy. The purposes of these acts are to communicate about the state of an organism (interpersonal ritual), about a social or public order (legal ritual), or about the external order that grants meaning to the social order (ceremony). Ritual does not have as its main function the transfer of unique information; it involves a fixed arrangement of elements, time and place, and performance. Manning adds that "ceremonial information tends to be more certain, more invariant, and therefore more predictable than any given item of information and any individual repertoire."

Courtrooms are places of legal ritual (the law is applied) and of ceremonial (justice is seen to be done, or demonstrated as done). In the courtroom ritual, participants express the relationship of their decision making to LPS and to the ideals of justice. The legal ritual tends to be more meaningful to the courtroom decision-making personnel, while the ceremonial or dramatic elements of courtroom-activity are more apparent to the observer. In addition, the courtroom personnel enact interpersonal ritual during court hearings of which the observer will be unaware.

Legal Ritual: The Wendy Poe Case, a Habeas Corpus
Writ Hearing Transcript

A major ritual function of the courtroom is to demonstrate coherence between case decision making and the mandates of LPS. Such coherence is demonstrated by a verbal ritual which has both written and spoken elements. To illustrate the legal aspects of courtroom ritual, I quote an entire case transcript[1] from Department 1—a habeas corpus hearing on "Wendy Poe."

Wendy Poe, *habeas corpus* petitioner, walks to the witness stand in Department I. Walks is not exactly the right word; she slouches and shuffles to the stand, shoulders hunched, eyes down, feet slapping in bedroom slippers. She looks incongruous in what seems to be a bathrobe. On the stand she can barely speak at first, due to drugs or "mental disorder," but later she becomes talkative.

METROPOLIS, CALIFORNIA, TUESDAY, AUGUST 18, 1976, 11:15 A.M.

THE COURT: In the matter of Wendy Poe

IVOR WALLACE *called as a witness, was duly sworn, and testified as follows:*

MR. WALKER: Will counsel stipulate as to the doctor's qualifications?

MS. MORLEY: So stipulated.

DIRECT EXAMINATION BY MR. WALKER

Q: Doctor, in your capacity as a physician and psychiatrist, did you examine Wendy Poe?

A: Yes, I have examined Miss Poe yesterday at the hospital.

Q: As a result of said examination, were you able to form any opinion as to her present mental condition?

A: Yes. My opinion is Miss Poe is still mentally ill, schizophrenia of the chronic undifferentiated type, and she is gravely disabled at this time.

Q: What do you base all that information on?

A: The history and examination. The history indicates that according to the patient she has just been released from State

1. This case transcript was selected because (*a*) it has no especially unusual features, and (*b*) it came to hand without cost. Transcribed versions of court hearings are extremely costly.

Hospital. She has been in State Hospital at least four times during the past three years. After her release, and that is according to the patient, she stayed with a boyfriend because she has no interest in family. She has six children who are all in foster homes for reasons unknown to me. She was arrested and placed in jail on Easter Sunday and while in jail she was found to be psychotic and was transferred to County Hospital. When she came to the hospital she was hallucinating, bizarre, irrational, belligerent, and hostile. She is taking medication by mouth, Mellaril, and Prolixin by injection. She has calmed down considerably. However, her thinking is very greatly disturbed and disorganized and inappropriate. She lives on ATD. I feel because of this rather severe thought disorder that she is still gravely disabled.

MR. WALKER: Nothing further.

CROSS-EXAMINATION BY MS. MORLEY

Q: Doctor, did you talk to any other family members?

A: No. No, I have had no chance to talk—

MS. POE: No.

MS. MORLEY: Did you talk to her boyfriend at all?

A: No.

Q: How long did you talk to Ms. Poe?

A: Until I am satisfied. That I couldn't tell you exactly.

MS. POE: About ten minutes. He didn't talk long. Okay, I can't say anything.

MS. MORLEY: Not yet.

MS. POE: Okay.

THE WITNESS: It varies from patient to patient.

MS. MORLEY: Excuse me?

THE WITNESS: I talk to them and look at the record until I can form some opinion.

MS.MORLEY: And how long did you talk to Ms. Poe, if you remember?

A: I don't remember. About half an hour.

Q: How many prior hospitalizations did you say she has had?

A: Four in State Hospital.

Q: And has she had any others?

A: Not as far as I know.

Q: Doctor, did you state a diagnosis, or did you form a diagnosis?

A: Yes. Chronic undifferentiated schizophrenia.

Q: What kind of medication is she on?

A: She is on injectable Prolixin and Mellaril by mouth in considerable dosage. She gets 400 milligrams of Mellaril a day and Prolixin Deconate once a week.

Q: Now, was Dr. Mendez her doctor at State Hospital?

A: She mentioned the doctor.

MS. POE: I told him everything he is saying.

MS. MORLEY: Did you talk to Dr. Mendez at all about her mental condition?

A: No.

Q: Do you have any idea whether she was a voluntary or involuntary patient at State Hospital?

A: I don't have the record from them.

Q: Do you have any idea when or why she was admitted to State Hospital?

A: I have no records.

Q: What medical records did you review?

A: Only the records which are available at the hospital, her present admission, and that is all I have.

Q: So you reviewed the County Hospital records for a period of a few days, is that correct?

A: That is correct.

Q: You state she does have ATD income of $235 a month?

A: She told me that she has ATD, yes.

Q: Do you know whether she has funds in the trust office at County?

A: I don't know whether I have this here. On admission to the hospital, she was unable to give any information, so I don't have any.

MS. MORLEY: Thank you, Doctor. I have no further questions.

THE COURT: It is not clear to me what were the circumstances of her admission, Doctor.

THE WITNESS: She was transferred to the hospital from Women's Prison.

THE COURT: Was this a 4011.6?[2]

THE WITNESS: No.

MR. WALKER: I have no way of knowing, Your Honor. Apparently not.

THE COURT: Transferred from Women's Prison. Do we know, is there a pending criminal case?

THE WITNESS: No. From what I have read it is all traffic violations.

MS. POE: I don't have any. Never.

THE COURT: And what were the facts that supported the three-day—I take it it started with a three-day?

THE WITNESS: She was hallucinated, bizarre, and irrational.

THE COURT: That is at the admission?

THE WITNESS: On admission, yes.

THE COURT: You may proceed.

> WENDY ALICE POE *called as a witness of her own behalf, was duly sworn, and testified as follows:*

---

2. Transfer from correctional institution to mental hospital.

DIRECT EXAMINATION BY MS. MORLEY:

Q: Ms. Poe, if you were to be released today, do you have a place to go?

A: [Nodding]

Q: Speak out loud.

A: Uh-huh. Yes.

Q: Where is that place?

A: 1003 East 92nd.

Q: And do you have any income?

A: My ATD checks.

Q: Where is that? Do you know?

A: At 1003 East 92nd, apartment 5, I think.

Q: Is anyone living in that apartment now?

A: I don't know.

Q: When did you rent that apartment?

A: I didn't rent it. Mr. Simmons did, but he let me stay in it until I could get on my feet again.

  I woke up in the morning with pneumonia, and I almost died from it, so I went to the campus to Dr. Oxford at emergency, 24-hour clinic, and got an injection for pneumonia. That is where I was going, from, then on to the campus [i.e., prison] pharmacy.

  I went back to State Hospital for the reason I was sick again from sleeping with no clothes on because I didn't have all my clothes with me.

  All my clothes got burned up last year in June or July, and I still don't have enough clothes to keep me warm and to keep me from catching death of cold again.

Q: Now, has Wendell Simmons come to see you in the hospital?

A: No. No visitors except yesterday.

Q: Who visited you yesterday?

A: A lady from Halfway House in El Centro, California.

Q: Now, who was your doctor at State?

A: Dr. Mendez, I told him.

Q: Did a Dr. Mendez say you could leave State?

A: Uh-huh. I was discharged. Then they brought me—I was going to friends Sunday morning, but my sister-in-law told them not to open the door, and when the police came in they asked me if I was a lesbian, and I'm no lesbian because I have six children here and I know I take care of them.

Q: Where are your children now?

A: They have been in foster homes. I moved the baby. She is not feeling well.

Q: That is—

A: She was born here, unit 1 or unit 2. She was Sylvia June Poe, and I am a patient here.

Q: Is there anything else you would like to tell the Judge?

A: Well, anything else he wants to know I'll tell him if he asks me.

THE COURT: He may wish to ask you questions.

MR. WALKER: I don't care to.

MS. POE: You don't care. That is what they all say I do about my family and everything else.

THE COURT: Counsel, what do you think?

MS. MORLEY: I have no further questions.

THE COURT: Any comments?

MS. MORLEY: I will submit it, Your Honor.

THE COURT: Any comments?

MR. WALKER: Submit it.

THE COURT: Are you going to ask for a conservatorship?

DR. WALLACE: The hospital hasn't asked for a conservatorship yet, but it is probably indicated.

THE COURT: I'm not sure. When was she brought over?

DR. WALLACE: On the 10th of August.

MS. POE: I got my medication at home, too. I know what I take. Mellaril, not no Thorazine, and all that medicine, and injections. I'm sore from being shot.

THE COURT: I want to have somebody come in that will indicate that Ms. Poe can stay with them. Can you get in touch with this man whose apartment you have been staying in with him?

MS. POE: I just got in touch with my sister-in-law and she is at the beauty shop, and she is going to see if she can find the man. The phone number is 832-9900.

THE COURT: When did you get out of State Hospital?

MS. POE: I don't know the exact date, because I have been since the 10th of August in there.

THE COURT: Was it two days?

MS. POE: About a week before I got out. About a week before I entered County before they had the lady's funeral. I know the lady, but I didn't know whose funeral they had because the man told me they should have told me. I only have a dime. That is what I had when I went in.

THE COURT: You came out to go to that?

MS. POE: No. I couldn't go to the funeral. I didn't have anything to wear. They were dirty clothes. I didn't make it home. They just took me to the house to pay respects and don't nobody care.

THE COURT: I'm going to deny the writ, but if this man that you have been staying with will come in—

MS. POE: Could bring—

THE COURT: If this man that you have been staying with will come in and say he is willing—

MS. POE: Well, he has my check and my I.D. card. I don't know why he wouldn't bring it out there.

THE COURT: You better get in touch with him.

MS. POE: Can I go call now?

THE COURT: You will be permitted to call from the hospital. Under the law you will be permitted to make calls there.

MS. POE: The social worker can't get him to call there.

THE COURT: If you don't have anybody—

MS. POE: Well, I have somebody. I will call her.

THE COURT: You can file a paper again as soon as you have somebody who will come in here.

MS. POE: As soon as I finish. I got a check. I have to go to the bathroom. I have to use the restroom now.

THE COURT: Remanded for the balance of the treatment without prejudice to renew the writ.

As the psychiatric aide approaches her to transport her back to the hospital, Wendy Poe bursts into tears and screams, "I don't want to go—what are they doing to me?" The sheriff comes to the help of the aide, and Wendy Poe is removed from the court.

In hearings such as Ms. Poe's, courtroom decision making is ritually related to mental health law. Some of the content of this transcript serves to record that LPS has been implemented. Complying with LPS is demonstrated:

PSYCHIATRIST: My opinion is Ms. Poe is *still* mentally ill [thus liable for a 14-day as well as a prior 72-hour hold], schizophrenia of the chronic undifferentiated type (a diagnosable mental illness), and she is gravely disabled at this time (assertion of the behaviorally relevant component). . . .

THE COURT: And what were the facts that supported the three-day—I take it it started with a three day? [probe for the legitimacy of the earlier 72-hour hold].

THE WITNESS: She was hallucinated, bizarre, and irrational [assurance of legitimacy through display of extreme symptoms]. . . .

MS. MORLEY: Ms. Poe, if you were to be released today, do you have a place to go?

MS. POE: [Nodding]

MS. MORLEY: Speak out loud.

MS. POE: Uh huh, yes [attempted demonstration of adequate shelter, continued below, thus nongrave disability].

MS. MORLEY: What is that place?

MS. POE: 1003 East 92nd Street [end transcript quote; parenthetical comments added].

Legal rituals in the court are intended to demonstrate compliance with procedural rules as well as with substantive law. Case transcripts such as the above are not only rituals of content (compliance with the law is demonstrated), but they are also rituals of form (e.g., the correct mode of transcription and participant reference). Finally, the ritual activity of court reporting in the courtroom produces the documentation of documentations—in the court reporter's transcript, which is a document, there is recorded, permanently, the document of compliance with substantive and procedural law.

The form of recording and transcription in the courtroom is standardized carefully to conform with procedural requirements. The only error in the legal form of the Poe case, so far as I can see, is that the court reporter has left the day's date blank on her certification that, more than a year after the hearing, she transcribed the testimony for some legal purpose. The ritual of form, in any court, is a ritual of demonstrating adherence to procedural rules.

Santos (1977) comments that the ritualistic writing down of legal material serves the function of ensuring participants' adherence to courtroom decision making beyond the immediate situation. He states that "a written formulation of will creates a particularly firm sense of commitment. . . . Writing is a ritual with its own dynamic, oriented to the creation of a mythic legal fetish which it superimposes upon the material base (the elements of the contract, the paper, the writer)" (p. 47).

Abel (Santos 1977) adds that "typed documents have other symbolic features. Typing produces uniformity in the shape, size and spacing of characters, which increases the fetishistic nature of the typed document, and its power to command a uniform response from people. The electric typewriter takes this one more step, since it produces letters that are uniform in darkness as well. Printing lies still further along this continuum, which explains why lawyers use printed forms and fill in blanks. . . . Typing also eliminates errors, which means that the document is infallible, and cannot be questioned" (p. 48n.).

The spoken component of the legal ritual orders the proceedings into a set of priorities compatible with the relative power of the courtroom actors. In these hearings, the psychiatrist is sworn in as the "people's" witness, and the district attorney gives the first direct examination, as in the Poe example. Then the public defender may cross-examine the psychiatrist. Sometimes, the petitioner testifies on his or her own behalf, and does so—in mute testimony to relative status—after the psychiatrist. The judge (vested with symbolic authority in transcriptions as "the Court") has the authority to intervene with questions at any time; others who interrupt the ritual by speaking out of turn are liable to reprimand, as Ms. Poe, despite her supposed disorientation, seemed rapidly to learn.

The ritual of word order is even more precise than the hierarchical arrangement of speakers. This order is prescribed by common usage and custom, and in itself serves to demonstrate the orderliness and thus the justice of the proceedings. In the typical habeas corpus writ hearing the psychiatrist is asked for his or her diagnosis of the patient's medical condition, then for the basis of the diagnosis, and finally for the basis of the 14-day hold. The evidence presentation and questioning sequences for other witnesses follow similarly predictable designs.

The case transcript is a documentary product of one of the nonverbal rituals of the court: court reporting. The legal ritual of court reporting is one of immediacy and infallibility, connecting the present moment in the courtroom inextricably with a reinterpreted past and a prescribed future. Only an instant intervenes between the spoken word and its written translation into hieroglyphs which can be interpreted only by experts. The act of court reporting crystallizes past and complex events into a clear and simple present: the case.

Court reporting provides a linkage between the law and the written word; once crystallized, the court record can be used for future appeals, scrutinized for technical or procedural errors. Other nonverbal rituals in the court bridge the legal with the ceremonial through symbolism. The physical arrangement of the courtroom and of the participant is one such set of symbols. The judge in his robe and on his platform, the audience beyond and below, the plaintiff surrounded by attorneys, are all part of the courtroom's symbolic apparatus.

Some nonverbal acts, such as ear scratching, are random rather than ritual, just as some spoken asides are not recorded by the court reporter because they are perceived as outside the ritual. Still other nonverbal acts are legally significant as information transfer but are not ritualistic; such acts must be transformed into verbalizations through the act of court reporting:

"Is your psychiatrist present in court?" asked the Commissioner. The petitioner pointed silently to a man in the jury box. "Let the record show that Mr. Smythe pointed at Dr. Andreas," the Commissioner instructed the court reporter.

In the Wendy Poe case, the petitioner had to be coached into the world of the courtroom, where nonverbal gestures have to be verbalized:

Q: Ms. Poe, if you were to be released today, do you have a place to go?
A: [Nodding]
Q: Speak out loud.
A: Uh huh, yes.

Courtroom Ceremonial

As indicated earlier, a unique feature of courtroom decision making is that justice must not only be done, it must be seen to be done. Unlike organizations whose decisions are made in private, the court is always open to the scrutiny of outsiders, who are referred to contemptuously by court personnel as the "looky loos." For the outsider, the sociologist, the journalist, the student, the relative, and assorted other looky-loos, the ritual of the court is rather mysterious, unless the observer has a more than usual knowledge of substantive and procedural mental health law. But the ceremonial or dramatic aspect of the ritual is quite striking—that combination of verbal and nonverbal cues that is supposed to demonstrate publicly that justice is done.

To the newcomer, the entire ritual of the courtroom appears as what Garfinkel (1956) has called a "degradation ceremony." Garfinkel views the court and its proceedings as a dramatic ceremony in which the total identity of the defendant is transformed publicly into a deviant one, by the denunciation efforts of persons acting in their public capacity to reflect the moral indignation of the community as a whole. He specifies that both the defendant and his or her behavior "must be removed from the realm of their everyday character and made to stand 'out of the ordinary'" (Garfinkel 1956). Furthermore, the denouncer must not seem to be acting out of personal motives but, rather, as a denouncer for the whole community and drawing upon the topos ("communally entertained and verified experience"). The procedure of denunciation must set a moral distance between the deviant and both the denouncer and the audience (Garfinkel 1956).

To the outsider, walking into the court the first few times, the spoken and documentary rituals and nonverbal symbols of the court signal a ceremony guided by persons whose interests lie outside the mundane and the personal. Garfinkel's analysis of the court as drama is most relevant from the perspective of the visitor, to whom the denouncer appears to be acting publicly and the defendant appears to be undergoing identity degradation. Both these perspectives—on the denouncer and on the petitioner—change as the observer becomes familiar with the court.

As I became familiar with Metropolitan Court, I came to realize that the rituals of the courtroom were legal in nature (linking decisions to aspects of LPS) but that the decisions being made were affected by considerations personal to the judge, such as mood. In one case, for example, the judge became angry at the defendant's description of her insanity as a "voyage," and declared from the bench that she was self-deluding and should not be released (see also Chap. 7). This case was one of the rare occasions on which the denouncer did not even *portray* himself as not "acting according to his personal, unique experiences." In general, while the portrayal followed the ritual, the private motivations which also entered into the decisions were communicated only after the hearing, to trusted intimates and unimportant strangers.

With regard to the defendant, Blumberg (1967, pp. 88–93) questions Garfinkel's view of the court as a setting for public denunciation and identity transformation (even from the perspective of the denouncer, let alone the petitioner; see Chap. 3). He interprets the degradation ceremony as a "cop out" ceremony in which the defendant or petitioner has a cynical view of her or his identity transformation, while the degraders are simply doing a routine job: "The 'cop out' is in fact a charade, during which an accused must project an appropriate and acceptable degree of guilt, penitence, and remorse. If he adequately feigns the role of the 'guilty person,' his hearers will engage in a fantasy that he is contrite and thereby merits a lesser plea" (Blumberg 1967, p. 89). According to Blumberg, in the criminal court it is the routine process of plea bargaining followed by a cop-out ceremony of guilt which keeps the court calendar moving (see also Sudnow 1965).

In Metropolitan Court, since what is on trial is not crime but madness, the petitioner attempts to project not guilt but innocence—innocence of the charge of mental disorder, dangerousness, or grave disability. If he or she adequately projects innocence, there is some chance of release from hospital. But court personnel view this innocence labeling as a charade also:

> The judge had just released a middle-aged man who had managed to keep fairly quiet on the stand. He had been brought in for insisting that he was Jesus; on the stand he insisted he wasn't. After the case, the public defender walked through the judge's chambers muttering, "crazy as a loon," and the judge commented, "We'll be seeing him again within a week."

The discrepancy between Garfinkel's, Blumberg's and my view of courtroom ceremony is not just a matter of court case content, it is a matter of perspective. To the stranger (particularly a middle-class one), the courtroom ceremonial is one of degradation. But to the personnel performing the ritual and making the decisions, the activities within the courtroom are a particular extension of the whole organizational project of doing their job and keeping cases moving (see Chap. 8). And, as a routine organizational work setting, the courtroom has its interpersonal rituals, understood only by the participants and by anyone with whom they choose to share their information.

Interpersonal Ritual and Routine

Interpersonal, or what Manning (1977) calls personally indexical ritual, takes place in the public courtroom outside the range of meaning of the audience. These rituals are intended not as an exchange of information but to symbolize aspects of the relationship between participants. Information exchange, which may be embedded in the legal ritual and pass unnoticed by the audience, extends the routine organizational understandings about decision making into the courtroom. For example, several aspects of the Wendy Poe case involve a routine demonstration to the judge of matters which the judge deems important, and which the district attorney or public defender has attempted to bring out. For example, Ms. Poe said her address very carefully (see above, and Chap. 3), demonstrating her reality orientation to the judge. She was asked by the DA about her shelter and income, and the psychiatrist was asked for a diagnosis, in the attempt to make a case for her grave disability under LPS (legal ritual). But she was also asked about her children and about her willingness to take medication, since the attorneys are quite aware that the judge sentimentalized children and that he measures "grave disability" in part by refusal to take medication (see Chap. 7).

Interpersonal rituals which are not information giving have nothing to do with the law, although they might seem to have. They are games between participants; a form of play which has evolved into an institutionalized and repeated event. From the Wendy Poe case, off the record:

> JUDGE: [to Wendy Poe]: "How old are you?"
> With this question he directs a slight, sideways grin at the
> court reporter, which she returns. After the hearings are completed, he says, "Well?" and she replies, "I said 45." The judge
> comments, "My guess was 35; she was actually 42. You win."
> By now I had learned that this was a regular ritual of court
> reporter and judge; each would guess the age of a petitioner,
> then they would compare notes and congratulate the person
> who came closest.

Feeley (1979, p. 259) reports similar interpersonal rituals between participants in a lower court, interestingly enough also between a male judge and one of his female subordinates.

Summary and Discussion

Justice, as Feeley (1979, p. 22) comments, "presumes a process which bases decisions on general, *universalistic* principles, not *particularistic* or situational criteria." For observers of courtroom decision making, what offends their sense of justice—what makes justice seem not to be done—is particularism, situationalism, or arbitrariness. In Metropolitan Court, what makes justice seem to the nonparticipant audience not to be done is the obvious lack of correspondence between what trials are supposed to seem like and what they actually are.

The everyday personally indexical rituals of the court take place simultaneously with the ritual and dramatic aspects of the legal process. The intent as well as the statutory language of LPS, compliance with the ritual requirements of transcription and recording, and obeisance to the ceremonial are the dialectics of courtroom legal ritual. Discussions of personal affairs, side bets on age, and joking relationships are equally part of the court's ritual, interwoven with the legal and ceremonial aspects. The audience are not always aware of these interaction rituals. These appear as inappropriate informality, and an interference, by unseriousness, with the appearance of justice.

A second interference with the appearance of justice, for the observer (the topic of the next chapter), is the lack of correspondence between decision-making practices in the court and the legal categories supposedly guiding that decision making. The legal ritual observed by my students and others I took to the court was viewed as ritual empty of meaning, just as the ceremonial was seen as damaged by interpersonal ritual.

A third source of a sense of injustice was the prominence of the topos of mental illness in decision making. The topological structure underlying legal reasoning is quite evident to knowledgeable observers of any courtroom, but in Metropolitan Court it assumed such prominence that it was evident also to the casual observer. Embedded in the concept of justice, in addition to universalism, is the requirement that the law stand above and beyond the world of everyday life, with its commonsense interpretations of events. Justice is sought in the application of special legal rules, without special favor, to the chaos of events.

The ritual character of the courtroom functions to reassure the observer symbolically of the dominance of rationality and universalism. But the intrusion of interaction rituals into legal ritual and ceremony, and the invocation of the topos, threatens the sense of legal dominance which the ritual symbolizes. As Santos notes, this dialectic is inevitable:

Ever since the Greeks, Western thought has distinguished between two modes of reasoning (and of knowledge): apodictic reasoning, seeking to demonstrate necessary proofs in the form of logical deduction or empirical experimentation; and the dialectical and rhetorical reasoning, seeking to deliberate about or argue for what is credible, reasonable, plausible or probable, by means of dialectical and rhetorical proofs that reason from generally accepted opinions and arguments (*topoi*). . . . Today lawyers and legal scholars emphasize the elaboration of general principles of an axiomatic nature, from which necessary legal solutions can be deduced logically within the premises of a closed system. . . . both historically and structurally . . . [but] legal reasoning always has been, and still is, dominated by rhetorical elements. [Santos 1977, pp. 14–15]

Thus, the search for justice in the courtrooms of Metropolitan Court contains built-in contradictions. The law is supposed to, and cannot, be completely rational and universal in application; commonsense, particularistic, arbitrary, and situational criteria will inevitably enter into decision making. But if these elements are seen to enter into decision making, they are seen as obstructions of justice. The law's erroneous claims (by virtue of the legal and ceremonial rituals, if not by verbal claims) to being outside the framework of everyday life renders it vulnerable to charges of lack of justice, cynicism, or even corruption (Manning 1977).

The next two chapters detail other aspects of court decision making which, if they come to the attention of observers, add to a sense of injustice. The gap between legal categories and decision making practices in mental health law is described and analyzed in the next chapter. In Chapter 8, the inter- and intraorganizational factors which structure decision making independent of the qualities of the petitioners to the court are discussed. And the qualities of the petitioner, such as social class, social marginality, and ethnicity which enter into decision making beside and beyond the law, are investigated.

The intrusion of particularistic criteria into courtroom decision making—social marginality, age, or ethnicity as the basis for involuntary civil commitment rather than mental disorder—can be seen as menacing the concept of justice in this court. This particular form of injustice is the target for those who seek revolutionary change in society; unless and until the social order is altered so that these particularistic criteria for judgment of any kind are no longer relevant, then justice in the courtroom cannot be done, and cannot be seen to be done.

7 Habeas Corpus Writ Decision Making

*I*n Department 1, habeas corpus decisions are made on a daily basis. The process is as follows: advocates of patients' rights at the state hospital and Mental Health Counselors employed by the court inform patients certified involuntarily on 14-day holds of their right to a judicial hearing. There is no way of knowing how many patients actually hear of their rights, but since the patients' rights advocates are fairly aggressive, most of them probably realize they have this right. In Los Angeles County in 1979, 2,796 patients out of 9,778 14-day holds filed writs. Of this number, 298 were released by the hospital, 282 changed to voluntary status, 40 escaped, 628 were discharged after the writ was issued, 620 were released on stipulation from the court (which means that there was prima facie evidence that LPS did not apply and thus that the 14-day hold was illegal), and 972 went to court. Of these 972, 57 were released without a hearing because the hospital did not provide information needed, 255 were released after the hearing, and 660 were not released after the hearing (see also fig. 2.1).

I was interested in the factors that went into the decision to release or retain persons in the mental hospital and that were used in evidence in reaching the decision. The basis for this analysis was a systematic collection of data of 130 writ hearings. An observational and multiple-regression study of the factors entering into the denial or granting of the writ was done on 130 cases, and an observational study was made of the factors entering into the labeling of 100 persons as mentally disordered, gravely disabled, and/or dangerous to self or others (see Appendix on Method).

Denial and Granting of Writs

The study of decision making in the granting or denying of habeas corpus showed that of the 130 writ petitions, 49.9% had their petitions granted and were released from the hospital, and 47.7% had their writs denied (the remainder were disposition unknown). Demographic characteristics of the total sample of 130 are described in table 7.1.

The study of the decision to deny or grant the writ proceeded from several theoretical assumptions which exist in the literature on criminal justice decision making. As indicated, the organizational perspective interprets the court as a system with its own goals and logics, whose decisions relate more to organizational imperatives than to features of the immediate courtroom situation; it will be considered in Chapter 8 (also see Blumberg 1967; Feeley 1979; Heumann 1977). The legal perspective views the seriousness of the offense

Table 7.1
Sample Distribution
($N = 130$)

Variable	N	%
Sex:		
Male (82)	82	63
Female (48)	48	37
Total	130	100
Age:		
Under 19 (20)	20	15
19–35 (69)	69	53
36–50 (24)	24	18
Over 50 (17)	17	13
Total	130	99
Ethnicity:		
Black (33)	33	25
White (74)	74	57
Other (23)	23	18
Total	130	100
Appearance:		
Middle class (48)	48	37
Lower class (52)	52	40
Counterculture (5)	5	3
Other (25)	25	19
Total	130	99[a]

Note: Table also illustrates the distribution of conflict variables.
[a]Does not total 100% because of rounding errors.

as a major criterion in the decision-making process (Hagan 1974; Rovner-Pieczenik 1976). Conflict theory relates courtroom and other criminal justice outcomes to structural variables associated with the defendant, such as socioeconomic class, ethnicity, age, and sex (Quinney 1974). What Gibson (1978) calls individual decision-maker theory focuses not on the defendant but on the individual judge: his or her attitudes, beliefs, and background.

In summary, the organizational perspective predicts courtroom decision outcomes based on court organization, the legal perspective predicts outcomes based on the law, the conflict perspective predicts outcomes based on qualities of the defendant, and the individual perspective predicts outcomes based on the decision-making judge. Table 7.1 illustrates distribution of cases seen in Department 1 by conflict variables, table 7.2 by legal-psychiatric variables, and table 7.3 by individual decision-maker variables (see below for an explanation of table 7.3). From each perspective we developed hypotheses that would predict outcomes in a particular direction.

Conflict Theory

Conflict theory is a social structural theory which predicts more judicial punitiveness toward those groups in society which have relatively lower amounts of power and other resources. Thus, minorities

Table 7.2
LPS Psychiatric-Judicial Criteria

Variable	N	%
Mental Disorder:		
Hallucinating and/or delusional	74	75
Not hallucinating and/or delusional	28	25
Total	102	100
Gravely Disabled:		
Conservatorship filed	27	82
Conservatorship not filed	6	18
Total	33	100
Danger to Self:		
Suicide attempt/threat	15	48
No suicide attempt/threat	16	52
Total	31	100
Danger to Others:		
Assault/threat of assault	11	68
No assault/threat of assault	5	31
Total	16	99

Note: *N* represents those cases on which information was available on both variables.

Table 7.3
Individual Decision-Maker Criteria

Variable	N	%
Will take medication[a]	29	60
Will not take medication	19	40
Total	48	100
Prior hospitalization	95	84
No prior hospitalization	18	16
Total	113	100
Family will take	32	47
Family will not take	36	53
Total	68	100

Note: N represents those cases on which information was available on both variables.
[a]As determined by court.

relative to white Anglos, the elderly or young relative to adults, women relative to men, the poor relative to the wealthy, and the lower class relative to the middle class would be expected to receive severer sentences in the criminal justice system.

In a study of adjudication (whether or not cases were dismissed) and severity of sentencing in a lower court, Feeley (1979, p. 133) found in his multiple-regression analysis that the structural factors of sex and race made no difference, when severity of offense was controlled, in either adjudication or sentencing. In fact, Hagan (1974) asserts that previous studies which found that blacks were more severely treated in the criminal justice system than whites were methodologically faulty in that none of them controlled for other factors such as severity of offense.

But the mental health system is not the criminal justice system; it can be viewed theoretically either as a punitive system like the criminal justice system, or as a social resource which would be expected to be more readily available to those with some preexisting power and resources. Given my experience of the courts and of the state hospitals which provide most of the court's clientele, my judgment is that the mental health system shares more of the characteristics of a punitive than a helping system. This is especially true in cases where commitment to it is involuntary, and socially marginal clients are seeking judicial release. Therefore, we predicted that:

1. *The petitions for release of the young and the elderly will be denied with greater frequency than the petitions of the middle-aged adult.*

2. *The petitions of females will be denied with greater frequency than the petitions of males.*

3. *The petitions of non-Anglos will be denied with greater frequency than the petitions of white Anglos.*

4. *The petitions of lower-class appearing and counterculture appearing persons will be denied with greater frequency than the petitions of middle-class appearing persons.*

Individual Decision-Maker Theory

As Reiss (1974, pp. 692–94) points out, "Judges are granted enormous discretion," including, in Metropolitan Court, the final disposition of all habeas corpus petitions. As Feeley (1979, p. 152) notes, "Perhaps decisionmaking is best explained by examining the attitudes, values and goals of the decisionmakers themselves." However, in his multiple-regression study of lower-court decision making Feeley included variables such as the judge's political party affiliation but not the meaning of decision factors to the judge.

It is uncommon for legal decision-making studies to take the meaning of decision factors to the decision maker into account. Gibson's (1978) work on racial discrimination in the courts did utilize judges' interpretive schemes as a key variable. He summarizes:

> Research on racial discrimination in the courts can be classified in terms of whether a societal or an individual perspective is adopted. . . . The first approach, prevalent among sociologists, begins with the argument that courts as institutions are systematically biased. . . . Discrimination is conceptualized as flowing from the *institutional structure.* . . . An alternative theoretical perspective seeks to explain discrimination in terms of the beliefs and values of the individual decisionmaker. . . . Most studies treat the court as the unit of analysis, rather than the individual sentencing judge. [Pp. 456–58]

In his research, Gibson found that "overall, the analysis supports an individual, rather than an institutional interpretation of discrimination" (p. 475), and he added that, "in the aggregate, the sentences imposed in the . . . Superior Court appear not to discriminate against blacks. However, this is largely due to the fact that anti-black judges are balanced by pro-black judges" (p. 475).

In the courtroom, individual decision-maker interpretive schemes mesh with organizational factors; because these schemes become known to other court personnel. Since a single judge made decisions in Department 1, both court personnel and researchers were well aware of the major criteria he used to decide cases. These were: (1) the patient's prior hospital record; (2) the patient's family willingness to take her or him back into the home; and (3) the patient's apparent willingness to take psychotropic medication, if released, to keep his or her condition stabilized (see table 7.3). We predicted that:

5. *Persons believed willing to take medication will have a lower proportion of writs denied than those believed unwilling.*

6. *Persons whose family will take them back will have a lower proportion of writs denied than those whose families will not.*

7. *Persons with prior hospitalizations will have a higher proportion of writs denied than those with none.*

Legal and Psychiatric Theories

A purely legal perspective would predict decision making based on what the law says, and on other legal criteria. In his multiple-regression study, Feeley (1979) found legal factors to be significant outcome predictors, although he warns that even the most significant factors account for only a "minute trace" of the variance (p. 142). Defendants with records of prior arrests and who possessed weapons at the time of their arrest all had higher conviction rates than those who had no prior convictions and no weapons; furthermore, as the number of prior convictions increased, so did the severity of the sentence.

Legal theory based on LPS predicts that those involuntarily hospitalized will be those who come clearly within the grave disability or dangerousness provisions of LPS; psychiatric theory predicts that those hospitalized will be those who are the most grossly mentally disordered (see table 7.3). In the psychiatric context, there was little variance in the attribution of mental disorder, since psychiatrists release patients they think are adequately reconstituted before the hearing. However, there was some variance in the severity of current symptomatology. We divided the sample into those with and those without current delusions or hallucinations and predicted that:

8. *Persons who were hallucinating and/or delusional at the time of the hearing would have a higher proportion of writs denied than persons not hallucinating or delusional.*

We also attempted to tap the use of the legal LPS criteria for commitment. Danger to others was measured by the reported presence or absence of threats of assault or of actual assaults on others. Danger to self was measured by the presence or absence of reported suicide threats or attempts. Grave disability was measured by the presence or absence of a recommendation for conservatorship. We predicted that:

9. *Persons who are not assaultive will have a higher proportion of writs granted than those who are.*

10. *Persons who are not suicidal will have a higher proportion of writs granted than those who are.*

11. *Persons who have not had conservatorships filed will have a higher percentage of writs granted than those who have.*

Outcomes

As table 7.4 illustrates, the petition is most likely to be granted when the family is willing to take the patient, and when the patient does not have delusions or hallucinations, is not physically assaultive, has not had a conservatorship filed, takes medication, has no prior hospitalization, has conventional middle-class appearance, and is white. These variables have a moderate relationship with the dependent variable (multiple r = .49) and, when taken together, can explain 24% of the variance in the outcome of the hearings.

Taking the groups of variables together in their theoretical contexts, the individual decision-maker variables and the legal-psychiatric variables are the most predictive of the outcome of habeas corpus petition hearings. With respect to judicial factors, willingness of the family to take the patient back is one of the most influential variables (beta = .33), and it explains 15% of the variance in the dependent variable. Willingness to take medication and lack of prior hospitalization together explain an additional 1% of the variance (beta = .13 and .09, respectively). The data support hypothesis 6 but give no support to hypotheses 5 and 7.

Three of the four legal-psychiatric variables are relevant to the outcome of habeas corpus petition hearings. Lack of delusions/hallucinations is one of the more influential variables (beta = .28), and it explains an additional 4% of the variance in the dependent variable. Not being physically assaultive and not having a conservatorship filed (betas = .19 and .14, respectively) are likely to result in a higher number of writs granted. The latter two legal-psychiatric variables

Table 7.4
Predictor Variables

Variable	Beta	Standard Error Beta	Multiple r	r^2
Willingness of family to take	.33	.22	.39	.15
Patient has delusions and/or hallucinations	.28	.25	.43	.19
Physically assaultive	.19	.14	.46	.21
Conservatorship filed	.14	.15	.47	.22
Takes medication	.13	.14	.47	.22
Prior hospitalization	.09	.32	.48	.23
Middle-class appearance	.11	.28	.48	.24
White	.06	.25	.49	.24

explain an additional 2% of the variance in numbers of writs granted. The data do not support hypotheses 8, 9, and 11. Male or female status had no relationship to writ-hearing outcome (hypothesis). Contrary to our prediction, age also had no relationship (hypothesis 1; see also Steadman and Cocozza 1974, pp. 154–55).

The minimal significance of petitioners' appearance could be a feature of the mental health court in its psychiatric aspect, since the court is prepared to observe all kinds and conditions of appearance without shock or comment. The minimal significance of ethnicity is perhaps a reflection of the combination of the psychiatric and judicial areas: in the criminal justice system, as indicated, blacks tend to be locked up more, as a sign either of more and more serious crime or of prejudice on the part of white soceity, but in the mental health system blacks may not be locked up because white society has minimal concern for their psychiatric treatment (Stone 1975).

The data indicate that judges pay attention to the law as well as to social factors. The importance of delusions and hallucinations in the decision-making process is well within the intent of LPS provisions for short-term commitment, since these commitments are supposed to provide some way of dealing with acute mental illness symptomatology. The limited evidence for the hypotheses related to grave disability and danger indicates that less attention is paid by the judge to the legal than to the psychiatric LPS criteria.

The decision-making criteria deemed important and used by the individual decision maker is a neglected area for research. In Metropolitan Court, during the time of my research, there was one judge who released about half of the petitioners who came before him (very close to the release rate of my nonrandom sample). In a later year, by contrast, with a different judge, the release rate was about a third of the petitioners. Some of this difference could be accounted for by factors relating to the two judges.

Attaching importance to the family of the petitioner by the judge echoes other findings in the psychiatric literature concerning family as an important determinant of the handling of patients. Speculations concerning the reasons for the importance of family are discussed by Greeley (1972) who noted that family desires for release of patients were predictive of release when perceived seriousness of mental illness on the part of the treating psychiatrists was controlled for. He attributed this relationship to family pressures on the psychiatrists.

Steadman and Cocozza (1974, pp. 154–55), in their study of criminally insane persons released from New York's Dannemora Hospital, also found that the family was a central factor in release decisions. Steadman and Cocozza note:

> One possible explanation for the importance of family interest for release, given that psychiatric evaluation has also been found highly related, is that the latter leads to the former—that is, families are interested in patients who are well, as reflected by the psychiatric evaluation of improved, and families are less likely to be interested in those patients who seem to be doing poorly. If this were the case the presence of the interested family rather than independently affecting release would actually be related to release only because of its association with improved psychiatric status . . . this is not the case. Psychiatric evaluation and the presence of interested family members are not significantly related, and therefore, influence the release decision independently of one another. [P. 127]

We were able to tap the reasons behind concern for "family willingness to take," through the participant observation of process, just as we could tap the fact that it occurred, through quantitative measurement of outcome. The judge's reasoning with respect to family willingness—particularly in the case of grave disability—was that if the family will take the patient he or she is provided with food, clothing, and shelter, and is not gravely disabled. As a fiscal conservative, the judge was extremely concerned about the cost of mental health care to taxpayers and would shift the burden of payment to the families whenever possible. In this example, the significance of an individual decision-maker variable is stressed at the same time as it is shown to be related to other significant variables such as the (conflict) variable of petitioner background and the (interorganizational) variable of California state mental health law system.

Decision making in Metropolitan Court is a complex and shifting interplay of factors which are of varying importance in predicting habeas corpus writ outcomes. The variable most predictive of outcome is the willingness of the family to take the patient; the most predictive theories are the individual decision makers and the legal-psychiatric.

Mental Disorder and LPS Labeling

But decision making in Department 1 is not limited to denying or granting writs; in Department 1, people are labeled as mentally disordered and given specific diagnoses, and are labeled as gravely disabled, dangerous to self, and/or dangerous to others. Specific rationales are given in court in support of these labels. Some of the rationales are within the intent of LPS: some are more tenuously related to the statute. In Metropolitan Court, divergence from the statute took two principal forms. Evidentiary standards actually used for the assessment of the three conditions—especially grave disability and danger to others—were not those provided under LPS. And the basis for commitment in the habeas corpus hearings was "bargained down" from that used for the earlier 72-hour commitment, generally from danger to others to grave disability.

Mental Disorder

As table 7.5 indicates, the finding of mental disorder was routine and illustrated the accepted practice of using psychiatric testimony to establish mental disorder in law. Fifty-two percent of the diagnoses made by psychiatrists were of schizophrenia, either paranoid or undifferentiated. Psychiatrists rarely testified that the individual was not mentally disordered (11% of the cases). This is not surprising since, if the psychiatrists regarded the petitioner as cured, in remission, or for some other reason not mentally disordered, the psychiatrist should already have released the petitioner, thus sparing the state the cost of the habeas proceedings and sparing the petitioner trauma.

In practice, district attorneys and public defenders rarely challenged psychiatric diagnoses and findings of mental disorder during habeas hearings; controversy focused upon the other LPS conditions. In this

Table 7.5
Psychiatric Diagnoses of Mental Disorder

Mentally Disordered		Not Mentally Disordered	
Diagnosis	$N (= 100)^a$	Diagnosis	$N (= 11)$
Paranoid schizophrenic	30	Adjustment reaction to adult life	3
Schizophrenic	22	Explosive personality	1
Drinking/drugs	14	Mental confusion	1
Neurosis	9	Isolated incident	1
Manic depressive	8	Depression	1
Psychotic episode	7	Drugs/drinking	1
Adjustment reaction to adult life	3	Character disorder	1
Psychopath	2	Ambivalent	1
Explosive personality	1	Mild paranoid schizophrenic	1
Postpartum psychosis	1		
Acute environmental stress	1		
Thinking disorder	1		
Anhedonia	1		

[a]There were 89 individuals; multiple diagnosis accounts for $N = 100$.

court, most of the petitioners were represented by public defenders, who generally refrained from vigorous advocacy of their clients' legal rights under LPS. Therefore, as indicated by tables 7.6, 7.7, and 7.8, the amount and variety of evidence introduced by the public defender to demonstrate the lack of grave disability or dangerousness is less than the amount and variety of evidence introduced by the district attorney to demonstrate the presence of these qualities.[1] A phrase used by all types of personnel in the court to refer to the nonadversary nature of the proceedings was: "we all work together here" (see Chap. 8).

Grave Disability

Grave disability is defined operationally in this court by a number of diverse criteria, only a few of which relate directly or indirectly to the statutory standards concerning food, clothing, and shelter. Other criteria viewed as significant by the court relate to the defendant's relationship with his or her family, as indicated above, and prior involvement in the mental health system (see also Mendel and Rappaport 1969).

Prior hospitalization relates both to prior involvement in the mental health system and to prior functioning in the community. The petitioner in involuntary commitment proceedings is not given the right (granted to accused criminals) to exclude past records from evidence. Prior hospitalization, the evidence most frequently offered to show grave disability (70% of the cases), has no necessary connection with *current* inability to provide food, clothing, and shelter. Therefore, it seems to relate more to functioning within the mental health system than to functioning within the community at the time the writ is filed. This emphasis on functioning within the mental health system also characterizes other kinds of evidence frequently cited: not taking medication, denial of illness, lack of cooperation in hospital, and conservatorship proceedings.

Of the 60 persons initially committed as gravely disabled, 45% were alleged by the district attorney to have refused to take their medication, usually on the basis either of psychiatric evidence or of prior incidents of going off medication. Of those 35 persons whose

---

1. The evidence in tables 7.2, 7.4, and 7.5 pertains to standards of commitment used after mental disorder was established. We also attempted to keep evidence of grave disability and of dangerousness separate in those cases in which a person was held under more than one provision. This meant, for example, that if a person had been held for grave disability and danger to others and refused to take his or her medication, we included that person in all three tables but listed the refusal to take medication under the grave disablement standard. However, if the individual was held under danger to others and was noted as refusing to take medication, we included the refusal as a criterion for dangerousness to others.

writs were denied, 37% were alleged to have refused to take medication; of those 25 persons whose writs were granted, only 8% were so charged; thus refusal to take medication again appears as a significant factor in the outcome of habeas corpus hearings. In both informal conversations and in courtroom encounters the judge repeatedly emphasized this factor:

> JUDGE: I will not let him go. When he refuses to take medication he is gravely disabled.
> PETITIONER: I am not going off it again.
> JUDGE: Remanded. I don't care what you say, it is your track record. Remain in hospital and see that you take your medication.

Like refusal to take medication, denial of illness implies an unwillingness to adapt to the mental health system (see also Hart 1974, p. 121). Denial of illness was used as evidence of grave disability in more than a quarter of the cases:

> JUDGE: If he had sound judgment he would say that he wants to get well.
> DISTRICT ATTORNEY: That is not what the legislature had in mind for "gravely disabled" [off the record].

In an illustrative case, the judge denied the writ because the petitioner would not acknowledge her illness despite the evidence of an outpatient organization that she was doing well with them. This case was in clear violation of the least-restrictive alternative doctrine implied by LPS:

> PUBLIC DEFENDER: On what subject is your Master's thesis?
> PETITIONER: The metaphysics of insanity—personal experiences in the area of my own insanity—although I don't call it insanity—
> JUDGE: I may say, counsel, you have aptly demonstrated this organization is very thoughtful, concerned, and that she [the petitioner] is a hard worker—a massive case of self-delusion—she has taken enough of the state's time—the writ is denied—you're fooling yourself, madam.

In nearly a quarter of the cases lack of cooperation in the hospital during the 72-hour hold was used as evidence of grave disability. Cooperation in the hospital appears to have been a significant factor in the denying or granting of the writ. Of those whose writs were denied, 22% were "charged" with not being cooperative in hospital; of those whose writs were granted, only 2% were so charged. In an extreme instance of the misuse of such evidence, an individual was committed to a hospital for 14 days and then recommitted on another 72-hour hold "because his lack of cooperation during the first commitment constituted grave disablement" (psychiatrist). The judge granted his writ on the grounds that such a procedure was a gross violation of the LPS Act.

The Uses of Conservatorships

In about a third of the commitments evidence was elicited (generally by the judge's questioning) that conservatorship proceedings by the public guardian were being initiated or were already underway. LPS provides that a court may declare persons who are gravely disabled to be wards of the public guardian or of a private conservator (generally a relative) (LPS par. 5355). The individual may then be placed in a hospital or board-and-care home, or cared for in a private setting at the conservator's discretion (LPS par. 5358).

The appointment of a conservator for a person makes it irrelevant whether or not the habeas corpus writ is granted, since the mental health system retains its control. Sometimes, therefore, the fact that conservatorship was in effect, or proceedings had begun, meant that the individual could be released on the writ, since released made no difference. On the other hand, if conservatorship proceedings had not yet been initiated but were expected to be shortly, or if they have been initiated but the outcome was uncertain, then the writ was more likely to be denied on the grounds that the proceedings themselves were a sign of grave disability, thereby maintaining continued control.

Lamb et al. (1981) make a similar point concerning the uses of conservatorships in California as a whole. They state that one "abuse" of the conservatorship process is to hold patients in hospital beyond their 14-day holds. The hospital applies for a temporary conservatorship, which is granted by the court prior to the actual hearing, supposedly so that an investigation can be carried out. But about half of these temporary cases are discharged before the hearing, and the case is dropped. The purpose of this procedure, they say, is to ensure continued medication.

In this court, in summary, denial of illness, refusal to take medications, prior hospitalization, and conservatee status are used as indicators of grave disability. If people cannot function without coming to the attention of the mental health system, they are gravely disabled:

> JUDGE: He is unable to remain in the outside world because of his own conduct, therefore he is gravely disabled.

As indicated earlier, sponsorship of family members willing to care for the patient was a significant factor in the granting of the writ, while rejection by the family was an important reason for denial (see also Greeley 1972; Steadman and Cocozza 1974, pp. 125–27). Family rejection was sometimes an indirect means of demonstrating the lack of ability to survive; at other times, however, family evidence related to the inability of the mentally disordered person to get along with his or her family, either permanently or temporarily. Twenty-two of the 70 petitioners about whom there were data had been brought to the hospital for a 72-hour hold by family members; in another 11 cases the family called the police; thus families initiated nearly half of all commitments. Part of the function of the mental hospitals in the area was to act as a kind of safety valve for the families of mentally disordered persons, who could obtain relief from the problems of dealing with recalcitrant members for three, and possibly as long as 17, days. Therefore, the court took note of the willingness of the family to take the member back and, conversely, of its need to have some additional peace (see also Stone 1975, p. 45).

Residual Deviance

As indicated in table 7.6, several of the criteria used in habeas corpus hearings relate directly to grave disability standards regarding food (3%), clothing (12%), and shelter (7%). One individual, for example, was said by the psychiatrists to be unwilling to eat; another was allegedly dehydrated from all inadequate intake of liquids. However, cases that were clearly within the statutory category of grave disability were in the minority. Other testimony was not within its provisions: evidence was introduced in one case that an individual's clothing was "bizarre," and in another that the petitioner walked around in various military uniforms; several people were found wandering around in the street but had just come from homes; at least one person was found gravely disabled on the ground that her home was dirty. Some situations were neither clearly within or clearly outside the category of grave disability, since the standard of adequate food, clothing, and shelter is open to a good deal of interpretation.

It is analytically often difficult to separate people who are gravely disabled within the intent of LPS from others who are merely social pests. As the judge frequently repeated, persons who annoy others to the point where they are forcibly removed to a mental hospital are by definition unable to function in the community. Thus psychiatrists (and occasionally other hospital personnel, such as nurses) sometimes testified to the petitioners' residual deviance (Scheff 1966) or violation of folkway norms. Dancing in the street, parading around in military uniform, yelling and screaming, moving furniture, reciting on a street corner, standing on the street corner trying to hail a taxi, being obese, being transient, and having a dirty home were among the folkway violations used as evidence of grave disability.

Table 7.6
Civil Commitment on Grounds of Gravely Disabled

	Cases		Writ Denied		Writ Granted	
	N	%	N	%	N	%
Evidence for commitment:						
Previous hospitalization	42	70	30	50	12	20
Will not take medication	27	45	22	37	5	8
Family rejects	26	43	23	38	3	5
Conservatorship proceedings	18	30	13	22	5	8
Denies illness	17	28	10	17	7	12
Can't manage/no money	16	27	13	22	3	5
Takes drugs/drinks	14	23	9	15	5	8
Uncooperative in hospital	14	23	13	22	1	2
Inadequate/inappropriate clothes	7	12	4	7	3	5
Annoys people	4	7	3	5	1	2
Inappropriate living place	4	7	3	5	1	2
Won't eat, drink	2	3	2	3	0	0
Evidence against commitment:						
Relative will take care	13	22	5	8	8	13
Will take medication	8	13	4	7	4	7
In remission/improved	8	13	0	0	8	13
No prior hospitalization	5	8	3	5	2	3
Outpatient care	6	10	1	2	5	8
Not mentally disordered	5	8	2	3	3	5
Has money	3	5	2	3	1	2
Improper commitment	2	3	0	0	2	3
Criminal charges filed	3	5	0	0	3	5
Untreatable	1	2	0	0	1	2
Total	60	100	35	58	25	42

Note: Percentages throughout expressed as a portion of total cases: percentages sum to more than 100 because multiple categories of evidence are offered in many cases.

Residual deviance and the unwillingness of relatives to provide for the individual were used as indirect evidence of the inadequacy of food, clothing, and shelter. Another form of indirect evidence was financial and employment status. One quarter of the petitioners had money problems: they were unemployed, they had no source of funds, or they were unable to manage their money. Among the unemployed were many who received public assistance, social security in particular. Those individuals who could document such a steady income had an enhanced chance of release. Others had no financial resources outside their family; if their relatives rejected them, they became "gravely disabled" by definition. Still others had money but spent it "inappropriately." In one case, the district attorney argued that the petitioner was gravely disabled because "she spends all her money on books instead of necessities."

Danger to Others

The major focus of recent debate over civil commitment has been on danger to others rather than grave disability (see Chap. 1). From table 7.7, it appears that the most frequently used criterion for assessing dangerousness was prior hospitalization. However, since many persons judged dangerous to others were also found gravely disabled, it is difficult to assess the relevance of the prior hospitalization for that small sample of persons found only dangerous to others. Similarly, denial of illness, being troublesome in hospital, refusal to take medication, and refusal to take the patient back into the home were offered as evidence on this ground as well as the previous one. But the behavior said to constitute dangerousness, and the seriousness and imminence of that behavior, is relevant to the "danger to others" standard. Such behavior includes threats of violence, assaults, attacks on property, history of violence, and reckless driving (see table 7.8).

Table 7.7
Civil Commitment on Grounds of Danger to Others: Nature of Threats and Violence

	N	%
No violence/threats specified	17	43
Threats to kill (with bomb, knife, hammer):		
Family/friends	6	15
Strangers	6	15
Social control agents	3	8
President/vice-president	2	5
Other threats:		
To kidnap	2	5
To rape	1	3
Violence against:		
Family/friends (beatings, knifings, and chokings)	7	18
Unspecified	3	8
Strangers	1	5
Total	40	100

Note: Data from mental health reports (see table 7.3). *N* is different from danger to others totals in table 7.4 because of missing data. Percentages expressed as a portion of total cases. Absolutes and percentages sum to more than *N* (100%) because of multiple allegations in many cases.

Table 7.8
Civil Commitment on Grounds of Danger to Self

	Cases		Writs Denied		Writs Granted	
	N	%	N	%	N	%
Evidence for commitment:						
Suicide attempts	20	67	11	37	9	30
Prior hospitalization	13	43	9	30	4	13
Family rejects	9	30	9	30	9	0
Suicide threats	6	20	5	17	1	3
Reckless driving	3	10	3	10	0	0
Evidence against commitment:						
Family will take care	8	27	3	10	5	17
Will take medication	7	23	3	10	4	13
Not mentally disordered	5	17	1	3	4	13
Outpatient care	4	13	0	0	4	13
Not suicidal	4	13	3	10	1	3
No prior hospitalization	3	10	3	10	0	0
Cooperative in hospital	1	3	0	0	1	3
Total	30	100	17	57	10	33

Note: All percentages expressed as fraction of total cases; both absolutes and percentages sum to more than N (100%) because of multiple allegations in most cases. In three cases (10%) there was no evidence, and the writ was granted.

Threats of violence are the most common means of proving, in habeas corpus proceedings, that the petitioner is dangerous to others; they are alleged in nearly half the cases (see table 7.8). These threats are both verbal and written and are directed to specific persons or to society at large.

Only one individual was adjudged dangerous on the basis of a writing—letters threatening the murder of a previous employer. All other threats were oral, directed at famous people, strangers (including police), family, and friends. Threats against family members were both verbal and physical, and often serious:

Mother brought him to. . . . Had been threatening members of the family with a knife and made gestures as if to stab himself in the stomach [dangerous to self, to others, and gravely disabled].[2]

2. This case shows an overlap, common to many cases, between threats and assaults, since the verbal threat in question was backed up by the presence (but not the use) of a weapon. In this analysis, the category "threats" includes cases in which the use of a weapon was threatened, while "assaults" includes only those cases in which there was contact between the individual and his or her victim, with or without a weapon.

Threats to strangers were made either against specific people or whatever audience happened to be nearby:

> Police officers were called to the district office of the Welfare Department where a man was creating a disturbance by claiming to be James Bond, Agent 007. He said he was working undercover for the CIA, claiming that he usually carried a machine gun but not that particular day. He said he was at the Welfare Office to see a supervisor and kill him [dangerous to others and gravely disabled].

> Man placed a suitcase on the gas pump at the station and said he was going to blow everyone to bits [the suitcase was later found to be empty].

Two individuals made verbal threats to the lives of the president or other political figures. In both cases, the judge denied the writs on the ground that a mistaken prediction of nondangerousness was too risky in the climate of public opinion following two recent attempts in the same state to assassinate the president. The judge added that he would not hesitate to deny the petition of anyone who threatened a public figure, no matter what the evidence.

Less than one-third of the petitioners had physically assaulted another person. Those assaults that did occur were mainly on family members. Many of the assaults appeared serious in intent; some involved knives, hammers, and other weapons:

> Parents had called police because he was beating mother with belt. Upset because his parents had put the house up for sale. . . . Officers had to subdue him. Has beaten up parents in past [dangerous to others].

> Police called to home regarding a family disturbance. She was observed trying to choke her father. She was hallucinating, and was religiously preoccupied about the Lord, the Holy Spirit [dangerous to others, herself, and gravely disabled].

Other assaults had the character more of quarrels or accidents:

> The father was vacuuming the hall. R. could not stand the noise and tried to stop the vacuum by grabbing the cleaner away from the father. They tussled. Sister ran to help father, got hit and fell [dangerous to others, and gravely disabled].

In most cases, the public defender did not act as an advocate for the petitioner but worked together with the other participants in the hearing to come to what all could agree was the "right decision" for the individual and for society. Therefore, the fact that most of these patients had little or no prior history of violence did not appear in evidence. It was argued in only four cases and did not affect release.

However, prior possession of a gun was introduced as evidence of dangerousness in four cases, although in none was there any evidence that the gun had been used.

Attacks on property have been suggested as a criterion of dangerousness by a minority of experts, but this is rejected by many more (Monahan 1976; Wexler 1981). Such attacks were alleged as evidence of dangerousness in 17% of the cases, although in several of these the property belonged to the patient (the ownership of the property was not always clear and was not often made an issue):

> Called by apartment manager, the police found apartment a mess, broken furniture, wall plaster broken, etc. Said police had been hurting his brain with some kind of electrical device. They were creating mosquitoes to magnify their noise.

An interesting and unexpected feature of prosecutorial construction of all three LPS standards was the significance of the automobile in one way or another. Reckless driving, for example, was used as evidence of both danger to others and danger to self, even though the relevant driving incidents had occurred long before hospitalization:

> He has an extensive arrest record and about three months ago was in an automobile accident where he went through a red light and was hit. He had been drinking. Police report suggested he was suicidal.

Imminence and Seriousness of the Danger

Besides evidence concerning the prior dangerousness of the petitioner, LPS requires evidence concerning the imminence and seriousness of future danger. These criteria were simply ignored in most of the 100 habeas corpus proceedings we observed. One case in which these issues were debated at length was the highly atypical incident where the petitioner had threatened a previous employer by mail. This petitioner had been in prisons and mental hospitals on threat charges for seven years, was represented by private counsel appointed by the court, and had attained a degree of local fame (he was released; see Chap. 2).

Imminence and predictability became an issue in this court only if two or more psychiatrists testified and their testimony was contradictory. In the case mentioned above, not only did the psychiatrists disagree but the petitioner's private attorney took a strongly adversarial stance in his behalf. In this court both dedicated advocacy and psychiatric disagreement were necessary conditions for thorough proof of all the requirements of LPS.

Much current research is directed toward constructing scales and measures that will predict the level and imminence of danger more accurately (see Meehl 1970; Monahan 1976; Steadman and Keveles 1972). The assumption of these efforts is that if such scales were made available they would be used in both hospitals and courts. If courts avoid the issues of seriousness and imminence because they are too problematic, then indeed the scales might be welcomed and used extensively, and their construction would be extremely significant. But if the courts avoid these issues for organizational reasons, then the scales would probably not be put to use[3] (see Chap. 5).

Danger to Self

Persons committed on the ground of danger to self—particularly if also committed as gravely disabled and dangerous to others—constitute a somewhat different population and represent a somewhat different application of LPS standards. Unlike most other petitioners, those who had attempted or threatened suicide (nearly 90% of the petitioners fell into one or the other of these categories) were nearly all young, and fewer had previously been hospitalized (see table 7.8).

Hospital and court personnel displayed more sympathy for these young, troubled patients than for those who were older, more institutionalized, and stereotypically "mentally ill." Cooperativeness with hospital staff and willingness to take medication were used more frequently in favor of, and were not used against, the petitioner. More of these petitioners were receiving outpatient care (13%) than the gravely disabled (10%) or the dangerous to others (0%).

Family rejection was a significant factor in the denial of writs in danger to self cases, probably because so many of the suicidal petitioners were adolescents. In one-third of the danger to self cases the patient's family refused to take him or her back, and in all cases the writ was denied.

As indicated in table 7.8, a fifth of the petitioners had made suicide threats, and another two-thirds had made suicide attempts shortly prior to hospitalization. In many of the suicidal cases the act was defined by the psychiatrists as a gesture rather than an attempt.

> PSYCHIATRIST: He made a suicide attempt, crashed at [hospital]
> after taking an overdose, he said, it could have been
> lithium . . . 18 past suicide attempts as a result of frustration
> of his hedonistic needs. Not a heightened suicide risk in my
> opinion, except accidentally he might succeed, but he does
> not select methods which are lethal . . . as an overdose.

---

3. There is some evidence that hospital personnel might avoid the use of such scales, since they often use involuntary hospitalization to get patients to "needed treatment" (see Wexler 1974).

However, the judge was fearful that this and other suicidal patients, if released, would commit suicide; he therefore tended to be over-cautious:[4]

> JUDGE: He either is mentally ill or he is maligering. It is not for a judge to say if he is malingering—it is up to him to take into account the behavior of the individual.
> PUBLIC DEFENDER: I ask the court to grant the writ because the doctor has said he does not fit the categories [writ denied].

The court paid greater attention to the legislative standards in applying the category of danger to self than it did in construing either of the other categories, partly because of the characteristics of the patients diagnosed as suicidal. This is particularly interesting in the context of the theory behind LPS, which links grave disability to dangerousness to self as *parens patriae* provisions, and distinguishes dangerousness to others as an aspect of the police power of the state.

Summary and Discussion

Application of the mental disorder, dangerousness, and grave disablement criteria under LPS were examined in 100 habeas corpus proceedings in one metropolitan court. The major finding was that statutory criteria for civil commitment, which in any case tended to be vague, was not strictly applied. Diagnoses of mental disorder were overwhelmingly schizophrenia, either paranoid or undifferentiated. Few persons were labeled "not mentally disordered" by psychiatrists. However, in a minority of cases the same label—for example, "adjustment reaction to adult life"—was used to indicate both mental disorder and its absence.

Grave disability standards dealt less with food, clothing, shelter, and finances—functioning within the community—than with functioning inside the family and the mental health system. This suggests that considerations of individual rights and the protection of society are displaced in this court by considerations of the relief of family tensions and the smooth functioning of the mental health system.

Danger to others is mainly a matter of threats and assaults within the family, sometimes quite serious; in this it resembles justice-system patterns of criminal assault. Threats to public figures, though rare, are treated as being politically explosive. The greatest deviation from LPS standards was the failure even to try to predict the imminence and seriousness of danger to others. Continued commit-

---

4. The judge's fear of the possible subsequent suicide of a released petitioner indicates a fear of false negatives in cases of danger to self as well as danger to others.

ment for danger to self, on the other hand, focused directly on threats, gestures, and attempts at suicide.

An outcome study using 130 habeas corpus writ hearings found that about half had their petitions for release granted, and about half had to return to the hospital to continue their 14-day certification. The most important determinants of outcome using a multiple-regression study were those relating to the individual decision maker and to LPS rather than those relating to the social characteristics of the petitioner.

An anticonflict theorist might conclude from these findings—and from similar findings reported by Feeley (1979) and Gibson (1978)—that a conflict perspective on rule enforcement is not a useful one; that the labeling of deviance takes place within the rule of law, unaffected by social class and race bias. I think this would be a misapprehension. In my view, the symbolic interactionist and structural levels of analysis are intertwined; rule enforcement according to existing laws is enforcement of laws framed by powerful groups seeking their own goals and interests. Furthermore, the biography of the judges making the decisions—like the biography of the sociologist reporting those decisions—is shaped by social class and other sociohistorical forces. The relevance of macro conflict theory to rule enforcement is not direct; it is indirect, mediated by the interpretive schemes adopted by the decision makers.

The relationship between social systems and interpretive schemes is also reflexive. Not only is the judge's biography shaped by the collective history, but also there is a certain facticity to what the judge is faced with making decisions about. One of the things he is faced with in Metropolitan Court is a socially marginal clientele with few resources and alternatives—a material determinant of his decision making which influences his interpretive schemes. Another thing he is faced with is a society in which extended family structures rarely exist to support deviants; for the chronically mentally disordered there may be no family supports. So his interpretive and evaluative interest in getting family members to take responsibility for these petitioners is moderated by the factual difficulty of the social and personal isolation of so many of them.

8 The Court and the Interorganizational Network

*M*etropolitan Court is an organization within a network of mental health law organizations. As Feeley (1979, pp. 18–20) notes, drawing on contemporary organization theory, courts are part of open rather than closed interorganizational networks.[1] Weber's analysis of bureaucracy envisaged such networks as closed, with shared and followed rules and goals, a clear hierarchy, and rational authority structures. Contemporary organizational theory, in classifying social control networks as open systems, acknowledges the importance of fluidity and flexibility in organizational authority, hierarchy, rules, and goals. This fluidity is in part a product of the interdependence of the organizations in the network, and in part a product of the existence of individual, interpersonal, and nonbureaucratic interests in organizational decision making.

System interests, organizational interests, the interests of subgroups within the organization, and self-interest all play a role in the decision-making process at Metropolitan Court. The interests involved are material—related to economic, personal, and professional survival—and ideal—related to ideas about justice, mental illness, and the law. Furthermore, these material and ideal interests have individual, interactional, and external elements: organizational decision makers have their own views about justice, they share views with others in the organization, and they are in the position of responding to externally made decisions, such as new mental health legislation. And people have their own material and professional

1. Since this book represents an interdisciplinary endeavor, it is not possible to give complete coverage to the varieties of organizational theory that have relevance to this chapter.

177

self-interest, they take action in concert with others, and they operate within resource and other practical constraints imposed from outside the organization. Thus the decision making in the court reflects the ideal and the material, and the group, societal, and individual levels of social action.

The deviants about whom decisions are being made disappear when the organizational context of decision making is the major focus. The relevance of their social marginality and other characteristics remains as a social structural reflection; the relevance of their existence as a client resource, which must neither disappear or enlarge beyond capacity remains as an item for interorganizational analysis. But at least for the purpose of this chapter, the mentally ill are not the most significant factors taken into consideration in organizational decision making.

The Mental Health Law Interorganizational Network

Using an inductive, symbolic interactionist perspective, and moving outward from the court into the interorganizational network, my view of the mental health law network I studied is somewhat incomplete. I refer to it as a network rather than as a system because I conceive of a system as *more* complete and derived deductively from the most external shell (in a conflict framework, the political economy). I have mapped, in figure 8.1, the parts of the interorganizational network with which Metropolitan Court had frequent transactions. The extension of the network beyond this model to the political and economic structures of society is assumed as a background feature of this analysis as a whole.

The connections between the interorganizational units on the diagram represent personnel who act as liaisons between them; for example, public defenders from the court sometimes visit mental hospitals to see clients, while state hospital psychiatrists come into court to testify. There are some personnel within the network who have specialized liaison roles, for example, the MHCs (see Chap. 1), and the psychiatric technicians from the State Hospital whose job it is to transfer patients who have filed writs back and forth from hospital to court.

The other modes of interorganizational communication are interorganizational meetings, letters, memos, and telephone calls. I frequently attended meetings of court personnel, psychiatrists, hospital administrators, and local health department bureaucrats, which were held at the court. I did not have routine access to the other forms of communication; however, the judge would often copy for me any memos and letters he thought might interest me.

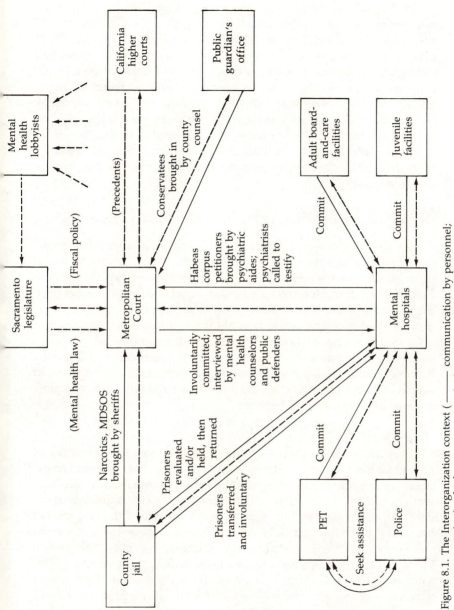

Figure 8.1. The Interorganization context (——— communication by personnel; ‑‑‑‑‑► communication by letters, memos, telephone concerning policies, precedents).

Interorganizational communication has a quality different from intraorganizational communication which makes it more inaccessible to the researcher. Within organizations, much decision making is done in casual interactions accessible to the researcher rather than in formal meetings, which in some organizations function more as rituals than as decision-making forums. Interorganizationally, however, meetings, memos, and phone calls may be the only source of communication, since the people involved do not run into one another casually on a day-to-day basis. The exclusion of outsiders from these more private or formal channels makes it more difficult to observe interorganizational than intraorganizational decision making.

Interorganizational Factors in Mental Health Court Decision Making

There are two ways in which to analyze the impact of interorganizational factors on the decision making of one organization: through tracing resources—which include money, personnel, and clientele—or through analyzing interactions between personnel from the different units and relating those interactions to decision outcomes. The first approach is crucial for a macrosystems approach to interorganizational decision making, and also quite useful as a background factor from a symbolic interactionist perspective. I am able, however, to make only a few generalizations about fiscal resources in courtroom decision making, and these are mediated through interactional and interpretive factors.

Resource Allocation

The allocation of resources occurs at three levels: at the level of policymaking (federal, state, and county), within the interorganizational network, and within each organization of the network. If money is the resource, for example, a given amount is allotted to some part of the mental health system (the state mental hospitals, or the community mental health service centers, or the mental health court), and different amounts and classifications of funds to different types of organizations within these subparts. Resources form a structural constraint upon decision making which may also become an interpretive constraint; as indicated in Chapter 7, for example, the judge of the court made some decisions based upon his perceptions of strained state resources.

Clients are resources, as well as money, but they have different implications. A working, adequate number of clients is a desirable resource; none, and the organization might not exist, too many, and it might be overwhelmed (see Chap. 2). With money, on the other hand, there seems to be no upper limit of desirability. Clients to mental health court come from mental hospitals in the surrounding county, mainly the state hospitals, but sometimes also from private and VA hospitals.

Personnel, as indicated in Chapter 1, include judge and commissioner, district attorneys and public defenders, mental health counselors, and support staff; in addition, psychiatrists are appointed temporarily on a fee basis. Like all courts, there is a complaint from the various personnel components that there are not enough workers to perform the job properly; the public defender's office has doubled its staff over the past four or five years, and the DA's office has added two members.

Like the criminal courts, Metropolitan Court and the mental health law network are open systems; one of the things the network must be open to is change in the substantive and procedural law by which decisions are to be made. Therefore, the mandate of Metropolitan Court is to make decisions concerning release from involuntary confinement in the context of (1) an ever-shifting array of legal requirements, (2) resource allocations which come from different sources than the law, and (3) a clientele which comes from a part of the network—that is, the mental hospital—governed by laws, policies, and resource constraints which both overlap with and differ from those of the court. Conflict as well as consensus in decision making interactions within the network is, therefore, to be expected.

The relationship between governmental resource allocation and organizational aspects of decision making is of great significance, but at the same time it is quite difficult to study empirically (because it is expensive and difficult, if not impossible, to obtain the necessary budgetary data) and to make causal connections between resource allocation and decision making (because only correlations can be made at this macrolevel of analysis). For example, during the period of my research the state made sweeping cuts to the state mental hospital budgets for staff and patient care. During the same period of time there was an increase in the number and percentage of habeas corpus writs granted (a correlation). It is possible that the hospitals were encouraging more patients to file writs, and/or that the court was cooperating with the beleaguered hospitals in releasing more patients—or neither, or some alternative explanation.

When symbolic interactionist analysis is added to structural, it becomes more feasible to make causal statements by asking those involved in the decision making which, if any, of the hypothesized factors entered into the decision. In the instance noted above (similar to one analyzed only at the structural level by Haney and Michiellute [1968]), I asked the judge (the sole ultimate decision maker in habeas corpus cases) what factors entered into his decisions during that time. He did not include state budget cuts among his list of factors.

It is also possible to discover the ways in which fiscal and other resource considerations enter into the decision-making process as subjectively relevant factors (the complement to the macroconflict approach to the political economy as a factor in decisions). The judge of Department 1, for example, often trailed—put off until later—a decision on habeas corpus hearings in the hope that the care of the petitioner could be transferred to someone other than the state, usually a relative. He commented: "I trail them until a family member can be found. If they are gravely disabled their family should take care of them. There is no reason that the state and the taxpayers should take care of them." Feeley (1979, pp. 196–97) documented a similar type of fiscal concern on the part of judges in a lower-level criminal court. Some judges appear to see themselves not only as responsible to the community for the decisions they make but also for the resource cost of those decisions.

Implementation and Interorganizational Networks

Given shifting mandates and varying resource allocations, organizations within open systems face the challenge of implementing the law in concert with the other organizations, but with a minimum of conflict (Bardach 1977, p. 9). Bardach summarizes interorganizational implementation: "Implementation politics is, I believe, a special kind of politics. It is a form of politics in which the very existence of an already defined policy mandate, legally and legitimately authorized in some prior political process, affects the strategy and tactics of the struggle. The dominant effect is to make the politics of the implementation process highly defensive. A great deal of energy goes into maneuvering to avoid responsibility, scrutiny, and blame" (p. 37).

Van Dusen (1981) has developed a predictive theory of the implementation of legislation such as LPS based on (1) the degree of mandate, (2) the philosophic resonance of the law's provisions with those practitioners who must implement it, (3) the shifts in power between interorganizational units and in discretion vis-à-vis clients, and (4) incentives in the form of money and increases or reduction in paperwork processing. Combining Van Dusen's theory with Bardach's insights, the interorganizational level of implementation decision making is characterized by all units attempting to appear to fulfill the law's mandates (if it is mandated, as the LPS provisions I am concerned with in this book are), with some practitioners and organizations philosophically against one or more parts of the mandate, with differential or frequently altered access to resources, power, and discretion, and with attendant organizational inertia, interpersonal squabbles, resentments, evasions of blame, shifting of responsibility, or whistle blowing.

Organizations within the network which are philosophically resonant with the legislation are in a good position in the struggle to appear to be fulfilling the legislative mandate, because they also want to do so. As Bardach notes, "Participants who favor the policy goals of the mandate use the existence of the mandate as a moral and sometimes legal weapon in the emerging struggle over the terms on which policy is effected" (1977, p. 43). For example, the patients' rights advocacy programs created by Governor Brown of California following the wave of media scandals over hospital conditions in the early 1970s were on the side of the legislative attempt to extend rights to the involuntarily committed. Since their beliefs were consonant with the law, they could carry out their activities with a certain amount of moral smugness. However, these advocates were intensely disliked by some of the other practitioners in the network—for example, state hospital psychiatrists who were not philosophically in favor of the expansion of legal rights for the mentally disordered. Characteristically, morally resonant interorganizational units whose philosophies are feared or disliked by other units will turn to the media for exposure of the others' "incorrect" activities and for public validation of their own "correct" ones.

Organizations within the network which receive higher increments of interorganizational power or discretion as a result of changes are also in a good position vis-à-vis those units which have been relatively deprived. Power and discretion can both increase further opportunities for more of the same and protect practitioners from scrutiny and blame. Conflict in interorganizational networks will occur when laws are passed which favor some units over others.

In general, material and ideal consensus and conflict in interorganizational networks have consequences for decision making within that network. Network implementation analysis is highly complex; the relationship between implementation and decision making can best be understood by examining instances of consensus or conflict over decisions between the court and other specific network units, for example, the mental hospitals and parts of the criminal justice system.

The Court and the Mental Hospitals

Throughout the course of my research, the relationship between Metropolitan Court and the private and VA hospitals could be characterized as a hostile truce, while the relationship between the court and the two large state mental hospitals was more routinely and smoothly cooperative. Conflicts and disruptions of established patterns of relating occurred from time to time; conflicts and disruptions which had an impact on habeas corpus and other decision making within the court.

The court depends upon access to hospital records of the involuntarily committed in order for public defenders to make a case for the petitioner's release (the records are available to the people, i.e., the DA's office, through the people's expert witnesses, the hospital psychiatrists). But the private and VA hospitals in the county, seeking to keep control of their patients, routinely refused to give the public defenders access to their records. The attorneys and MHCs who were supposed to look at the records or talk to patients consistently found themselves frustrated. In a typical instance, the access of a mental health counselor to an involuntary patient, Mr. Smith, was blocked by the private hospital's personnel. The MHC wrote in a report to the court:

> I the undersigned received at least six, possibly ten telephone
> messages at my office indicating Mr. Smith's desire to petition for
> a writ of habeas corpus. . . . I was not permitted visitation with
> Mr. Smith because as stated by a nurse, "There are new regula-
> tions on visits by attorneys and others." However, Mr. Smith ap-
> proached me in the hallway and stated, "I'm still being held
> here." At this point, the nurse remonstrated with Mr. Smith that
> he could not talk to me. The nurse then led me out of the ward to
> the social worker's office, stating that the social worker had to
> interview me before I could visit with Mr. Smith. The social
> worker refused admittance to her office, saying that she wanted
> the doctor present before she would talk to me. She said the doc-
> tor was not available. I . . . called the public defender, explained
> the circumstances, and requested that a petition for a writ of ha-
> beas corpus be filed on behalf of Mr. Smith. My telephone con-
> versation was monitored by the nurse and a male attendant
> standing next to me.

This interaction is typical of the defensive truce established between Metropolitan Court and the county's private and VA hospitals. In general, private mental hospital personnel perceive themselves as "treating" needy patients and view legal procedures as an unwarranted interference with this. The VA hospitals are afraid of legal problems which might result from the release of patients' confidential records to the court. Both private and VA hospitals insist that patients' records are confidential and that the court should not have access to them. The court, therefore, stays away from these hospitals except in those cases where the patient is extremely insistent, or where the public defender's office wants to make an issue of a case for some organizational reason.

The court and the private or VA hospitals sometimes became involved in more overt conflict. In one instance a public defender was arrested and jailed on the complaint of hospital staff that he was "trespassing" on hospital grounds at night. The court retaliated by making a test case of one patient, who was dragged reluctantly from the hospital to demonstrate in person the staff's obstinacy in refusing to release records:

> A young man who had signed a writ from Monte Lake private hospital came into court in a very bewildered state, saying that he did not know what was going on, and that he wanted to go back to the hospital. He had entered the hospital voluntarily, he claimed; the public defender claimed that the man had been coerced into signing the voluntary papers. The judge demanded to see the records, since if the patient was actually voluntary the writ was inappropriate. The public defender reported that he had been denied access to the patient's papers, and that he had thought it best to clarify the patient's status in open court. The judge granted the writ (thereby releasing a person who had expressed a desire not to be released and who did not remember filing the writ), and thundered to the audience: "You can go back to that hospital and others we have trouble with and tell them if they won't give us access to the records I will order the release of all the involuntarily committed patients in the hospital." All the patients sitting in court cheered loudly.

The two public hospitals in the county provided more of the business of the court than all the private and VA hospitals combined, both because of their greater volume and (to a lesser extent) their cooperativeness. The attorneys and MHCs from the court were greeted in a friendly manner at the public hospitals; reciprocally, the public hospital psychiatrists were a part of the everyday life of the court. Access to public hospital records was routinely granted to the court.

In the one instance of overt conflict between the court and a public hospital which I heard about during my research, the public defenders' office, with the full approval of the judge and the nonprotesting knowledge of the DA, "punished" three public hospital ward psychiatrists for not releasing the "correct" number of patients who filed writs prior to their court appearance (thus avoiding a hearing). Their "punishment" for this offending behavior was the court's insistence on a strict implementation of LPS.

LPS requires the testimony of "treating"—that is, ward-based rather than administrative—psychiatrists to testify to the patients' mental status in the writ hearing. However, the public defenders' office had agreed to "stipulate" that nontreating psychiatrists could testify instead. This meant that the hospitals had to send only one or two (not 8 or 10) psychiatrists into the court to testify.

In return for the privilege of retaining their psychiatrists on the wards, the state hospitals were expected to release patients whom they though the judge would release anyway *prior* to the hearing, thus not overloading the court with "unnecessary" cases. The PD's office made an "informal analysis" of the percentage of writs granted to patients from the different wards at the state hospitals, and found that patients coming from three particular wards were being released on writ at a higher rate (about 80%) that patients in "average" (about 50%, see Chap. 7) wards. The PD's office interpreted this "deviation" to mean that the three ward psychiatrists were being stubborn and purposely ignoring interorganizational norms. The PD's office sent one state hospital a letter which read in part:

> . . . The purpose of this letter is to draw your attention to particular difficulties which surround habeas corpus proceedings . . . and to demonstrate why certain procedures now followed must be changed.
>
> Section 5276.1 of the Welfare and Institutions code provides that the person requesting release may, upon the advice of counsel, waive the presence at the evidentiary hearings of the physician who certified the petition and of the physician providing intensive treatment.
>
> This procedure has been generally acceptable. . . . But it is apparently the policy of the hospital that a patient is not discharged if the treating physician advises against discharge, even in cases where the psychiatrist who will testify in court advises release. . . . *such a procedure results in unnecessary work for the court and court officers.*
>
> In the future there will be no waiver as provided in Section 5267 (WIC).
>
> We have been compiling data on the outcome of writ hearings for patients on various wards in the hospital, and have found that the rate of discharge on writs for three wards exceeds 80%, which contrasts with 50% for all wards.
>
> Our purpose in insisting upon compliance with the statute is not to hinder the hospital in providing services to the patients, but rather to make the psychiatrists on these wards accountable for their actions.

In Metropolitan Court, the PD's action in insisting upon the presence of more psychiatrists from the one hospital became known as the "PD's Operation," and lasted for several months. In fact, the ward psychiatrists rarely appeared to testify; therefore, since the testifying psychiatrists were legally not qualified to testify, most patients from that hospital were released outright. One PD who kept a running tab estimated that there was an increase in the rate of writ granting of about 50% during the two months of the operation. The judge regarded the matter good humoredly, and released patients whenever a PD refused to waive the presence of the ward psychiatrist—although personnel sometimes forgot the "Operation":

[The judge calls the first case.]
JUDGE [to PD]: Do you waive the presence of the treating doctor?
PD: Yes.
JUDGE: What?
PD: I mean no.

The Court and the Criminal Justice System

In addition to the hospitals, the court had to deal with parts of the criminal justice system as well as other parts of the mental health system. In the majority of the involuntary hold cases in the State of California, police bring persons to the hospital for the 72-hour hold (Teknekron 1978; Warren 1979). In some of these instances—particularly family disputes—hospitalization is initiated because the police know that charges will not be filed against an offender, or because they have inadequate evidence for a criminal conviction; in these instances they use the 72-hour hold as a convenient short-term sentence. However, since LPS came into effect it has become increasingly difficult for police to convince intake psychiatrists to admit just anyone; such admissions should become even more difficult as psychiatrists come to bear more legal liability for their actions (Brooks 1974, pp. 1123–24; Urmer 1973).

Persons committed originally to jails or prisons also appear in Metropolitan Court. Both jail and prison personnel are empowered, under LPS, to transfer an inmate to state hospital for 72 hours of evaluation and treatment. There is a similar provision for juvenile correctional facilities. Hospital personnel express resentment that the jails "dump" troublesome inmates into the hospitals, and assert that many of these jail transfers do not fulfill psychiatric criteria of mental disorder (although they may fulfill legal criteria of danger to self or others).

In a typical instance, a man was booked into jail for throwing rocks at passing cars from a freeway bridge. In jail, he "annoyed" the other inmates and jail personnel, then was taken to the nearest state hospital on a 72-hour hold. The MHC recommended in a later writ hearing that the writ be granted because "he is not mentally disordered." The MHC also noted that if released "there is a hold on him from County Jail where bail was set at $250." The writ was granted, and the petitioner returned to jail. This cyclical transfer and retransfer of inmates expresses the hostile but not overtly conflictual truce between the correctional and mental health systems.

Some persons enter the mental health system prior to criminal labeling, then move into it upon the granting of the writ. In one case of kidnapping and assault, the young man involved was transported to a state hospital and certified for 14 days, whereupon he filed a writ. The MHC commented: "Mr. Jones, when interviewed, was mildly contrite about his acting out behavior, astonished to find himself in a mental hospital, but grateful he is not in jail. There is no indication of thought disorder. It is respectfully recommended that the writ of habeas corpus be granted."

During the writ hearing, the DA asked that the petitioner be released on the writ directly into the custody of the police, who wanted to arrest him. The judge granted the writ, but would not release the petitioner to the police since "this court is not in the criminal business." However, the man was in fact arrested after he left Metropolitan Court, since a DA had alerted the police via an informal telephone call.

Intraorganizational Decision Making

The fate of habeas corpus writ petitioners and other clients of Metropolitan Court depend upon intraorganizational as well as interorganizational factors. Outside the courtroom ritual, most traces of adversary behavior on anyone's part disappear. "We all work together here" is a phrase heard often in the hallways of the court and repeated proudly to the questioning researcher. The phrase symbolizes the way in which the different persons and groups at Metropolitan court interact as a unit, preserving the organization from potential threats from outside and from within. It symbolizes the subordination of sectarian and individual differences to common interest in the fitting together of interaction patterns into the day-to-day routines of the court.

Organization Inertia and Defensive Politics

This tendency for organizations to develop routines to which there is general adherence has been referred to as organizational inertia. As Seidman and Chambliss (1974, p. 657) point out, "The system of courts is an organization" and one characteristic of organizations is that "the ongoing policies and activities . . . are those designed to maximize rewards to and minimize strains on the organization." But both public and private organizations today are faced with the almost constant necessity to respond to external pressures to change.

Courts are at the vortex of reform legislation, policy maneuvering, and assorted external forces. The result is often an intraorganizational search for ways to minimize the impact of legislative change upon routines. "Defensive politics" (Bardach 1977, p. 43) intersects with organizational inertia to produce innovative ways of getting around legislation.

As one example, the court responded as a unit to a case ruling in California, *Michael E*, which would have disrupted several routine practices. The *Michael E* case established, in the early 1970s, that minors had the right to file writs of habeas corpus on their own behalf, even if committed to a mental hospital by a parent (which is legally a voluntary commitment, although commonsensibly it would be recognized as an involuntary commitment). At the time of the research there were several thousand teenagers committed to mental hospitals either by parents or state agencies acting in *parens patriae*.

In the initial attempt to implement *Michael E* by releasing children on writs, court personnel came under pressure from irate parents and juvenile workers. The judge, district attorneys, public defenders, and MHCs of Metropolitan Court—members of the organization cooperating as a whole—embarked on a search for a legal way to evade the problems attendant upon implementing *Michael E*. A public defender, while flipping through the statute books during a meeting called for the purpose of planning evasive action, found the solution: by using conservatorship proceedings for juveniles, under which patient-initiated review could take place only once every six months. As indicated in Chapters 2 and 7, conservatorship is the usual route of LPS circumvention efforts.

Court personnel seeking *Michael E* loopholes were quite open in describing this search as their purpose. One meeting participant described the process as "tinkering with" the new precedent until it "came out right." Reasons for the need for tinkering cited in the meeting included not only the parents' and guardians' wishes and the welfare of the children but also the inconvenience of having to develop a system of response to the new precedent.

Conflict over Routines

Organizational inertia and defensive politics interact to produce consensus and cooperation among intraorganizational working units. However, where there was not consensus—say, when one unit had an interest in implementing a new rule and another an interest in evading it—various types of conflict would arise between the units. If the units involved were the judge and anyone else, the unit which preferred not to do as the judge said would generally engage in

evasive tactics rather than in overt verbal conflict. With more equal-
ity between the various interests, the potential for overt conflict increased.

In an example of judicial ordering and subunit evasion, the judge
changed a longstanding policy of not requiring MHCs to notify all
involuntary patients of their right to file a writ. Prior to this change
(which the judge promoted in response to external pressures), both
judge and MHCs had agreed informally that there were too many
patients and not enough MHCs to carry out the letter of LPS:

> MHC: They say we're supposed to see everyone and tell them they
> can file a writ. There are so many patients that it's impossible.

During the second year of my research, patients' rights groups
stationed workers at the mental hospitals to inform the patients of
their right to file writs. This practice incensed both the mental hospitals and the judge. To forestall the impact of the patients' rights
advocates, the judge called the MHCs in and insisted that they be the
ones to do all the advising, thus upholding the function and honor of
the court. But the MHCs, convinced of the impossibility of the task,
continued to inform some patients as they had before, while verbally
reassuring the judge that everything was being taken care of. Such
evasive tactics in response to an authoritative command are only
possible for those segments of a unit's activities which are relatively
invisible to the authority in question.

Consensus on Routine: The Myth of Advocacy

Organizational viability depends upon a minimum level of cooperation between units, although these units may experience varying
conflicts of interest at times. In the public imagery of the ideal courtroom, fostered by exposure both to ideals of justice and to Perry
Mason, the prosecution and defense are pitted against one another in
a struggle over case outcome. This imagery does not reflect the practice in Metropolitan Court or in other courts (Blumberg 1967; Feeley
1979; Sudnow 1965).

Both lawyers and researchers are interested in the problem of how
to get advocate public defenders and district attorneys who represent
the people to work together to ensure organizationally appropriate
outcomes for the flow of cases. A considerable body of legal literature
is devoted to the question of why public defenders in mental health
courts do not act as strong advocates for their clients (see Chap. 7).

There is indeed a conflict between the medical and legal views of
human action in the realm of ideas. In practice, however, the conflict
tends to vanish. One reason is the shared commonsense conceptions
of mental illness elaborated in Chapter 3. Another reason is that

lawyers and psychiatrists in the court work together over long periods of time; the psychiatrists become familiar with legal practices and adapt to them, while the defense attorneys temper their advocacy with psychiatric sympathies.

As indicated, the personnel of Metropolitan Court spoke of their clients as crazy, weird, or some functional equivalent (see Chap. 3). The judge justified the lack of an adversary approach to justice in mental health law on the grounds that the role of the defense attorney was to be "a reflection of the client's personality" rather than a vigorous advocate. If the client was crazy, then this should not be concealed by the defense attorney.

The practice of allowing chronically or floridly schizophrenic patients to testify on their own behalf was one way in which defense attorneys could at one and the same time ensure that many patients were not released (since they made such a crazy spectacle of themselves on the stand) and still give the appearance of following due process (since persons have the right to testify on their own behalf). The judge supported these tactics by encouraging patients to testify on their own behalf and assuming, if they did not, that they were too crazy to do so.

The second major reason for the lack of advocacy was the organizational "we all work together here." Like most lower-level courts, Metropolitan Court has developed the smooth, rapid, and routine mode of processing referred to as "assembly line justice" (see also Feeley 1979). In such a system, the judges, defense attorneys, public defenders, and psychiatrists act within routinized expectations that include a relaxation of advocacy on the one hand, and a stable release rate on the other. The institutionalization of the nonadvocate expectation was highlighted dramatically when it was violated by a new public defender (see below).

Thus, an intraorganizational unit—the public defender's office—which could in theory have disrupted the even flow of patients back into the hospital refrained from doing so, in part for organizational reasons. As Rovner-Pieczenik notes of the (criminal) court,

> The goals and objectives of the court become speed and ease, that is, efficiency, in case adjudication . . . informal agreements . . . simplify decision making and limit adjudicatory uncertainty. Although each subunit (defense, judge, and prosecution) works within a varying set of constraints, functional interdependence in adjudication and agreement upon the goal of efficiency in administration promote the emergence of a consensus on case evaluation. . . . A shared normative consensus on case disposition overrides the partisan group interests of judge, prosecution and defense, limiting uncertainty of adjudication outcome and facilitating decision making. [1976b, p. 463]

"Plea Bargaining" in Mental Health Court

The records of writ petitioners to the court show that there is a change of label from the 72-hour hold to the 14-day hold, usually from all three behavior categories to "gravely disabled" alone (see table 8.1). This change in designation occurs because the hospital believes the patient to have "calmed down" after three days of medication and also because the grave disability designation can be used to prolong involuntary commitment (see Chap. 2). Some bargaining took place between the intraorganizational units on what category or categories would best fit the patient, that is, enable a case to be made for his or her retention. Very occasionally, this type of bargaining was carried out in the courtroom, on the record. The petitioner involved had been committed on grounds of danger to others and not grave disability:

> JUDGE [cannot read the LPS standard under which the petitioner is committed]: As far as I'm concerned, we'll treat it as dangerous to self and others [the petitioner has threatened to kill the police with a hammer and has pushed his mother through a window].
> PSYCHIATRIST: At the present time he is not a heightened danger to others. I don't know if he returned home—he was cooperative on the ward, but denying, not assaultive, he admits to the threat to kill the police.
> JUDGE: Where is he going to go? I'm not going to send him home, I'd sooner order a new 3-day on gravely disabled . . . I have no choice but to have him start a new 3-day, if he's taken back to his family with a hammer I can't do that.
> PSYCHIATRIST: Is he more dangerous to self than others? We can do a 14-day on that.
> JUDGE: How? It is limited to suicidal. I have to read the law fairly, I have to find one of these categories. They merge of course. If you say he is not now a heightened danger to others, I have a problem. Dr. Araji wants him back at state hospital.
> PUBLIC DEFENDER: We could stipulate that the writ is amended to grave disablement since that would prolong his hospitalization.
> JUDGE: I think that's right, the court accepts amendment to grave disablement. I think we have all the testimony we need on that one. [Writ denied.]

Many of the decisions sealed in the courtroom had already been made in informal discussions between the participants in chambers before the hearing. Researchers who measure the time taken by cases in mental health and other courts should be aware that a number of those cases which take only a few minutes have been effectively settled in advance (see, e.g., Miller and Schwartz 1966; Scheff 1964).

Table 8.1
Standards for Commitment

	N	%
Mental health report:		
Dangerous to others + dangerous to self + gravely disabled	36	44
Gravely disabled + dangerous to others	11	14
Gravely disabled	9	11
Gravely disabled + dangerous to self	7	9
Dangerous to others	3	4
Dangerous to self	1	1
Dangerous to others + dangerous to self	0	0
Missing cases	14	17
Total	81	100
Habeas corpus writ hearings:		
Gravely disabled	42	52
Dangerous to self	12	15
Dangerous to others + dangerous to self + gravely disabled	10	12
Dangerous to others	5	6
Dangerous to others + dangerous to self	4	5
Dangerous to self + gravely disabled	4	5
Gravely disabled + dangerous to others	4	5
Total	81	100

Under the prevailing consensus on the use of grave disability as the "best" label, all intraorganizational units receive some benefits. The public defenders' office reduces the likelihood of their clients being labeled as dangerous. The district attorney's office does not have to show imminent and predictable danger to others. The judge is not required to release most of the petitioners (which he might if the dangerousness label were retained), and the psychiatrist is enabled to return patients to "needed treatment."

De Facto Continuation of Pre-LPS Standards

These uses of the grave disability label demonstrate a de facto continuation of the more psychiatric and less legal involuntary commitment standard that prevailed in California prior to LPS: the need for care and treatment (see Chap. 2). Hart (1974) and Shah (1974) note that psychiatrists may seek to prolong the hospitalization of persons who are not dangerous and many be able to take care of themselves in order to continue "needed treatment." Like the defense attorneys, the judge of Metropolitan Court acquiesced to the topos of madness in his judgment that the persons processed through his court are indeed crazy and need help. He was therefore willing to facilitate their continued hospitalization when this appeared commonsensically necessary.

The second way in which the use of the grave disability label facilitates the use of pre-LPS routine practices is through conservatorship proceedings. One intent of LPS was to limit the use of long-term confinement. Danger to self carries an upper limit of 31 days' confinement; and danger to others 90 days, renewable. The grave disability label, however, provides the sole legal route to the semipermanent conservatorship process. The cooperation of intraorganizational units and of the interorganizational network in this matter has the effect of making easier both long- and short-term involuntary commitment.

Individuals and Decision Making

The petitioners processed through Metropolitan Court have been invisible in this discussion; in a sense, so have the people who staff the deviant-processing organization. Individuals have been quoted or mentioned only as they represent some organizational or interorganizational role; organizations have been discussed as if they had perspectives or activities independent of the persons who comprise them. In a concrete sense, organizations do not exist apart from individuals. But organizations and networks become real as they are symbolized in the consciousness and interaction of individuals; laws and ideas become real as they are conceptualized by individuals in their decision making. Ultimately, decisions are made by individuals: "By itself the systems perspective cannot *explain* decisions; it can only establish the *context* of decisions. Decision making in the criminal process is purposive and presumably principled. In order to come to grips with these factors, it was necessary to consider the values, incentive, and concerns of the individuals who compose the court" (Feeley 1979, p. 279).

Individuals make decisions on the basis of what factors in the environment, as interpreted by them, are relevant to them. These systems of relevance are both shared with others in the organization and unshared; they are both hierarchical and shifting, and they are both situational and transsituational. These systems of relevance include (but are not limited to) organizational loyalties, adherence to abstract justice ideals, and personal self-interest, including not only material self-interest and role performance but also such matters as emotion and mood.

Individuals may have predominant systems of relevances—the

"organization person" or the "advocate attorney"—or they may be more situational in response. But all displays of self in organizational decision making are relevant to the process, whether directly or indirectly. Indirectly, the "goof off" worker may process far fewer clients than the "hard worker." Directly, the attorney who makes a decision to ask for a jury trial may justify the decision on the basis of an abstract ideal of justice.

The Relevance of Justice Ideals

Decision makers may be influenced by loyalty to abstract ideas; in the case of courts, this is often an ideal such as justice or advocacy. One public defender who was hired during the period of my research, Mr. Simmons, had a considerable impact on the proportion of writs granted at Metropolitan Court for about three months, because of his dedication to the letter of LPS and strong advocacy and justice ideals. Since I had access both to the statistics showing writ-granting outcome, and the decision-making rationales of the judge during that period, I was able to make the causal connections in this instance.

The new, aggressive, advocate defense attorney was a common organizational problem at Metropolitan Court. The expectation was that such a person would arrive, would learn the ropes, and would become socialized to the way things are done—to the practical ideal of all working together here. At first, Mr. Simmons aroused comment typical of such persons; both his current idealism and his projected future organizational loyalties were taken for granted:

> JUDGE: That new public defender, Mr. Simmons, is feeling his oats—but he will soon settle down.

"Feeling his oats" or "acting like a law school graduate" were the terms used to discuss, and dismiss, new advocate attorneys. But Mr. Simmons both started and persisted in the behavior common to new advocates: he persuaded a number of his conservatee clients to ask for jury trials, thus tying up Department 2 for days on end. He also spent hours studying and arguing on habeas corpus hearings, committing what was probably the most egregious organizational faux pas, talking at length to clientele. Unlike his predecessors, Mr. Simmons did not modify this behavior over time, let alone cease and desist. After a few weeks, the judge became angry:

> JUDGE: Mr. Simmons is still holding jury trials.
> RESEARCHER: What are you doing about it?
> JUDGE: It is taking too much of the state's money. If he is assigned to a writ, I just grant it automatically.

As an organizational deviant, Mr. Simmons succeeded in raising the proportion of writs granted, and conservatorships terminated, for a period of several months. The judge was displeased with him, and his fellow public defenders did not come to his defense:

JUDGE: I am going to have Mr. Simmons declared incompetent.
PUBLIC DEFENDER: That Bill Simmons is an ass.

Bill Simmons was fired from his job after about three months; when I asked another public defender why, he replied, "Oh, that guy—because he was stupid."

Vested Interests

Other decisions were made on the basis of interests vested in an organizational, interorganizational, or extraorganizational audience. In one incident, a psychiatrist acting for the moment on the basis of organizational interests came into conflict with the judge who was at that same moment responding to an extraorganizational attentive public.

During a habeas corpus hearing, a state hospital psychiatrist gave the very unusual testimony that the petitioner, James Ellis, was not mentally disordered or dangerous. This testimony was unusual because psychiatrists rarely take to the witness stand to assert that petitioners are not mentally disordered (see Chap. 1), and also because the behavioral evidence fit LPS criteria better than most cases. James Ellis had made 18 suicide attempts or gestures, and had threatened the life of the president, in writing. The judge denied the writ and returned the petitioner to the hospital—all with an air of some amazement.

After the case, in an informal exchange, the judge asked the psychiatrist "how on earth" he could have testified that Ellis was sane and not dangerous. The psychiatrist replied that Ellis was so much trouble on the ward he wanted to get rid of him. In this situation, the psychiatrist's most important relevance in the system he was using was organizational.

The judge, on the other hand, found his conception of the attentive public relevant in coming to this particular decision. Two attempts on the life of the president had been made, in recent weeks, by Californians; the judge said that he was "not about to release anyone who threatens the president." This particular case was an exacerbated example of a more general response to the attentive public's fear of false negatives and the court's fear of accountability for releasing dangerous persons.

The public commonly links mental disorder with dangerousness and, as indicated in Chapter 3, fears the release of dangerous mental patients (Monahan 1976). As the judge sometimes commented, his decision making in danger to others cases was directed toward balancing the interest of the attentive public with the implementation of LPS:

> JUDGE: The radicals think we don't release enough people and the public thinks we release too many. We try to release just the right amount.

Self-Interest in Decision Making

As Kanter (1975, p. 49) notes, individual self-interest is relevant to organizational decision making. Self-interest may be conceptualized as those personal relevances which are more tied to biography than to shared ideals or concrete groups. In Metropolitan Court, self-interest both indirectly and directly affects the labeling of patients and the granting, denying, or trailing of writs, and thus the lives of those labeled mentally disordered.

Self-interest is intertwined with the other forms of interest through the concept of role; since personnel in the court make decisions based on their role within the organization, the role becomes the place where biography meshes with structural or external influences. It does not, for example, take extreme cynicism to conclude that the judge in the dangerousness case described above was concerned with his self-interest—in this case his reputation as a judge—as well as with the protection of the community.

The judge in this example was acting from what might be termed rational self-interest—self-interest related quite directly and logically to the way the role is played and the outcome of the decisions made. However, the judge, and to one extent or another all decision makers, are affected by another form of self-interest: emotional self-interest. Both judges and other court personnel made decisions or gave testimony on the basis of feeling, mood, or momentary whim.

The concept of role can also illuminate the relationship between emotion and praxis in decision making. At the intersection of job performance and the emotional self is the question of style or personality in the performance of work—a question much discussed and seen as of great practical importance in the workplace but not given much academic credence in studies of decision making.

Since "personalities" are often the subject of talk in organizations (Kanter 1975), the researcher learns about them much as do other members: through observation of personal styles and through the talk of others. For example, one MHC assigned to a state hospital (Joe) was known as a lazy person who did not take his work seriously. He was frequently observed coming to work late, leaving early, and hanging around the court rather than going to interview patients. Another MHC (Amy), assigned to the other state hospital, was known as a hard worker who took her work home at night. She was observed by all coming to work early, leaving late, and industriously interviewing patients at the hospital (this latter activity assumed by court personnel and observed directly by me). Correlatively (and in this instance I cannot say causally), there was a higher proportion of writs filed at Amy's than at Joe's hospital. Personal styles of workers can affect the fate of deviants in deviance-processing organizations in ways that both add to and transcend organizational roles.

Selves in organizations make decisions on the basis of systems of relevance that have some fixed and some shifting elements. The concept of role fixes such elements as what audiences will be relevant (organizational, interorganizational, and extraorganizational), and what sets of ideas, ideals, and law will be applied. The concept of personal style ensures that the praxis of decision making will have idiosyncratic as well as role-related elements, and will contain unpredictability as well as predictability.

All displays of self through and in organizations are powerful, since organizations and networks are powerful—and, ultimately, organizations and networks are not abstractions but are the summations of the consciousness of individual actors. The interorganizational, organizational, and personal power of action and consciousness in decision-making agencies has a profound impact on the lives of processed deviants and, reflexively, in the cumulative relevance of that decision making for future policy and practice. For law and situations do not exist independently or in a vacuum. If selves in organizations respond to law, then, equally, law grows out of the everyday practices of selves in organizations. Organizational practice is a process of sedimentation by which everyday decisions pile upward, affecting not only the persons of the moment but the future lives of the organization, its clients, and the law.

Summary and Discussion

When looked at as the product of organizations, decision making has both upward and downward dimensions. Downward, in the direction of the influence of social structure and history on decision making, the interorganizational networks which affect decisions are themselves products of prior sociohistorical decisions made by groups powerful enough to create and sustain policy and social control systems. The interorganizational network is constrained both by the allocation to it of a specific quantity and quality of resources, and for its mandate to operate within a specific set of legal, procedural, and cognitive assumptions.

The organization within the network is subject both to these same types of direct material and ideal constraints, and to the indirect effect of the interorganizational network that influences the flow of clientele and other resources. Just as the organization is the best place to observe the general praxis of decision making, the worker role within the organization is the best place to observe the interaction of role- and biography-related factors in individual decision making.

The idiosyncratic and organizational features of decision making in Metropolitan Court are obvious to the long-term observer to the court, and may be evident even to the casual observer. The idiosyncratic and organizational elements in decision making add to the sense of justice not done in Metropolitan Court, to the topos and informal ritual of the court (Chap. 6), and to the particularism of decision making (Chap. 7).

Organizational variation in decision making accounts for local variation; without the unpredictability of organizations, the same social structure could be expected to produce the same, determinate kind of decision making. As indicated in Chapter 2, Lamb et al. (1981) found considerable variation by county in California in the degree to which state hospital populations had actually declined. Teknekron (1978, pp. 128–29) found similar variation in the counties in the implementation of LPS provisions from the 72-hour hold through conservatorship proceedings. Teknekron concluded that this variation illustrates the arbitrariness of mental health justice in California.

The court operates as the location for decision-making praxis in an open interorganizational network, where ideas and material interests intersect with clientele. The decisions made in the court, in that they both affect persons and are seen to affect them, are of sociological and scholarly importance as one way in which labeling and social control are effected, and of legal and practical importance as part of the general problem of justice.

In the next chapter, I summarize and discuss the process of decision making in Metropolitan Court both as a social problem and a sociological problem. Mental health law is an arena for the development and application of scholarly thought and empirical evidence; it is also an arena in which the fate of people is decided, and, as such, its assessment goes beyond the scholarly and the empirical into what both Morse and Zusman call a "matter of values."

9 Mental Health Law and Social Policy
Summary and Discussion

*D*ecision making in mental health court is part of a multifaceted system of mental health law involving both sociological and social or policy problems. As a sociological problem, decision making in mental health court is multilayered: seen through the framework of labeling theory its determinants are the sociohistorical or structural context, the organizational network, and the individual in interaction. As a social problem, decision making in mental health court has two aspects: as a problem of the doing of justice, and as a problem of the seeing of justice done.

As Gusfield (1975, p. 285) points out, social problems such as mental illness involve two levels of perceived responsibility: "cognitive responsibility" which "explains why the problem occurs," and "political responsibility" which "indicates who is obliged to solve the problem." Both cognitive and political responsibility involve the formation and entrenchment of interest groups: categories of persons who "own" the problem and/or its solution. Much of the problem of mental illness in both its aspects has been vested in psychiatrists and allied experts, while part of the intersection of mental illness and the law is the provenance of attorneys and judges.

Outsiders to the system such as myself who undertake to study decision making in mental health law take on, by that undertaking, a share of cognitive and political responsibility. As I discuss further in the Appendix on Method, the findings of social scientists are used directly in the formation of mental health law policy; the ideas generated by academics, even if they have no such direct influence, entail cognitive responsibility to the degree to which they purport to explain the problem theoretically.

I have endeavored to fulfill my cognitive responsibility by presenting not only the data and the theoretical perspective but also the biographical and philosophical elements which entered into the data's interpretation. I want to fulfill my political responsibility in this chapter by indicating my support of continued involuntary commitment and the general grounds for this support—a critique of the social order which supports mental health law.

Summary

As a sociological problem, decision making in mental health court illustrates the operation of labeling by audiences at several levels of analysis, in both the ideal and the material arenas of social action. The most external ideal layer which must be understood to make sense of decision making is the formation and sedimentation of sociohistorical categories which define, and provide the social grounds for, the recognition of madness. These categories form the background for current legislation, scholarly theories, and policy debates about mental illness, the law, and involuntary confinement.

This background to decision making involves the interplay of material conditions with the world of ideas. The ideas within which mental illness is interpreted and the laws by which the mentally disordered are processed are products of the activities of historical and contemporary interest groups. The ways in which the laws and ideas are applied are products both of social policies promoted by the rule makers and of the activities of the rule enforcers.

The process of labeling is most easily verifiable at the level of rule enforcement in social control organizations. As an organization, Metropolitan Court was an ideal place to study the praxis of decision making—the intersection of the ideal and the material which gives rise to socially meaningful practices in interaction. The organization is both a structural and an interactional phenomenon; it exists as a social control agency developed by those in power, and as a site for rule enforcers to interact and produce decisions in concert with other rule enforcers.

Decision makers in the court act within their roles and from their self-interest as individuals in that interaction. Both role- and self-interest have structural as well as interactional implications: role-interest through the placement of the tasks within the organization and the network, and self-interest through the sociohistorical structuring of biography. Decisions in mental health law are affected by organization persons in roles and as persons.

The court and its background are imposed upon the lives of another set of selves who, in this study, are somewhat shadowy: the mentally disordered and involuntarily committed, and their significant others. Labeling theory predicts correctly that those mentally disordered processed through the court will be socially marginal; thus only some of them have significant others. Those who do, and who are labeled as mentally ill by those others as well as by social control agents, may or may not transform their essential identities to mentally disordered.

I found labeling theory to be an inadequate explanation of mental disorder, although it is an entirely adequate perspective on the societal reaction to mental disorder, since it can encompass both the interactional and the structural components of that reaction. I believe mental disorder to be a condition of some sort independent of labeling, a condition which can involve the subjective sense of loss of control. The experience of madness may or may not lead to self-identification as mad, to seeking or acceptance of the sick role, or to social labeling as mad.

Mental Health Law and Social Policy

A social policy statement on madness is ultimately grounded in value choice. As both Morse and Zusman note in their chapters, despite their opposed conclusions, any position on the retention or abolition of involuntary civil commitment is also a value choice, regardless of the trappings of law and medical science which can be invoked in a mythology of objectivity. My position on involuntary civil commitment, given the evidence I have presented and my critique of the social structure, is that it should be retained in a form more or less like LPS.

Neither Morse nor Zusman fail to recognize the existence of a profoundly difficult human problem. The difference between them lies in their conception of the cognitive ownership of the problem—whether or not it is a problem of mental illness—in the solutions to the problem which flow logically from the chosen conception, and in the assignment of moral responsibility for the solution.

Morse views mental illness labeling as arbitrary, and moral responsibility for behavior as the only basis for interfering with personal freedom. Zusman, on the other hand, argues the LPS case: that moral responsibility for behavior is equivocal and problematic, that mental illness labeling is partly arbitrary and partly reflective of some actual condition, and that the placement of persons in the sick role to enable them to express and meet dependency needs is appropriate social policy.

I would agree with Zusman's position on the question of involuntary civil commitment at the present time in history. I believe that

moral responsibility for behavior is an ideal and that personal freedom is a value that could perhaps be expressed within some social
order but cannot be expressed within ours. Dewey used the concept
of effective liberty to describe the hiatus between personal freedom
and an unfree social order:

> Effective liberty is a function of the social conditions existing at
> any time. . . . as economic relations become dominantly control-
> ling forces in setting the pattern of human relations, the necessity
> of liberty for individuals which [the liberals] proclaimed will re-
> quire social control of economic forces in the interest of the great
> mass of individuals. Because the liberals failed to make a distinc-
> tion between purely formal or legal liberty and effective liberty of
> thought and action, the history of the last one hundred years is
> the history of non-fulfillment of their predictions. [Dewey 1963,
> pp. 34–35]

In a society in which the economic conditions were such that personal liberty had effective meaning, then I would take the position
adopted by Morse. However, in a society in which the effective
meaning of liberty for the involuntarily committed is social marginality, deprivation, and despair, I am reluctantly committed to the
Zusman position on social policy.

As indicated in Chapter 1, my perspective on this social order is
more critical and conflict-oriented than it is functionalist. I see the
sociohistorical conditions for the handling of madness as alienated
conditions. The general critique of capitalist society by Marx is
well-known and has been applied extensively to the criminal justice
system by radical criminologists. With reference to the mentally disordered, I view capitalist society as alienated in structure, as one in
which individualism and profit making take precedence over supportive networks and human needs. The system for handling the
mentally disordered, therefore, will have the same characteristics:
entrepreneurial social control and a denial of human needs.

One argument advanced by Morse for the abolition of involuntary
civil commitment is that such commitment is nonlegal social control
disguised as treatment. I agree. However, I do not agree with one
possible implication of this statement: that if involuntary civil commitment is abolished, then there will be no further social control
(unless crime is committed, in which case the criminal justice system
will come into operation).

Social Control and Entrepreneurship

As indicated in Chapter 1, social control in capitalist society takes the
form of controlling not only those who commit predatory crimes but
also those who are socially marginal and economically useless

(Foucault 1965). The degree of control over the mentally disordered, and the age, sex, or ethnic categories selected for control from among the mentally disordered, vary with the shifting interests of powerful groups.

In recent decades, there has been a social policy shift in the juvenile, criminal, and mental health fields referred to as "de-institutionalization." De-institutionalization involves the relaxing of the ultimate form of social control—total institutionalization. De-institutionalization, therefore, appears as a humane social policy shift. But is it?

It is true that there has been less control through certain types of institutions—for example, state juvenile and adult mental hospital facilities. However, there is evidence from the juvenile and mental health areas that what has occurred is not so much de-institutionalization as "transinstitutionalism" (Altman 1979; Guttridge 1981; Guttridge and Warren 1981; Lerman 1980; Warren 1981).

A set of figures published by the Task Panel on the Scope of Mental Health Problems by the President's Commission on Mental Health shows that there was a drop of 47.3% in the population of mental hospitals between 1950 and 1970 (Teknekron 1978, pp. 20–21). However, "the total rate of institutionalization was higher in 1970 that it had been in 1950. . . . Three . . . categories . . . rose consistently between 1950 and 1970. Those three categories are . . . chronic disease hospitals, homes for the aged and dependent, and homes and schools for the mentally handicapped" (p. 20).

As Stone (1975, p. 10) says, "The mental health system as it empties its megainstitutions both because of the new law and administrative policy, creates a burden for the welfare system." What seems to have happened to the chronic schizophrenics that used to be in the state hospitals is that they have moved into for-profit board-and-care or nursing homes which are supported by the residents' welfare checks (Emerson et al. 1981). Stone (1975, p. 12) adds that there is a "functional interrelationship between the welfare, mental health and legal systems" at the national level, which "also can be seen as filling a function in modern society which might once have been attributed to the family." Also at the national level, Morris (1978, p. 231) summarizes the gross statistical evidence for transinstitutionalism in the mental health system and comments: "The report of the United States Subcommittee on Long-Term Care attests to a nationwide trend of reducing state mental hospital populations. During a five-year period, the average daily census of these institutions declined forty-four percent, from 427,799 patients in 1969 to 237,692 at the end of 1974. This policy of deinstitutionalization has resulted in placing patients in for-profit homes or boarding homes which are ill-equipped to meet their needs."

Studies in New York have shown that there are an estimated 25,000–40,000 ex-patients living on welfare, about 6,000 of them in for-profit board and care homes (Altman 1979; Herman 1979a, 1979b; Stone 1975, p. 93). These homes collect their residents' SSI payments and provide for basic needs. An audit found that most had daily costs of less than the SSI rate and made a sizable profit, in some cases more than $100,000 per year.

A study in Hawaii showed that the reduction of the state hospital population in the early 1970s resulted in a 63% decrease in that population between the late 1950s to the early 1960s, but also a "proliferation, with the explicit encouragement of the state mental health division, of unlicensed boarding homes for the placement of ex-hospital patients" (Kirk and Thierren 1975, p. 211). The authors of the study assert that, at least in Hawaii, the Community Mental Health movement has brought about four "myths" rather than the proposed four realities: rehabilitation, reintegration, continuity of care, and monetary savings can be translated into survival-level existence, transinstitutionalism, fragmentation of care, and a shift in (nondeclining) total mental health costs from the state to a federal welfare/entrepreneurial system.

There is also some evidence for transinstitutionalism and a shift to welfare/entrepreneurial care of chronic mental patients in California. Rose (1979, p. 451) comments that one board-and-care home chain of 38 institutions in California and 25 elsewhere reported revenues of $79.5 million in 1972. Emerson (1981) notes the expansion of private—and increasing large-sized—board-and-care homes for ex-mental patients in California.

These data from New York, Hawaii, California, and other states (Scull 1981) mainly concern the fate of those poor and/or elderly mental patients who have been de-institutionalized from the state mental hospitals (Estes and Harrington 1981). However, the poor and the elderly are not the only "social junk" who can be transformed "into a commodity from which various 'professionals' and entrepreneurs can extract a profit" (Scull 1977, p. 120). Adolescents—both from poor families and from the not-so-poor—can also be socially problematic and candidates for social control.

In recent years, there has been a movement to deinstitutionalize juvenile delinquents in a manner parallel to the de-institutionalization of state mental hospital patients. Ironically, one result of the de-institutionalization of delinquents from justice facilities has been their transinstitutionalization into mental hospitals (Guttridge 1981; Guttridge and Warren 1981; Lerman 1980; Warren 1981).

Like poor or elderly chronic mental patients, adolescents also have elements of social inutility. In an era of high unemployment, adolescents have exacerbated unemployment. Families are increasingly fragmented and are both unwiling and unable to cope with adolescent misbehavior. And the numbers of juvenile wards of the court "de-institutionalized" from juvenile correctional facilities exceed the numbers (and tolerance) of those foster and group homes available to care for them. Mental hospital transinstitutionalism is one outcome of these trends.

Adolescents are being hospitalized in public psychiatric facilities in increasing numbers at a time when adults are being released (Gallagher 1980, p. 231; Lerman 1980, p. 286). In addition, in California at least, private (profit and nonprofit) adolescent psychiatric hospitals are big business. In addition, the adolescents subjected to hospitalization are, in the main, not diagnosed as schizophrenics or psychotics as are adult inpatients. In one California study of 1,116 patients aged 12–18 years in four hospitals, nearly 70% were diagnosed as antisocial, depressed, runaway, or personality disorder (Guttridge 1981).

While the poor and elderly chronic mental patients are transinstitutionalized within a welfare/entrepreneurial system, adolescents are transinstitutionalized within an insurance/entrepreneurial medical system. There has been a proliferation, in California, of private profit (owned by corporations such as the Charter Company) or private nonprofit (owned by groups of psychiatrists and other professionals) mental hospitals or wings for adolescents.

Payment to these private concerns for services rendered is often made through third-party insurance arrangements; some take Short-Doyle funds, or Medi-Cal, or both, while others avoid state payment systems and thus avoid some degree of state control. The private hospitals which accept public patients on contract from the state must be nonprofit. However, there are income and tax benefits to be derived from nonprofit hospitals; thus, in California, one of the striking features of the contract system is its program entrepreneurship (Teknekron 1978, pp. 9–10; see also Warren 1981).

Entrepreneurship also operates at the level of legislative lobbying. During the past five years there has been a mental health lobby in Sacramento which presses for the expansion of the rights of patients. One policy unit which found favor with this lobby was a proposal to change board-and-care homes for mental patients into boarding houses; the salient part of the change was to remove the supervision of medication from a nursing staff and restore it to the patients. By virtue of their interest in patients' rights, one group in favor of this boarding arrangement was NAPA, the National Association for Patients' Rights. But other lobbyists were hoteliers and construction interests, who foresaw a new market in the construction of homes and in the conversion of unprofitable hotels and motels to boarding houses for the mentally ill. One of the state hospitals in California already contracts with a motel across the road to take in excess patients, at a cost far less than the institutional rate.

To Becker's rule-making and rule-enforcement entrepreneurship in the area of deviance must be added social control entrepreneurship (Warren 1981). Like any other system in capitalist society, the social control system is one in which, given the market, there is money to be made. And there is a market; the social control of undesirable and socially marginal people is likely to be constant, taking the form of direct state control or of indirect state control in a combined welfare-entrepreneurial model.

One of the major reasons, then, for my support of involuntary civil commitment of the mentally disordered is because I believe the alternative to be worse. Care in a profit-making institution at a cost of $14.50 a day seems more treacherous and less human than care in a state institution at $31 a day (Rubin 1978). And the confines of the state hospital, for the dispossessed, seem to threaten effective liberty less vitally than the sidewalks, streets, and cheap hotels of the completely homeless.

Lack of Support Systems for Human Needs

A major problem produced by capitalism is that profit takes precedence over the fulfillment of human needs, and individual survival over collective responsibility. As Stone (1975) notes, the welfare, mental health, and legal systems have taken over functions once seen as the provenance of the family, the community, and other strong human support networks. No one takes care of the socially marginal in the true sense of the term "caring"; indeed, it could be argued that caring itself is a casualty of alienated society.

In Chapter 3, I discussed the ambivalence of Kenneth Donaldson concerning mental hospitalization, and the ambivalence about release I had observed among petitioners at Metropolitan Court. Such ambivalence, and the apparent "choosing" of the sick role (Braginsky et al. 1969), has both social structural and cultural roots. The social structural roots are the economically and socially deprived conditions of lower-class life. The cultural roots involve not only a lack of supportive networks to fulfill human needs but also a denial of dependency among adults. The "normal" adult in American cultural stereotypes is an independent and autonomous one—not incidentally, the qualities necessary for capitalist entrepreneurship.

In examining the case of Donaldson, Szasz (1976) finds support for his theory of the culturally arbitrary nature of mental illness labeling, and for his antagonism to involuntary civil commitment. He defines Donaldson's psychiatric problems as problems in living—specifically problems of housing arrangements—and suggests that the answer to these problems could be found in housing arrangements rather than in involuntary commitment:

> At the time of his commitment, Donaldson was a homeless, forty-eight year old man, divorced, unemployed, and living with his aged parents. It requires no great stretch of the imagination to see that this living arrangement might have been something less than ideal for both Donaldson and his parents. However, none of them faced this situation directly. Instead, all agreed to disguise it as a problem of mental illness. The father filed a petition to have his son declared incompetent and to commit him to the state hospital; mother and son consented unprotestingly. Once arraigned, Donaldson did ask for a lawyer, and pretended in other ways to protest his commitment. But these were merely dramatic gestures. In fact, he went along; he cooperated fully in the transfer of his residence from his father's home to the state hospital. [P. 354]

Szasz asserts that Donaldson's complicity in the commitment, and his actions before and after, indicate a desire for hospitalization denied, at the conscious level, by Donaldson:

> It seems likely that when Donaldson told his father that someone was poisoning his food, he knew that a possible, if not probable outcome of such a communication would be involuntary mental hospitalization. . . . Furthermore, Donaldson had ample time in which to counter such action by his father. He first told his parents of being poisoned in late November. However, it was not until mid-December that his father petitioned for a sanity hearing. Clearly then, had Donaldson wanted to avoid hospitalization, he could have done so, by ceasing to complain about being poisoned . . . it can be inferred that Donaldson made no serious attempt to avoid commitment, and thus indirectly asked to be treated as a psychiatric slave. To ignore that he did so is as absurd as to insist that because he did it was justifiable to treat him as one. [1976, p. 349]

Szasz takes the position that Donaldson chose to display psychiatric symptomatology as a way of obtaining a goal: involuntary confinement in a mental hospital. Like the lower-class patients studied by Braginsky et al. (1969), the state hospital seemed to Donaldson a better option than his current living conditions. But Szasz sees the personal liberty of Donaldson as a more important social value than his effective liberty. He adds:

> Whatever its purported aims, justifications or rationalizations might have been, Donaldson's original commitment was a solution to his problem of housing rather than to his problem of "illness." However, is compulsory housing a proper remedy for such a problem? I say that, in a free society, it is not. Housing qua housing may be offered and perhaps should be offered, to persons so disabled, but they should be left free to reject such offers, and to suffer the consequences. Those who want to remove members of their household (or others) from their homes (or society) by rehousing them in the warehouses now called mental hospitals should not have the option. Were the option of commitment removed, persons disturbed by so called mental patients would have to choose between living with them or "divorcing" them. The problem of justifying civil commitment would not then arise. [1976, p. 354]

I agree with Szasz that Donaldson's problems were in part housing problems, although I do not agree that this necessarily cancels out the psychiatric dimensions of the problem. I also agree that in a humane society, in which effective liberty and personal liberty were one and the same, the solution to material problems such as housing and poverty would eliminate much of the need for translating material problems into personal deficiencies. However, Szasz omits to mention that in addition to housing problems and psychiatric problems Donaldson's actions probably reflected unmet dependency needs, needs which would remain no matter whether his problems were defined as those of housing or of illness.

Szasz proposes that all persons, including mental patients, take responsibility for their actions and not retreat into the sick role. Nor should the families of the mentally disordered be relieved of their responsibility, even temporarily, by the state, or by defining a member's problems as one of sickness. He implies both by his view of the sick role and his automatic denigration of Donaldson's living arrangements that dependence is reprehensible. In this implication, he supports prevailing cultural evaluations of adult autonomy and dependency needs.

Just as there are cultural stereotypes of the mentally ill learned from the media and elsewhere (see Chap. 3), there are cultural stereotypes of the mentally healthy and normal, learned through the same sources. For both women and men in our society, the autonomous person in the independent nuclear family unit is the ideal. For males, the ideal is the working man who supports a wife and children and is not dependent on the state for survival or on extensive networks for emotional support. For the woman, the ideal is support by the husband rather than by extensive networks, or, secondarily, self-support. As Gove (1972) notes, the ratio of unmarried men to unmarried women in institutions reveals a greater number of men, while the ratio of married men to married women reverses the relationship. It appears that the hospital functions to fulfill dependency needs for those persons who cannot get them met elsewhere—unmarried men and married women.

Coupled with the negative cultural evaluation of dependency and the glorification of individual or nuclear family independence is a conventional wisdom antagonistic to the state's purportedly rehabilitative services—prisons, jails, mental hospitals, and so on. I am not suggesting that this cultural wisdom is necessarily undeserved—indeed, the reverse is probably true. I merely want to underline the double difficulty of admitting dependency needs and asking the state to fulfill them, in the absence either of supportive networks or legitimation of human needs.

Although the literature is suggestive rather than definitive, it appears that for many of the socially marginal the conditions in hospitals are preferable either psychologically (providing for dependency needs) and/or materially (providing for survival needs) to conditions on the outside. But at the same time, it is culturally inappropriate for lower-class people (especially males) to express dependency needs or approve of institutions. Segal et al. (1977) note that, like Kenneth Donaldson, the "psychologically disturbed street people" (DSP) they studied displayed great admiration for independence:

> DSPs, after all, do survive. They make do; they get by. Just as with their "normal" counterparts, survival becomes their badge of competence and autonomy. The high value street people, and thus DSPs, place on self-sufficiency and autonomy cannot be overemphasized; combined with their powerless status it creates an abiding hostility to psychiatric and social service institutions. . . . DSPs experience involuntary commitment as a serious affront to their sense of competence and autonomy. [1977, pp. 394–95]

As Goffman (1961) notes, patients in mental hospitals have "sad tales" to account for their presence, not in terms of their own sickness or dependency but in terms of the nefarious actions of spouses or others. In my own visits to hospitals, I noted the same phenomenon; in addition, some patients, apparently ashamed to be defined as such, defined themselves as other than patients. They were CIA agents, or FBI agents, or aides, or public interest lawyers, or visitors to the hospital. But still other patients come to accept and recognize their dependency; these patients will not be found among those who continuously file writs in the court of last resort, nor will many of them be found involuntarily committed:

> A patient at a private hospital I visited had the following exchange with the doctor who was showing me around: "I'm going to kill my brother!" DOCTOR: "I'm going to release you!" They both laughed. The doctor explained that this patient could have been released some time ago but they let him stay; any time he got wind of plans to release him he threatened to kill his brother—perhaps knowing that a threat of this type could get him back in under LPS.

> A voluntary patient at a private hospital replied to my question about when she was leaving: "Why should I leave? The insurance pays for it. I get three squares and people pay attention to me."

In cases like the latter, "normal" dependency may be exacerbated by institutionalism. Institutionalism creates a new or additional pattern of dependence in addition to preexisting dependence. Thus, putting the needy into institutions may both fulfill existing dependency needs and foster additional needs.

Despite the fact that mental hospitalization is in part a response to nonpsychiatric housing and other problems of social marginality, and despite the risk of institutionalism, I would argue for the retention of involuntary civil commitment under present socioeconomic conditions. Combined with the problem of social control entrepreneurship mentioned above, the problem of a lack of supportive networks to fulfill (or even a cultural validation of the existence of) human needs makes a system of compulsory assistance necessary.

Justice Observed

Justice is not done in involuntary civil commitment, and yet I would argue for its retention. In Metropolitan Court, decision making is particularistic, situational, and arbitrary rather than universal and fair; medical theories posture as proven facts, and organizational needs take precedence over legal and psychiatric requirements. And yet in the existing social system, I believe, human needs are better served by involuntary commitment than by the most probable alternatives: abandonment to the streets, or subhuman existence in uncontrolled for-profit institutions. Personal liberty, in my view, is a chimera where there is in truth no effective liberty.

The last three chapters detailed the reasons for justice not done and for justice not observed to be done. These reasons include the precedence of organizational and interorganizational needs over the needs of clientele, the intrusion of clients' social structure rather than psychiatrically relevant characteristics into decision making, and the appearance of the topos of mental illness and of interpersonal rituals among the formalisms of the courtroom. I would argue that the first and second reasons are products of the existing social structure and are potentially changeable in content, and that the third is probably transhistorical and therefore unchangeable.

At the simplest level, unless justice is an automatic response to a particular rule violation, it will always involve judgments concerning the law violator as well as the violation. But it is not necessary that the characteristics of the law violator or mentally ill person given social prominence through social arrangements be social marginality, minority ethnic status, old or young age, or gender. Other social systems could take other characteristics into account, such as degree of need, presence of support systems, adequacy of education, and other factors which could be related more logically to the commission of offenses or to mental disorder.

The prominence of organizational and interorganizational factors is more complex. If organizations exist, then we would expect such phenomena as organizational inertia and defensive politics to shape decision making in addition to factors more closely related to clientele. However, it is possible to minimize the growth of organizational vis-à-vis clientele importance by minimizing the procedural complexity of the system and its dominance by an ever-increasing corps of experts.

The degree of procedural complexity of LPS seems adequate to the twin tasks of facilitating involuntary commitment and preventing gross abuses. Such increases in procedural complexity as requiring judicial review for all 72-hour holds, or even all 14-day holds (see Chap. 2), seems quite excessive. While a legal check is perhaps necessary to psychiatric enthusiasms, psychiatric checks might be seen also as beneficial to legal enthusiasms.

However, my view is that there is too much of both types of expertise in the existing system, and I would argue for a more administrative, lay-dominated involuntary commitment system. In a more humane world of supportive community networks, all participation in decision making would be both lay and voluntary. In the absence of such a world, the inclusion of lay personnel in decision making would both inhibit organizational dominance and challenge the pseudoscientific rhetoric presently involved in the expert-witness system.

In addition, I would recommend short-term assignment of judges and attorneys to courts such as Metropolitan Court in order to minimize assembly-line justice and a sense of "we all work together here." It is not that I would expect much change in outcome if organizational inertia were somewhat disrupted; I do not believe that the decisions made in the court are erroneous, given the structural constraints already discussed. It is just that a little less inertia would, in my view, allow the shock of the condition of the mentally disordered in our society to be experienced a little more often by a few more people, and thus make the *process* of decision making less impersonal and routine.

Finally, I do not regard the use of the commonsense conceptions of mental illness in mental health law decision making to be harmful; in fact, I see the reverse as true. As Santos (1977) notes, the law and the topos exist in a dialectic in legal decision making—a dialectic that cannot be altered by making finer and finer legal distinctions. Indeed, just as I would argue for lay participation in mental health law decision making, I would also argue that the use of commonsense notions of mental illness is just as legitimate as the use of unproven psychiatric or genetic theories, or contextually absurd legal assumptions concerning rationality, choice, and free will. Both the topos and the interaction rituals of the courtroom seem inevitable trappings of courtroom justice and, if justice is indeed done, should not interfere with the sense of justice seen to be done.

Justice cannot be seen to be done where it is not done, and it cannot be done in an unjust society. Decision making in Metropolitan Court is not faulty social policy by virtue of the individuals or the interactions which bring it about. It is yet another manifestation of the basic social fault that structures all of our interaction with one another at this sociohistorical juncture: an alienated society.

Appendix on Methods

Any sociological study combines two elements: the data, and the means by which the data were gathered, analyzed, and presented. Thus, the sociological product is one which should be evaluated in the light of the sociologist's perspective: in the case of nonteam participant observation this perspective is that of the single observer. But what does it mean to say "someone's perspective"?

An observer's perspective is a complex and multilayered phenomenon. First, it is biographical: it is the perspective of one who has lived a certain set of experiences. But biography is sociohistorical as well as experiential. The observer's perspective is in part a product of such conventional sociological categories as social class, gender, and ethnicity, which, in turn, are reflections of the political and economic arrangements of our society.

The observer's perspective and the data combine to produce a work of sociology. The process by which sociology is done is one in which methodology, theory, perspective, and findings are inextricably interwoven, separated only by an ad hoc, conventional arrangement of topics selected for presentation, in specific ways, by the sociologist as data presenter. Choice of research topic, entree, data collection, data analysis, and data presentation must be seen as intimately related to the chooser, enterer, collector, analyst, and presenter, even at the risk of a seemingly faddish and unnecessary confessional style.

Entry into the Court of Last Resort

There are many ways in which biography intersects with setting to produce interest in a specific research topic: the sociologist may have easy access to the setting, may be secretly or overtly a part of it, may

215

enjoy or be titillated by the topic, may dislike the topic and want to be desensitized—the possibilities are many. I chose to study the mental health court out of professional and economic considerations rather than any inherent interests; from this inauspicious beginning came a personal and professional fascination which, in one form or another, seems set to last me for many years.

In 1973, I was a member of NIMH's Crime and Delinquency Review Panel, an experience I not only enjoyed but one which gave me assorted insights into the previously mysterious world of grant writing and grant getting. One of the priority areas for research in the crime and delinquency area was dangerousness, especially dangerousness in the contxt of mental health law ans what in effect was the preventive detention of involuntarily committed mental patients.

As a researcher into homosexuality and other aspects of human sexuality, I had no interest whatsoever in the problem of dangerousness and how to construct scales to measure it, which seemed to be one of the hoped-for outcomes of the priority area; nevertheless, I had for some time realized my professional obligation to get a research grant. I would be coming up for tenure in a couple of years, and, as my department chairman pointed out to me, although my publication record was quite good, my research grant–getting record was not. So I constructed a participant observation proposal to study the way in which the mental health court appeared to define dangerousness; the proposal was funded, and the observations began.

I selected the court as the site of the dangerousness study (something relevant to the priority area could, e.g., have been done in the mental hospital or with the police) primarily because a courtroom is a public arena, and I tend to be rather reluctant about such matters as obtaining bureaucratic permission to enter nonpublic settings. I selected participant observation as my major method because I am a participant observer, and because I have some belief in the greater validity of observational than statistical modes of studying social reality. At that time I would probably have referred to myself as either a phenomenologist or an interactionist in perspective: I viewed the court microsocially, as a place where meanings were constructed, as a good site for an isolated ethnography, and as a source of possible dramaturgical insights about frontstage and backstage performances. I had also occasionally watched Perry Mason.

These intersections of biography, sociological preferences, and priority areas would be expected to structure what was initially noticed in the setting: attributions of dangerousness to the clients, departures from Perry Mason-like dramaturgy, backstage performances frontstage, and generally what was more closed and micro about the setting. To a degree, this was what occurred. Since my perspective was ethnographic, I tended to assume that everyone I saw around the court belonged to the court and not to somewhere else (like a psychiatrist from the mental hospital, or a visitor from the Sacramento legislature). My microperspective in part structured the court, for me, as a microsetting.

But, on the other hand, a setting can be rather obdurate by its very strangeness: parts of it cannot be coped with by previously learned categories and meanings. The obduracy and mystery of a setting can be expected to vary with its proximity to or distance from the previous biography of the researcher: the anthropologist's primitive tribe is at one end of this spectrum, and an attempt to study one's own family or sociology department at the other. While in part not strange (because of Perry Mason familiarity), the court was in larger part most exceedingly strange, because of my unfamiliarity with the categories of persons at work there or how to identify them and, at that early point, my unfamiliarity with law and legal procedures.

Put simply, most of the time in the first few weeks of observation I did not have any idea of what was going on, and what I put down in my field notes had no relation to dangerousness and little relation to what I later came to understand as normal procedure. I basically, and somewhat desperately, wrote down fragments of talk larded with half-heard and nonunderstood numbers (later recognized as Penal Code or Welfare and Institutions Code references), by actors whom I could not sort out one from another. I could manage to recognize the judge in his robe raised on his dais, the mentally ill defendant, the sheriffs and court reporters and clerks, but the district attorneys, public defenders, assorted testifying psychiatrists, and county counsel personnel who figured in the actual hearings took many weeks to identify.

Entry into a court as a visitor to cases is a public event, with no need for special permission. However, I also wanted to talk to various personnel and learn about the various groups in the court. Courts differ from most other types of organizational settings in that control of access to all but the courtroom is vested almost completely in the hands of one person: the judge.

The Judge as Key Informant

Access to the judge was obtained for me, initially, by one of my research assistants whose husband was a judge and who used the informal colleagueship network of high-status legal people to give us and our work legitimacy in the judge's eyes. Throughout the several years of research involvement, this judge of Metropolitan Court was unfailingly cooperative and courteous, ordering other categories of personnel, and other offices, to accept our presence and facilitate our work. He wanted me to sit during cases at a court clerk's desk placed next to his dais and, during cases, routinely handed me documentary information on the hearings. After each habeas corpus writ hearing, he instructed his clerk to Xerox a copy of the MHC's report on the patient, which included a current interview and general background information, where available.

The cooperation of this judge had both advantages and disadvantages for the research process. The advantage in terms of access everywhere and to everything was extremely useful, particularly for the narrow focus of the proposal on dangerousness. For example, I was able to read narrative descriptions of supposedly dangerous behavior as well as to hear the more truncated courtroom versions (see Warren 1979). But for the purpose of general ethnography, there was a distinct disadvantage: I was seen by other court personnel as the judge's own person, literally almost belonging to him. I was, therefore, not able to set up independent relationships with anyone in the court in relation to matters in which that "anyone" was at loggerheads with the judge:

> PUBLIC DEFENDER [coming out of judge's chambers]: Oh boy, is he crazy that judge, oh boy am I mad at him.
> RESEARCHER: What on earth happened in there?
> PD: We just talked about the Milani case—he's crazy, he insists that... well, never mind, I'm sure *he'll* tell you about it.

Entree into all subsettings was, thus, assured in a physical sense: the judge simply dragged me along behind him and told the office I was interested in, from the records office to the lockup behind the courtroom, that I was "Dr. Warren, here from USC to do some research on us, and I want you to help her all you can." However, this very physical assurance of entree at the same time assured that I might be denied entree into those symbolic meanings of the subsetting which revolved around conflict rather than consensus in relation to the judge's assessment of the law and the office's tasks.

To get around this problem of entree into meanings as opposed to settings I sometimes, when alone, approached people who did not know me and introduced myself. Without the authority of the judge, people were free, idiosyncratically, to cooperate with me or brush me off:

> I approached a psychiatrist from [state mental hospital] and asked if I could sit in on his patient interviews; he said no, this was against the law.

> I approached a rather busy looking public defender and asked if I could accompany him to interview a patient at [state hospital] and he said no, he did not have time to make that kind of arrangement.

> I approached a mental hospital counselor and asked if I could ride with her to [state hospital] and spend the day with her. She said

"sure," and we left almost immediately since that was where she was going as I caught her. . . . I spent the day trailing after her, watching as she talked with patients, and talking with her about the court's policies in the interim times.

Framing Strangers

The sponsorship of the judge gave persons aware of such sponsorship the impression that I was a sort of symbolic property of his. The precedent for such a sponsor-property relationship in the court is that between the judge and his or her law clerk or extern (law student functioning as a law clerk). During my research at the court and elsewhere, I have found that people have certain frames that they place on strangers, once they have noticed them and started to pay attention to whom they might be in the setting (a process by no means assured; in most settings there is much ignoring of strangers who do not look too strange to be there at all). One frame is: this person is what he or she looks like; the other is: this person is like me.

The "what he or she looks like" frame sorts the stranger as a member of the category operative in the setting whom he or she most reasonably might be. As a white, middle-class and relatively young woman wandering about the court in tow to a judge, one obvious classification was law student extern, a classification through which many of the court personnel related to me throughout the research process, despite any introductions the judge might give about research, sociology, or USC. As a person with those same characteristics wandering around the court by myself, I was taken by some to be various types associated with external roles: most usually a law student or a nursing student. Since the court is quite small and people usually knew each other, I was taken for an organization member only once or twice; rarely an attorney, never a judge, psychiatrist, or psychiatric technician. Some people classify strangers who might reasonably be like them as like them: one law student framed me as a law student, one psychiatric nurse as a nurse, and one psychologist as a psychologist.

In summary: entry can be public or facilitated by contacts, but it does not guarantee comprehension of what is entered into if the setting is to one degree or another mysterious. Entry is, as the literature on field research amply documents, a progressive and continually renegotiated process rather than a one-time shot. The sponsorship of powerful persons can facilitate physical entree but may damage entree into certain sectors of the meaning world. And, finally, gatekeepers of subsettings, and members of them, define the researcher in a variety of ways, some of them only tenuously related to information which has been given to them, most of them using models already available in the setting for deciding "who persons are."

Data Collection

The process of data collection goes on at two levels: the mechanical procedures involved; and the methodologically relevant analytic themes upon which the sociologist meditates, and sometimes writes about, during the process of the research. The primary data collection method was team and individual field research, supplemented by the collection of background documentary material.[1]

Team Field Research

The early qualitative data collection procedures involved observation and the development of coding sheets and was carried out using a team field research approach. My first research assistant, Elizabeth Thompson, and I took field notes and developed a face sheet for coding cases in the event we later wanted to use quantitative methods. Later, the now Dr. Thompson was replaced by Dr. Phillip Davis and Ms. Pomphylia Baker who continued to take notes and use the face sheets.

As a team, we eventually observed, using the coding sheet to systematize our observations, 130 habeas corpus writ hearings, and assorted other proceedings which we did not code, using them for background information. We also talked with personnel from all segments of the court—district attorneys, public defenders, mental health counselors, and clerks—and psychiatric technicians, psychiatrists, and others who came from beyond the court. Eventually we visited sites outside the court but connected by links of procedure, law, and finance—a research technique with profound ramifications for my future sociological biography, as will be noted below.

Data were collected individually and as a team. Sometimes, two researchers would simultaneously observe the same proceedings; at other times, the researchers operated in different parts of the setting at the same time. Teamwork enabled us to be flexible:

> As John Jones's case was finishing and another interesting one was starting, Jones fled from the court in tears. So Betty followed Jones out and listened to him, while I stayed.

Documentary Data

Throughout the data collection process we collected any documents that were given to us, for possible later use: MHCs' reports of their interviews with writ filers, 72-hour hold certification, the court's file of "crazy letters." Later, during the analysis phase, I used not only these documents but also others—at this point seeking them out, to fill in crucial gaps in my knowledge and understanding. In addition to the usual sociological practice of integrating the work of other sociologists into the final document, I included such items as the

1. Since the literature on such matters as research roles in participant observation is quite large, and my experiences with these matters were quite repetitive with others and my own, I have decided to omit them.

autobiographies of ex-patients (see Chap. 3), the Bay Area data on schizophrenic women (see Warren and Messinger 1980), and the work of Bardach, a political scientist, on the passage and implementation of LPS (see Chap. 2).

Since I wanted to provide a systemic as well as an ethnographic component to the study, I also utilized documentary statistical evidence to supplement my first-hand data sources. It will be noted that the data used come from a number of different years; this is because much of the statistical material used in this book was quite difficult to come by and had to be pulled together gradually over the years.

Symbolic interactionists have for decades—and quite correctly—been critical of the use of official statistics to predict or explain social interaction, since the purposes and methods of such statistics do not relate directly to the interaction. However, if the purpose of such statistics is simply to provide a broad and general background qualitative context, then their use—if some macrolevel understandings are sought—seems preferable to their nonuse.

The background statistical material I used was of two types:

1. California mental health law system trends statistics, such as the utilization of the state hospitals over time, and the proportion of involuntary to voluntary commitments: the use of these statistics was to provide most often a historical or contemporary context for the discussion of mental illness and the law in general (see in particular Chap. 2).

2. Metropolitan County mental health law statistics, such as the number of 72-hour holds, 14-day certifications, and habeas corpus writ hearings: these statistics were used to give some notion of the caseload and task scope of Metropolitan Court (see in particular Chaps. 2 and 7).

In addition to using statistics as background and books about mental illness and the law as source materials, I have drawn upon various bodies of literature for my theoretical context. These bodies of literature include the labeling theory debate, micro- and macrosociological frameworks, organization theory, and so on. Since this work is interdisciplinary, I was only able to draw upon the various theoretical sources sparsely; I suspect, therefore, that highly disciplinary critics will find the various segments wanting in theoretical completeness. In an interdisciplinary endeavor, so far as I can judge, this disciplinary slighting seems a bit inevitable.

Data Analysis: Methods and Substance

The analytic themes which press for notice in a given work are not necessarily orderly, progressive, or neat; in my experience, they start revolving in my consciousness until in some cases I write them down, and in still others I get so far as disseminating and even publishing them. Some of these analytic themes refer to methods, while others refer to substance. The substantive analytic themes I found of importance are represented in this work as a whole. The methodological themes I found interesting included the place of emotions in doing research, sex and gender in field research (see Warren and Rasmussen 1977), and the function of audiences in data presentation. In addition, in this section I present some materials on analyzing mental illness, qualitative data analysis as a process, and the quantitative data analysis methods.

Emotions and Sociological Research

Emotion is a powerful force in human life, motivating individuals to actions, and changing lives, events, and relationships. However, there is rarely any discussion in sociology of the role of emotions either in the context of its topic—social interaction—or in the context of its methods. In the mental health court, strong emotional reactions created new perspectives on the data or damaged harmonious research relationships in the team field research situation.

Hochschild (1975, p. 280) notes, "There is now no sociological theory of feelings and emotion," adding:

> Perhaps the main reason sociologists have neglected feelings is that, as sociologists, we are members of the same society as the actors we study, and we share their feelings and values. Our society defines the cognitive, intellectual, or rational dimensions of experience as superior to being emotional or sentimental. [Significantly, the terms "emotional" and "sentimental" have come to connote excessive or degenerate forms of feeling.] Through the prism of our technological and rationalistic culture, we are led to perceive and feel emotions as some irrelevancy or impediment to getting things done.
>
> Another reason for sociologists' neglect of emotions may be the discipline's attempt to be recognized as a "real science" and the consequent need to focus on the most objective and measurable features of social life. [P. 281]

Douglas (1977) points out that emotion, or "brute being," is the foundation of the interactions and relationships people have with one another. Like Hochschild, Douglas notes that sociologists generally ignore the importance of emotions in the respondents' lives. Johnson (1975, pp. 146–47) makes a parallel observation with regard to emotions in research: sociologists' feelings are edited out of methodological reports as so much extraneous material, as much in field research as in "traditional scientific" reports of method.

This is not to say that every passing emotion is significant either for social relations or for sociological endeavors. However, some emotions result in a modification of the research process, and this makes them significant elements in the methodology. In my experience with courtroom research, significant shapers of the research process included feelings of hostility, self-consciousness, and pity. The first one proved to be damaging to some sources of information, while the latter two created a context within which to interpret the court experience.

In my previous field research experience I found that the access respondents give to their lives generates at least a mildly positive degree of liking, independent of conditions that would arouse either a stronger degree of liking or various degrees of hostility. However, in my research on the court I had strongly negative feelings about a key person in the setting, feelings which had the potential for destroying the research process and/or collection of data. This person was the judge.

My early feelings with regard to the judge were mainly positive; as I look back over my field notes, the negative feelings began to emerge after about a month. Having catalogued all the judge's cooperative virtues, I added in a methodological note:

> On the other hand, Judge F—— became somewhat demanding. He asked me to attend an evening class in law he was giving; at this point I am wondering how he will react to the fact that I am not going to do so. He insists that I take the LSAT exam, and wants me to go to law school (his law school) three nights a week and become a lawyer. He says that I am a born lawyer—he says he can recognize born lawyers in an instant.
>
> Furthermore, like many of the other cooperative administrators I have worked with, he wants to control the dimensions of my study. He has said to me several times, "When are you going to limit your study—it is so broad—I will help you limit it." I just agree noncommittally, which is my general stance on everything.

About three weeks later when I made my next methodological summary notes, my feelings had become extremely negative:

> Relations between the judge and me are becoming ever so slightly strained. Today in court he chatted with Clara (the court reporter) about the movie "Jaws," San Francisco, Carmel, and did not chat with me besides one comment (in the middle of a case), "Carol, would you like to look at these?" [records]; ME—[of course]—"Yes."
>
> At 11:30 he retired to his chambers without inviting me to join him, and closed the door. I went out the main door and peered into his office; he was in conference with one of the public defenders. I wonder about why I am not invited, and conclude this is because of a faux pas I made last week (or it might have been the week before): Judge, K, and I were at lunch during the case—
>
> JUDGE [to me]: What do you think I am going to do with M?
> ME: Let him go.
> JUDGE: Why?
> ME: Because you said so yesterday.
>
> As soon as this came out of my mouth, I realized what a stupid faux pas, born of repressed hostility. Judges are not supposed to

have made up their minds before the case is even started.

JUDGE [huffily]: Oh well, I might change my mind when I have heard all the evidence.

A chill struck the interaction; I cursed myself inwardly.

As this example shows, my hostility had become so great—repressed in the service of research—that it has escaped my control for a moment. In the context of the court, a remark such as the one I made is enough to destroy—let alone damage—relationships with a judge. The actual effect was one of temporary damage rather than destruction because of *his* positive feelings toward *me*.

My hostility toward the judge was tempered by other, conflicting emotions such as gratitude for his amazing cooperativeness and an occasional ambivalent liking. I was able, therefore, to interact with him reasonably well most of the time.

During my first few weeks in court I recorded the following methodological observation:

One minor embarrassment which I am now used to is that during court proceedings the judge will turn to me and say things like, "Carol, why don't you have a look at this and see how we do things here"—then he will pass me a [confidential] mental health report. Once he asked me if I could guess his weight.

But I am more or less used to all this now; the court at first appeared formal to me, but today I realized how informal it now seems when I caught myself powdering my nose in the middle of proceedings.

The realization of self-consciousness, and its diminution, helped me to learn that the court is a formal system only to the observer—to the routine participants it is a work community with institutionalized informalities, joking relationships, and rituals. Thus, what might appear as callous disregard of the frightened and unfortunate defendant is literally a different mode of interpreting the setting.

Part of my developing understanding of the court as a nonformal system also came through my own reactions to the mental patients. When they came into court they appeared to me as nonpersons: I rarely felt sorry for them or concerned about them, even though some of their tales were quite pathetic. This did not really surprise me, since I am not in general given to the type of empathy with society's victims exhibited by Johnson (1975, pp. 156–58). On the other hand, on my second visit to a mental hospital I received a literal shock of pity:

After leaving the hospital I realized that I felt just ghastly. The sight of those zombie-like patients literally had made me feel ill. I wondered how it was possible for people to come or be brought—which is it?—to such a pass.

The patients in this setting—as opposed to the court—were figures of pathos and, as such, real and human. I realized that my own lack of feeling for the patients in court probably duplicated the perspective on them taken by court personnel. The setting structures the definition of the human being as a person or nonperson; in the court, the petitioners or defendants do not act but are acted upon. Thus, they are easily seen as objects rather than as subjects.

Without the experience of self-consciousness and pity, I would not have understood so easily the way in which the setting structures people's reactions to it. Had I remained a stranger to the court, impressed like Garfinkel (1956) with its awesome power to transform identities, I would not have been able to appreciate it as an informal system full of levity and banter. Had I not visited the mental hospital and experienced pity, I would not have realized that my own lack of emotion about patients in court was a feature of court structure, not my own personality.

Emotions, then, helped to create the picture of the court—the sociological story of it—that I am putting together. Hostility, on the other hand, proved a destructive force—damaging but not destroying a highly significant research relationship and nipping another in the bud. The damaging effects of my hostility were mitigated in the first case by the high value placed on me by the judge, and in the second case by the preexistence of a team rather than individual field research methodology.

Sex and Gender in Field Research[2]

The folk adage "first impressions are usually the best" suggests a commonsense understanding of the importance of the initial impact anyone makes when first meeting strangers. The individual characteristics which combine to create this impression include such things as age, sex, appearance, voice, style of dress, and manner.

One would expect that first impressions made in a setting would be of paramount consideration in field research. Field researchers are continually entering new settings in which the member's evaluation of them affects the quality and types of the information they gather at various stages of the research. Yet, first impressions and researcher characteristics have remained relatively unexplored in the research methods literature. I have found, in this and other research, that the researcher's gender, combined with considerations of age and sex-role styles, has considerable influence on data access and collection.

References to sex and gender in field research are mainly anthropological and concerned with females rather than sociological or concerned with males (see, e.g., Golde 1970; Warren and Rasmussen 1977; Wax 1979). Peggy Golde's collection of fieldwork ac-

2. The material in this section is taken from Warren and Rasmussen (1977).

counts by women anthropologists contains a variety of references to the importance of gender. Golde (1970) classifies these references into several themes, which include "protection" and "initial suspicion."

Protection, according to Golde, involves the cross-cultural view of women as more vulnerable and exploitable than men, therefore in greater need of aid and surveillance. In turn, women are less liable to initial suspicion than men, since they are less threatening:

> The fact that I was a young female and therefore viewed as non-threatening probably had as much to do with my eventual acceptance by the [courtroom] staff as any other factor. My presence was particularly noticeable in the male-dominated criminal court. [Rovner-Pieczenik 1976a; p. 468]

> Two women . . . made contacts seem easy and harmless, and consequently people were responsive and unguarded. [Codere 1970, p. 156]

As Codere and Rosalie Wax note, the nonthreatening aspect of femaleness can result in ease of access to information: "Friendly respondents now began to instruct me in some of the less confidential aspects and attitudes of center life . . . Issei men were more inclined to do this. My inferior age and sex status made them less hesitant to give instructions and offer advice" (Wax 1971, p. 77).

Some analysts have suggested that women are more "natural" field researchers since their traditional role in many societies is one of interaction and relationships (Golde 1970). Douglas (1976) advises that women be used as "sociability specialists" in team field research: "In most settings, the ultimate sociability specialists are women. These low-key women do not threaten either the women or the men. They are likely too commonly share intimacies with both sexes. Men are simply more threatening to both sexes, even when they are the most sociable" (p. 214). Nader (1970, pp. 113–14) notes: "[It is said that] women make a success of field work because women are more person-oriented; it is also said that participant-observation is more consonant with the traditional role of women" (pp. 113–14). On the other hand, gender may restrict the field of operation of women observers: to the world of other women (Golde 1970, p. 10; Marshall 1970, p. 181), old men (Marshall 1970, p. 182), the powerless (Fischer 1970, p. 283), and children (Golde 1970, p. 6). The age factor, added to gender, makes for further differences: older women in anthropological research may be "androgenized" and allowed access to the male worlds (Golde 1970, p. 6; Myerhoff 1974).

Protection, Golde comments, also refers to the fact that women are perceived as sexually provocative, especially if they are unmarried (1970, p. 6). This perception of sexual provocation can result either in ease of access to information (from males) or a sense of threat (to women) (Weidman 1970, p. 256). Anthropologists are aware of the importance of sexuality and marital status in field research (Fischer

1970, pp. 275–77; Golde 1970, pp. 80–88), and of the role of physical attractiveness (Golde 1970, p. 6). Sociologists, as Johnson (1975) points out, seem less attuned to the effects of sexuality: "Observers of all kinds have remarked about the strength and pervasiveness of sexual desire for aeons. . . . And yet when reviews the methodological writings of the social sciences, the implicit instruction is to believe one of two things about this: either one must be a eunuch to conduct scientific research, or . . . the desires of scientists involve only (or primarily) cognitive elements" (p. 166). With Johnson, I have found that sexual attraction, like gender, does play a part in the field research process, especially in such settings as courts and other organizations, where males and females interact continuously (Warren and Rasmussen 1977).

As Kanter (1975, pp. 51–55) points out, organizations are most frequently male dominated, with women providing the supporting services in roles such as secretary, nurse, or clerk. The gender of the researcher, therefore, is framed within the context of "appropriate" gender roles in the organization. In research on the police, courts, and other organizations, male and female researchers must negotiate with mostly male power groups, and sometimes with mostly female support groups who hold less apparent but often quite real power over records and day-to-day decisions. Most of the powerful roles in the court—judge, public defenders, district attorneys—are filled by males, and many of the supportive roles—secretarial and clerical— are held by females. I found that access to the private, negotiated aspects of court decision making was facilitated by being a woman: as Rovner-Pieczenik (1976a) also notes, "The fact that I was a young female and therefore viewed as non-threatening probably had as much to do with my eventual acceptance by the staff as any other factor" (p. 468). In such organizations as the court, women—in the shape of secretaries and other paperwork staff—traditionally women—have access to "confidential" data and activities. They are seen as not powerful enough to threaten the powerful males' jobs and positions. The female researchers can easily be categorized with the secretaries, particularly if she is young and attractive and willing to assume a traditional female demeanor. I found that the assumption of the traditional, nonthreatening female demeanor was a useful research strategy: "Time taught me to assume the female status and its typical, ascribed sex-related role when it was useful for securing interviews and information" (Rovner-Pieczenik 1976a, p. 486).

The "traditional female" role provides an interesting example of the interplay of taking roles, being assigned roles, and developing strategies from the intersection of assigning and taking. In the court I found that the males automatically cast me into the role of the traditional female—lower status than male, harmless, helpless, and, as Golde (1970) notes, in need of protection while not very threatening. Like other women automatically cast into the traditional role, I was faced with the choice of continuing to play the role or of fighting it.

I chose to play the role and gather the data rather than try to shape another role and risk alienating the traditional-male power figures in the setting. The amount of access to data gained by this developing strategy was always surprising; I realized that the word "trust" used in field research is sometimes, in the relation of male power holders to women researchers, a gloss for "arrogant." However, the emotional strain of having to continue playing the traditional female role was often rather great.

The traditional female strategy was inadequate to cope with the problem of "hustling," which occurred from time to time. I always left my marital status ambiguous by using the title "Doctor" and by wearing a wedding-finger ring with a stone; thus, respondents were often unclear as to my marital status. Relations with an MHC at the court were slightly strained after the following incident:

JUDGE [to male attorney]: Have you met Carol Warren?
MHC: Is it Mrs. or Miss?
WARREN: Doctor.
MHC: I see.

I would guess that the situation of males hustling females would have a different outcome in organizations such as the court if the female researcher adopted a "professional," "feminist," or other nontraditional female role. In all probability, the occurrence of hustling would be reduced; at the same time, however, access to data might also be reduced among those males who cannot cope with any but traditional-role females. In some organizations there are many such men around; in others, a more liberal ethos predominates—at least upon the surface.

First impressions are indeed important in doing field research, as they are important in every life. Among these first impressions are many which are virtually unchangeable: age, gender, attractiveness, ethnicity. Other impressions are more subject to management and modification: clothing and style, amount and quality of verbalization, traditional or untraditional sex-role presentation. From this mix of first impressions is developed a process of interaction between research and respondent: the respondent forms impressions and develops expectations of the researcher, while the researcher develops strategies from what she or he perceives these impressions and expectations to be, and blunders along from there.

I have focused on only two of the more significant elements of first impression in the court: the sex-gender dimension, and physical attractiveness. Other elements are undoubtedly important, but I cannot directly address them; for example, the influence on the field research setting of a much older researcher, or a married researcher, or of black or other minority researchers. If the method of team field research becomes more extensively used (see Douglas 1976), it would be interesting to study these further dimensions in a more systematic manner.

However, some of the relevances of sex and gender in research are quite clear. The gender of the researcher, as well as the role style adopted and the degree of attractiveness, can be very significant in obtaining access to data, as anthropologists have long realized (Golde 1970). Women are regarded with less initial suspicion than men in most organizational settings where men predominate as power figures and women as support staff, though an exception may be macho subcultures such as the police (see also Douglas 1972). Women researchers—like women police officers—may have more trouble than men in obtaining entree and in gaining acceptance in the police's all-male, macho-oriented work groups.

Data Analysis as Process

Data collection can be described and organized in a meaningful fashion after the fact, and can even be the subject of methodological "recipes," "warnings," and "advice" for future generations of participant observers. But producing sociological analysis is quite a different matter from engaging in interaction with respondents or taking field notes; it is a solitary and cognitive activity rather than an interactive and relational one. As such, it is a product of both the data collected and of the sociologist's powers of cognition.

The process of analysis is sometimes presented in logical terms—the positivist's deductive model or the interactionist's inductive, grounded-theory model. Traditional sociological research relies on preexisting theory, from which are deduced hypotheses, which are in turn tested, and, if one is lucky, the theory is not destroyed by the data but supported, modified, and extended. In the interactionist model, the researcher exposes him or herself to the data, letting the data "speak for themselves" as it were, and, as concepts and categories emerge from the data, these are worked into grounded theory usually of a typological but sometimes of an explanatory or consequential/functional nature.

In my view, the deductive model of the positivist is more valid as a statement of the relationship between sociological theory and data than the inductive model of the interactionist. It appears to me that the participant observer starts with a set of presuppositions—in my case, a mix of interactionist, ethnographic, micro, and dramaturgical notions—which shapes to some degree what is noticed, written down, and written about. In interactionist research, as in the positivist, sociological conceptual categories tend to come from other sociological conceptual categories. Knowledge seems no more deduced from preexisting knowledge, with some entrance of data into the process, than it seems derived from the data speaking to the researchers and producing its own inexorable conceptual categories.

As an example from my own research, Chapter 6 of this book is a product of several things related both to the court and to my own interests: my fascination with the experience of being singled out and spoken to casually in the middle of supposedly formal court proceedings and my embarrassed focus on myself and others who engaged in this informality; my discovery of the concept of "topos," during my writing of the first draft of that chapter; my preexisting microsociological and encounter level sociological interests; and my concern to understand the various levels of interaction and meaning that appeared to be going on during court cases.

At the same time, the book as a whole is an example of how a world I entered as a sociologist—a set of data, if you will—transformed my presuppositions in a reflexive manner. At the beginning of this research, as I indicated, I would have described myself as an interactionist or phenomenologist, with primary interests in ethnographic research in small, unitary, or manageable settings. At the present time, I would describe myself as an interactionist with an interest in levels of analysis which transcend interactionism; with an interest in the socioeconomic, historical, and political context within which interaction takes place. I would describe my interests as interorganizational, with a systems focus; I am at the present time interested in the mental health system, and in particular the ways in which social control and profit intersect through such developments as third-party insurance payments for psychiatric care, and the development of private, welfare-supported board-and-care homes to replace state hospitals.

In the first stages of the data collection process, I remained unproblematically an interactionist by training and persuasion, unconcerned with macrosociology—let alone the debates between the conflict and functionalist versions of the social order. As my research progressed, however, I became more and more aware of the interorganizational network as a crucial factor in decision making, and on the economic and political power interests at the outer boundary of those networks. In the sense that conflict theory is an antifunctionalist statement of the ultimately determinative nature of economics, I became—through the research, and inductively—a macroconflict theorist.

One frame for the research, then, is conflict theory. Another is an interdisciplinary interest; there are legal, medical, economic, historical, psychological, and political frames used to present the data in this book: its interdisciplinary nature is reflected by the multiplicity of methods and reliance on the work of other scholars; its conflict orientation is reflected in the structure of the book, which moves from ideal to real, from outward to inward, and then back outward again.

The sociologist shapes the data through her presuppositions; the data shape the sociologist through theirs. But this process goes through a transformation which involves still other processes which need to be understood: a transformation from life lived to the written word, from the dynamic sociological process to the fixed sociological product. As the sociologist transforms experience into the written word, he or she shapes it according to the audiences presupposed for it.

Analyzing Mental Illness

In studying or writing about mental illness, the scholar constructs a model which is created in part from elements of the observer's personal and disciplinary biography, and in part from observation of those labeled mentally ill. In the Rosenhan and Temerlin experiments (see Chap. 3), it was clear that observers differed in their readiness to attach deviance labels to others and that one dimension of this readiness was professional socialization and setting. Readiness to accept the medical or labeling explanations for the existence of madness is also individually variable.

My views of mental illness and the law, as they now stand—although stand seems not the appropriate word—have been shaped both by my sociohistorical biography and by my exposure to Metropolitan Court and the interorganizational system—to the data. When I entered Metropolitan Court for the first time, I accepted labeling theory as received wisdom; after some initial shocks, I "converted" to the medical model. Currently, I argue for a more mixed and multifaceted model (see Chap. 3).

Interestingly, those trained in the medical model may undergo conversion in the opposite direction—but also become ultimately more multivalent, or perhaps ambivalent. Braginsky, from an initial medical model stance, describes his conversion to a more societal-reaction perspective on mental illness and mental patients:

> As one who has been reared in the psychiatric orientation to deviant behavior, my own reactions can be sequentially described as apprehension, euphoria, and finally realistic appreciation. . . .
>
> My initial reaction of apprehension was rooted in the recognition that the ideas being proposed were a challenge to a "way of professional life" in which I had been trained and to which I was committed even though I recognized the limitations of the psychiatric model after a quarter of a century of involvement in a variety of psychiatric settings. . . .
>
> Once I was able to reduce my uneasiness . . . I found myself caught up in a state of euphoric excitement. . . . I now felt that I was observing the evolvement of a model of deviant behavior that could and would become the "new religion" for those having responsibility for deviant people. . . .
>
> Finally, I settled into a phase of more sober reflection that permitted me to more realistically assess the body of conceptualization reported [in his monograph]. [Braginsky et al. 1969, pp. 1–2]

Quantitative Analysis

Data were collected in narrative form and using a coded facesheet developed after several months of pilot observations. The data in tables 7.5–7.8 were developed from examination and tabulation of the narrative and face sheets on 100 cases. Code sheets on these 100 cases and an additional 30 cases were used as the basis for the outcome study presented at the beginning of Chapter 7. For the outcome study, we developed hypotheses from theories which were both grounded and the observations we had made, and derived from what seemed like plausibly related sociological theories.

The multiple regression data analysis on these 130 cases was performed by Elizabeth Thompson of the University of Southern California, and Joann S. Sandlin of San Diego State University. Although there is some debate in the methods literature concerning the use of multiple regression with categorical variables (for a summary, see Hiday 1981), its use is well represented in the literature on legal decision making. (e.g., Feeley 1979; Ryan 1980–81). Data analysis of the coded observation was by a stepwise multiple regression (SPSS) (subprogram REGRESSION) with a pairwise deletion of missing values.

The most problematic aspect of the method was the operationalization of variables from the four theories. Ideally, more than the two or three variables from each body of theory should have been used; however, constraints on obtaining additional data on other relevant variables prevented this. The variables were derived and/or operationalized as follows:

Conflict. Age and sex were taken from court records, ethnicity from observation. Lower-class, counterculture or middle-class appearance was judged by the "snap reaction" to petitioners' appearance of the two data gatherers (Warren and Thompson) on the grounds that they shared the middle-class biases of court personnel.

Individual decision. Individual judicial variables were derived from three years' intensive study of the court, and an analytic assessment of those factors verbalized by the judge as important to him. Refusal to take medication was evidenced by either the psychiatrist's or judge's statement that he or she believed the patient would not take the medication. The willingness of the family to take the patient back was brought out in direct questioning of family members in court or by phone. Prior hospitalizations were a matter of court record.

Legal-psychiatric. Legal-psychiatric variables represented what we believed to be the most stringent tests of statutory intent. Mental disorder was measured by the presence of the severer psychiatric symptomatology: hallucinations or delusions. Attributions of assaultiveness, suicidal intent or threat, or pending conservatorships were taken as measures of danger to others, danger to self, or grave disability. Legal-psychiatric variables were derived from court testimony and court records.

Data Presentation and the Audience[3]

Considerable attention has been paid in recent years to the issue of the effects of methodology upon data collection. However, there has been relatively little attention directed toward the issue of methodological effects upon data presentation. And yet, as Johnson (1975) notes, data are dependent not only upon the means used to collect them but also upon the means used to analyze and present them: "The factual realities reported as findings of a given investigation do not inhere in the research process as such. The factual realities must be organized and put together by the observer. Only the observer's intention . . . provides the apparently rational account of social order" (1975, p. 187). I contend that a major aspect of the development of sociological or anthropological "rational accounts" is the reactions of audiences. These reactions may be imagined and projected by the researcher, or take the form of actual responses— sometimes vociferous—to his or her work. The relationship between imagined and actual responses may be reflexive over time.

Respondent Audiences and the Ethics Debate

There has been some implicit recognition of the problem of audiences in connection with the current debate on ethics in sociology. As Becker (1964) notes, "Publication of field research findings often poses ethical problems. The social scientist learns things about the people he studies that may harm them, if made public, either in fact or in their belief" (p. 267). This potential harm is of three kinds:

1. Harm to individuals in interpersonal relations with others in a process of recognition of selves and others in reports.

2. Harm to individuals in the context of social control agents and the "general public" if such audiences "recognize" those individuals and stigmatize them in some way, or the members' conception that this might be so.

3. Harm to groups or communities in the sense of making their existence known or revealing collective secrets.

In the context of harm to respondents, the researcher conceptualized a double audience for her or his product. In the first instance, the researcher imagines that both the respondents and "the general public" will read the report and that the respondents will fear or perhaps even receive stigmatizing reactions from that public or specific portions of it. There are reports in the literature of fear of harm and of the actual occurrence of harm. Wax (1971), for example, states that many of her respondents feared that she would report their anti-U.S. sentiments or activities to the government during World War II internship. Wax also gives one of the few accounts in the literature of how she deliberately (and successfully) set about harming a respondent; in this case, someone who had been responsible for the death of a friend of hers.

3. The material in this section is taken from Warren (1980).

When I first published an article concerned with the mental health court, I projected a specific audience of colleagues of the respondents as the double audience. My research assistant on the NIMH grant was the wife of a judge who is a colleague of the judge whose court we were researching. It was conceivable to me that this judge (i.e., the judge of the mental health court) could be discredited in the eyes of his colleague (who read the research products) and, possibly, by a process of contamination, in the eyes of other judicial colleagues (depending upon their evaluation of what appeared to me as discrediting findings).

There are two ways in which I could deal logically with this potential harm to one of my respondents. I could say that the judge is outside my "moral community," therefore he is a legitimate target for harming (such a case could be made from some ideological perspectives). On the other hand, I could point to the fact that legal case argumentation proceeds by destruction and reconstruction of specific judges' arguments and that, furthermore, in legal writings the judges in question are named and are not anonymous. However, judicial arguments in the main confine themselves to public statements of judicial argument, whereas a sociological presentation perforce focuses heavily on private pronouncements as well, publication of which transcends the rules of judicial warfare.

A second problem of audience response in connection with this judge is related to the judge's own response and not to the response of the general public. I worried about his reactions to reports he might read of my "real feelings" toward him and my "real motives" for doing research, as outlined in documents such as this, as well as my "real evaluation" of court proceedings.

In the last matter, even material which appears "neutral" to the reporter will generally appear negative or discrediting to those unfortunate persons who constitute that data. Often, respondent-audience's complaints take the line that the portrayal of them by the sociologist is accurate but not the idealized one they prefer to present to outsiders. One of William Foote Whyte's Cornerville respondents notes: "The trouble is, Bill, you caught the people with their hair down. It's a true picture, yes; but people feel it's a little personal" (1964, p. 60). Gallagher (1964) comments on Plainville's response to a book about the community by West, a previous anthropological resident: "The town . . . developed a line on West that was consistent with their attitude of betrayal. This enabled many of the people to admit that West's analysis was essentially correct and at the same time strongly criticize him and his book because the latter 'didn't go far enough,' that is, it did not include their own self-image" (p. 294).

If the data do not appear neutral even to the researcher but are highly critical of the system, then the problem is obviously compounded.

The publication of negative emotions and mystified motives connected with the judge or other identifiable persons in a setting is discrediting not only to the respondent but also to the researcher. In outlining tactics of repressing emotion and mystification used on the judge in the research process, I discredit myself. In specifying negative reactions to the judge and others, I discredit him and his colleagues, at least to the extent that I present these negative reactions as grounded in his actions and being rather than my own.

In writing up research reports on this court I found myself weighing the probabilities of the report being read by the judge. I assessed the likelihood of his reading any future book as extremely high, since he is a voracious and informed reader. The likelihood of his reading any law-related publication is even higher, while the likelihood of his reading well-known sociological journals is lower but still possible. The likelihood, finally, of his reading lesser-known sociological journals seems very low. Therefore, the amount and depth of detail about the research I would consider for each publication is variable as well as the particular aspect of the research I would discuss. I have even considered preparing a separate and special "front" report for his consumption. Other researchers have noted the strategy of making up "front" reports to satisfy respondent audiences.

Why, however, had I to be concerned with these respondent reactions? Why not tell myself to tell the judge to go to hell? The answer is that my feelings for him were basically ambivalent, compounded by a perhaps inevitable feeling of gratitude for his extremely cooperative facilitation of the research and a feeling of guilt for deceiving him. I did not want to hurt his feelings, because I am not in fact malevolent toward him, and I know that I would feel personally very sorry and chagrined if he found me out and if he got his own feelings hurt (which is the outcome I imagine if he reads some of my reports).

A second answer is that the court is a source of data for myself and others in the future, and I do not want to "foul the pitch." To a small degree, the pitch has already been fouled. An article I wrote about the court for the *Law and Society Review* (1977) was quoted by California Supreme Court Judge Rose Bird in support of her opinion that the standard of proof for insanity cases should be beyond a reasonable doubt, not preponderance of the evidence. Eventually, that standard of proof became the one required for jury trials in the mental health court. In visits to the court since, I have been teased and mildly reviled as a "looky loo," "that person who writes false things about the court," and my students have been told, "don't take any notice of her."

Funder Audiences

The subjects of research are not the only audiences that a researcher takes into account when writing reports of field studies. An additional and important audience of the research report can be the source of funding for the research work itself. Senior researchers may be answerable to funder audiences if their research is on a contract or grant (Baker 1975). It is already fairly well documented that re-searchers doctor their research proposals in order to satisfy funder requirements. Wax (1971) notes:

> We knew all too well that no honest person could contract to do any specific kind of research in an alien community. "To prepare a detailed and itemized budget requires that one envisage a pre-cise and predictable future, whereas the essence of good and honest ethnographic research is flexibility." In order then to pre-pare an itemized budget Murray was forced to project a fantasy of what would be practicable and useful to be doing with an idealized staff, and then to estimate what this would cost, month by month, when, in fact, he knew all the time that in all prob-ability most of this elaborate structure was a delusion. The situa-tion wouldn't be what he expected it to be; the staff would have talents different from those he had anticipated; the subjects would have strong ideas of their own; and the research would inevitably be led to channels which neither he nor anyone else could foresee. Nevertheless, Murray went manfully to work and complied with every detail. [P. 285]

Similarly, I added a considerable quantitative element to my original proposal for field research in the mental health court in order to encourage funding.

The issue of funder-audience response may be complicated if the funder audience is liked and/or respected as career relevant to the research. As I indicated, my mental health court research was funded by a government agency. As an audience, this agency requires only annual reports of progress rather than a specific research document used by policymakers or practitioners as in the case of contracts (Baker 1975). I have considerable respect and feelings of friendship for the competent staff who funded the grant, and I would like to put them on my mailing list; however, they will probably receive only a few papers.

My unease with reference to the funding agents as an audience to the work is not from feelings that they are not getting their money's worth, which they are, but from certain deviatons I have made from the human subjects protection procedures I devised. I have the data in a locked file, as promised—but the file is sometimes unlocked. I had also proposed to take field notes without recording patients' names, a practice which I violated. First, it was impossible given the speed of recording necessary to keep up with court cases, and, sec-ond, it would have proved extremely damaging to a second source of data which we gained access to soon after the project started. We found that the judge was willing to provide us with photocopies of patients' mental health reports, which we could then match with the field note records of persons who had been in court. Names were essential to this process.

Effects of Audiences

The effects of audiences upon data presentation are many, and, with all kinds of other effects, vary over time and in the reflexivity of the imagining of audience response and their actual response or nonresponse. As Johnson (1975) notes, research is a multilayered process only part of which is the cumulation of data:

> Writing the research reports not only reflects the author's thinking at a given point in time but also serves as a stimulus for further thought and reflection. This writing process will, at the least, possibly result in several different "stories," as Fred Davis called them. When guided by the intention to build progressively more theoretical analyses which still retain the actor's perspective, however, hopefully the end result of this writing-reflection process will be a view (or views) which progressively illuminate(s) and encompass(es) the previous one. [P. 200]

In Johnson's comments, however, the salient influences upon the data presentation are the author and the actor—not the chorus of different interest groups that may enter into the researcher's "progressive illumination." When they do in fact enter, the effects are relatively unanalyzed in the literature. For me they include a withdrawal from progressive illumination of certain topics, omission, falsification, and a more general process of directionality.

One of the factors which influenced me to move from further research in sexuality or in homosexuality to the mental health area was the various forms of stigmatization exercised by colleagues and other acquaintances. I found that I had developed a clannishness about my research in the gay world which I do not have with respect to courtroom research: I select carefully the persons to whom I mention the former and tell anyone who is interested about the latter.

As Douglas (1976), Johnson (1975), and others have noted, researchers often omit from data presentation those items (generally methodological and personal ones) which might discredit them with some audience, in particular with the colleague audience. Lofland calls this methodological omission "reporting only the second worst thing that happens," although in my estimation it is likely to be the tenth or twelfth. Only Johnson (1975) and a few others (Vidich and Bensman 1964) have seen fit to publish methodological details at a somewhat higher level of discreditability.

As with omission, falsification is most likely to be of methodological details which might discredit the researcher, although it is possible to falsify data because of ideological convictions about respondents, or in order to provide data which will satisfy funding agencies. Douglas (1972), for example, reports a case in which data on prison recidivism were falsified in order to satisfy the sponsoring agency's illusions that their program worked. Because of the different expectations in field research, the problems of *this* type of falsification *may* be less salient than in statistical and policy-oriented research.

Much has been written on how values shape the choice of a research problem and the analysis and reporting of it—values which the researcher has learned in some social class, ethnic, or other biographical context. However, it is clear from a review of the (scanty) material on audiences that they are also significant shapers of the presentation of sociological research. Audiences help to shape the direction of sociological research both in the context of particular research endeavors and, over time, in the context of the researcher's career. The audience shaping of data presentation, like the effects of data collection upon findings, are essential and little-understood aspects of the cumulation of knowledge we call science.

Social Science and Social Policy

Mental health law is one in which there seems to be an unusual degree of attention paid by lawyers to the writings and findings of social science. Such compilations of law/mental health material as Brooks (1974) include extracts from, and references to, social science scholars, for example, Goffman, Scheff, and Szasz, in the mental health field. Rose Bird's citing of my article as empirical support for her legal position is not at all unusual in the mental health law field. Bardach (1972) describes, during the initial stages of planning for the passage of LPS, how the Sacramento Subcommittee on Mental Health Services members Jerome Waldie and Arthur Bolton

> needed, first, a concrete issue around which to coalesce a large number of interests and, second, a feasible reform program . . . [a] staff assistant arranged for Bolton to read a research report prepared by a student of Erving Goffman's. It describes the author's observation of "a county lunacy commission." . . . Bolton was much impressed by the findings: the average length of the commitment hearing was 4.1 minutes [etc.]. . . . During the next few months Bolton and Waldie obtained two more pieces of graduate student research. . . . Bolton and Waldie concluded that they had found their issue. [Pp. 101–2]

The usual social scientists' lament that policymakers take no notice of their research is the obverse of the truth in the arena of mental health law: empirical studies are seized on by lawyers and other practitioners and appear in law books and court decisions. The reasons for this somewhat unusual situation cannot be elaborated in this appendix; however, its consequences can be intimated briefly.

The most important consequence is that the social scientist may be blamed for his or her findings, or for policy decisions flowing from them, in ways that make no sense given the sociologist's own interpretation of the meaning of his or her work. In the Rose Bird example, I had never conceived my article to have anything to do with standards of proof in law. However, as indicated, the result of her opinion was that the district attorneys in the court now had to use a higher standard of proof than before to make their case; and they grumbled at me as one of those responsible for their extra workload.

In addition, the response of the public defenders to the same article was to interpret it as a critique of the way they do their job and as an attack on them. Although a critique of the PD's performance could easily be read into the article (unlike the standard-of-proof reference), that was certainly not the main point of the article as I wrote it, and it still does not appear to me to be the article's main message. But the PDs of the court, like the DAs—with one exception, a man who teases me about the research but is most welcoming and cooperative—complain to me and assail my work as inadequate and in error.

I do not think that the article, or subsequent pieces I have written in the mental health area, are inadequate or in error; although as I noted in the beginning of this appendix, they are products both of the data and of my biography, therefore cannot be conceived as objective facts. But, on the other hand, the heavy use of social science research to buttress ideological justifications of specific policy positions does make the social scientist particularly responsible for a clear presentation of findings which are as carefully handled as possible. Beyond this, there is nothing that seemingly can be done about the process by which such research findings are used in ways that have only very tenuous, if any, connections with the intent of the researcher in doing the research or in presenting the findings. In these ways, audience responses are only sometimes anticipated correctly; there are audiences to the research, and interpretations and uses made of it, that cannot be guessed at by the data presenter.

Statutory and Case Law References

Statutes

Cal. Welf. and Inst. Code §§5150, 5250 (West 1972 and Supp. 1978).
Cal. Welf. and Inst. Code §5358 (Deerings Supp. 1977).
Developmentally Disabled Assistance and Bill of Rights Act, 42
    U.S.C. §§6001–81 (1976) and Supp. (1979).
Iowa Code S229.1 (2) (a) (b) (West 1979).
Massachusetts General Laws annotated Ch. 123 §§5 et seq. (1970).
North Carolina General Statutes, Ch. 122 (1973).

Cases

Addington v. *Texas,* 441 U.S. 418 (1979).
A.E. and R.R. v. *Mitchell,* No. C-78-466 (D. Utah, June 16, 1980); 5
    Mental Disability Law Rptr. 154 (1981).
Colyar v. *Third Judicial District Court,* 469 F. Supp. 424 (D. Utah,
    1979).
Commonwealth v. *Mutina,* 366 Mass. 810, 323 N.E. 2d 294 (1975).
Estate of Roulet, 23 C.3d 219, 152 Cal. Rptr. 425, 590 P. 2d 1 (1979).
Flakes v. *Percy,* 511 F. Supp. 1325 (W.D. Wis., 1981).
Halderman v. *Pennhurst State School & Hospital,* 446 F. Supp. 1295
    (E.D. Pa., 1977).
Hirabayashi v. *United States,* 320 U.S. 81 (1943).
In re *Hatley,* 291 N.C. 693, 231 S.E. 633 (1977).
In re *Williams,* 157 F. Supp. 871 (D.C., 1958).
In re *Winship,* 397 U.S. 358 (1970).
Korematsu v. *United States,* 323 U.S. 214 (1944).
Lessard v. *Schmidt,* 349 F. Supp. 1078 (E.D. Wis., 1972).
Lynch v. *Baxley,* 368 F. Supp. 378 (M.D. Alab., 1974).
New York State Assn. for Retarded Children, Inc. v. *Rockefeller,* 357 F.
    Supp. 752 (1973).

O'Connor v. *Donaldson*, 422 U.S. 563 (1975).

Parham v. *J.R.*, 442 U.S. 584 (1979).

Patterson v. *New York*, 432 U.S. 198 (1977).

Rennie v. *Klein*, 462 F. Supp. 1131 (D.C.NJ., 1978); 653 F. 2d 836 (3d Cir. 1981).

Rogers v. *Okin*, 478 F. Supp. 1342 (D.C. Mass., 1979); 634 F. 2d 650 (1st Cir. 1980).

Stamus v. *Leonhardt*, 414 F. Supp. 439 (S.D. Iowa, 1976).

Supt. of Worcester State Hospital v. *Hagberg*, 372 N.E. 2d 242 (Mass.) 1978.

Wyatt v. *Stickney*, 344 F. Supp. 373 (M.D. Ala., 1972).

References

Abramson, Marc F. "The Criminalization of Mentally Disordered Behavior." In *Community Health and the Criminal Justice System*, edited by John Monahan, pp. 305–17. New York: Pergamon, 1976.

Affleck, Glenn; Peszke, Michael; and Wintrob, Ronald. "Psychiatrists' Familiarity with Legal Statutes Governing Emergency Involuntary Hospitalization." *American Journal of Psychiatry* 135 (1978): 205–9.

Alexander, Franz, and Selesnick, Sheldon. *The History of Psychiatry*. New York: Harper & Row, 1966.

Alexander, George, and Lewin, Travis. *The Aged and the Need for Surrogate Management*. Syracuse, N.Y.: Syracuse University, 1972.

Allen, Richard C., et al. *Mental Impairment and Legal Incompetency*. Englewood Cliffs, N.J.: Prentice-Hall, 1966.

Altman, Lawrence K. "Release of Mentally Ill Spurring Doubt." *New York Times* (November 20, 1979), pp. B1 ff.

American Psychiatric Association (APA). *Diagnostic and Statistical Manual of Mental Disorders*. 3d ed. Washington, D.C.: American Psychiatric Association, 1980.

Andalman, Elliott, and Chambers, David L. "Effective Counsel for Persons Facing Civil Commitment: A Survey, a Polemic, and a Proposal." *Mississippi Law Journal* 49 (1974): 43–91.

Appelbaum, P.S., and Gutheil, T. G. "The Boston State Hospital Case: Involuntary Mind Control: The Constitution and the 'Right to Rot.'" *American Journal of Psychiatry* 137 (1980): 720–23.

Arnhoff, F. N. "Social consequences of Policy toward Mental Illness." *Science* 187 (1975): 1277–81.

Bachrach, L. L. "NIMH Deinstitutionalization: An Analytical Review and Sociological Perspective." *Department of Health, Education and Welfare Publication* #ADM 76-351, 1976.

Baker, K. "A New Grantsmanship." *American Sociologist* 10 (1975): 206–19.

Bardach, Eugene. *The Skill Factor in Politics: Repealing the Mental Commitment Laws in California.* Berkeley: University of California Press, 1972.

———. *The Implementation Game: What Happens after a Bill Becomes Law.* Cambridge, Mass.: MIT Press, 1977.

Bayer, Ronald. *Homosexuality and American Psychiatry: The Politics of Diagnosis.* New York: Basic, 1981.

Becker, A., and Schulberg, H. C. "Phasing Out State Hospitals: A Psychiatric Dilemma." *New England Journal of Medicine* 294 (1976): 255–61.

Becker, Howard S. *Outsiders: Studies in the Sociology of Deviance.* New York: Free Press, 1963.

———. "Problems in the Publication of Field Studies." In *Reflections on Community Studies,* edited by A. J. Vidich et al., pp. 266–84. New York: Wiley, 1964.

Benedict, Ruth. *Patterns of Culture.* New York: Mentor, 1959.

Blumberg, Abraham S. *Criminal Justice.* Chicago: Quadrangle, 1967.

Borus, J. F. "Deinstitutionalization of the Chronically Mentally Ill." *New England Journal of Medicine* 305, no. 6 (1981): 339–42.

Bower, B. "Understaffing Severe in State Hospitals Nationwide." *Psychiatric News* (September 18, 1981), p. 1 at col. 1.

Braginsky, Benjamin M.; Braginsky, Dorothea D.; and Ring, Kenneth. *Methods of Madness: The Mental Hospital as a Last Resort.* New York: Holt, Rinehart & Winston, 1969.

Brakel, Samuel. "Legal Aid in Mental Hospitals." *American Bar Foundation Research Journal* (1981), pp. 23–93.

Brakel, Samuel, and Rock, Ronald. *The Mentally Disabled and the Law.* Rev. ed. Chicago: University of Chicago Press, 1971.

Braun, P., et al. "Overview: Deinstitutionalization of Psychiatric Patients: A Critical Review of Outcome Studies." *American Journal of Psychiatry* 138, no. 6 (1981): 736–49.

Brill, H., and Malzberg, B. "Criminal Acts of Ex-Mental Hospital Patients." *American Psychiatric Association, Mental Hospital Service, Supplementary Mailing no. 153* (1962).

Brooks, Alexander D., ed. *Law, Psychiatry and the Mental Health System.* Boston: Little, Brown & Co., 1974.

Brown, L. B., and Bremer, J. M. "Inadequate Means to a Noble End: The Right to Treatment Paradox." *Journal of Psychiatry and Law* 6, no. 1 (1978): 45–69.

Brown, Richard H. "Bureaucracy as Praxis: Toward a Political Phenomenology of Formal Organizations." *Administrative Science Quarterly* 23 (September 1978): 365–87.

Buttiglieri, M. W., et al. "Driver Accidents and the Neuropsychiatric Patient." *Journal of Consulting and Clinical Psychology* 33, no. 3 (1969): 381.

Chambers, D. L. "Community-based Treatment and the Constitution: The Principle of the Least Restrictive Alternative." In *Alternatives to Mental Hospital Treatment,* edited by M. A. Test and L. I. Stein, pp. 23–42. New York: Plenum, 1978.

Chodoff, P. "The Case for Involuntary Hospitalization of the Mentally Ill." *American Journal of Psychiatry* 133, no. 5 (1976): 496–501.

Cockerham, William C. *Sociology of Mental Disorder.* Englewood Cliffs, N.J.: Prentice-Hall, 1981.

Cocozza, J., and Steadman, H. "The Failure of Psychiatric Predictions of Dangerousness: Clear and Convincing Evidence." *Rutgers Law Review* 29 (1976): 1084–1101.

Codere, Helen. "Field Work in Rwanda, 1959–1960." In *Women in the Field,* edited by Peggy Golde, pp. 143–60. Chicago: Aldine, 1970.

Cohen, Fred. "The Function of the Attorney and the Commitment of the Mentally Ill." *Texas Law Review* 44 (1966): 424–60.

Committee on Research, Group for the Advancement of Psychiatry. *Pharmocotherapy and Psychotherapy: Paradoxes, Problems and Progress.* New York: Mental Health Materials Center, 1979.

Conrad, Peter, and Schneider, Joseph W. *Deviance and Medicalization: From Badness to Sickness.* St. Louis: Mosby, 1980.

Dershowitz, A. M. "Psychiatry in the Legal Process: A Knife That Cuts Both Ways," *Trial* 4 (1968): 29–33.

———. "Preventive Confinement: A Suggested Framework for Constitutional Analysis." *Texas Law Review* 51 (1973): 1277.

———. "The Origins of Preventive Confinement in Anglo-American Law—Part II: The American Experience." *University of Cincinnati Law Review* 43 (1974): 781–846.

Deutsch, Albert. *The Mentally Ill in America.* 2d ed. New York: Columbia University Press, 1949.

———. *The Shame of the States.* New York: Arno, 1971.

Developments in the Law–Civil Commitment of the Mentally Ill. *Harvard Law Review* 87 (1974): 1190–1406.

Dewey, John. *Liberalism and Social Action.* New York: Capricorn, 1963.

Diamond, B. L. "The Psychiatric Prediction of Dangerousness." *University of Pennsylvania Law Review* 123 (1974): 439–52.

Dickey, B., et al. "A Follow-up of Deinstitutionalized Chronic Patients Four Years after Discharge." *Hospital and Community Psychiatry* 32, no. 5 (1981): 326–30.

Dickey, W. "Incompetency and the Nondangerous Mentally Ill Client." *Criminal Law Bulletin* 16, no. 1 (1980): 22–40.

Donaldson, Kenneth. *Insanity Inside Out.* New York: Crown, 1976.

Douglas, Dorothy J. "Managing Fronts in Observing Deviance." In *Observing Deviance,* edited by Jack D. Douglas, pp. 93–115. New York: Random House, 1972.

Douglas, Jack D. *Investigative Social Research: Individual and Team Field Research.* Beverly Hills, Calif.: Sage, 1976.

————, ed. *Existential Sociology.* Cambridge: Cambridge University Press, 1977.

Eisenstein, James, and Jacob, Herbert. *Felony Justice: An Organizational Analysis of Criminal Courts.* Boston: Little, Brown & Co., 1977.

Emerson, Robert, et al. "Enterprise and Economics in Board and Care Homes for the Mentally Ill." *American Behavioral Scientist* 25 (July 1981): 771–85.

Ennis, Bruce J. *Prisoners of Psychiatry.* New York: Harcourt, Brace & World, 1972.

Ennis, Bruce J., and Litwack, Thomas R. "Psychiatry and the Presumptions of Expertise." *California Law Review* 62 (May 1974): 693–752.

Essex, M.; Estroff, S.; McLanahan, S.; Robbins, J.; Dresser, R.; and Diamond, R. "On Weinstein's Patient Attitudes toward Mental Hospitalization: A Review of Quantitative Research (Comment on Weinstein, *Journal of Health and Social Behavior,* 1979)." *Journal of Health and Social Behavior* 21 (1980): 393–96.

Estes, Carroll L., and Harrington, Charlene. "Fiscal Crisis, Deinstitutionalization, and the Elderly." *American Behavioral Scientist* 25 (July 1981): 811–26.

Feeley, Malcolm H. *The Process Is the Punishment: Handling Cases in a Lower Criminal Court.* New York: Russell Sage Foundation, 1979.

Feighner, T., et al. "Diagnostic Criteria for use in Psychiatric Research." *Archives of General Psychiatry* 26 (1972): 55–63.

Fein, S., and Miller, K. S. "Legal Process and Adjudication in Mental Incompetency Proceedings." *Social Problems* 20 (Summer 1972): 57–64.

Fichter, J. H., and Kolb, W. L. "Ethical Limitations on Sociological Reporting." *American Sociological Review* 41 (1953): 96–97.

Fingarette, H. "Disabilities of Mind and Criminal Responsibility: A Unitary Doctrine." *Columbia Law Review* 76 (1976): 236–66.

Fingarette, H., and Hasse, A. F. *Mental Disabilities and Criminal Responsibility.* Berkeley: Univ. of California Press, 1979.

Fischer, Ann. "Field Work in Five Cultures." In *Women in the Field,* edited by Peggy Golde, pp. 267–89. Chicago: Aldine, 1970.

Foucault, Michel. *Madness and Civilization: A History of Insanity in the Age of Reason.* New York: Vintage, 1965.

Fox, Richard W. *So Far Disordered in Mind: Insanity in California, 1870–1930.* Berkeley: University of California Press, 1978.

Frank, J. D. *Persuasion and Healing: A Comparative Study of Psychotherapy.* New York: Schocken, 1973.

Frederick, Calvin J. "An Overview of Dangerousness: Its Complexities and Consequences." In *Dangerous Behavior: A Problem in Law and Mental Health,* edited by Calvin J. Frederick. Washington, D.C.: Government Printing Office, 1978.

Gallagher, A., Jr. "Plainville: The Twice-studied Town." In *Reflections on Community Studies,* edited by A. J. Vidich et al., pp. 285–304. New York: Wiley, 1964.

Gallagher, Bernard J., III. *The Sociology of Mental Illness*. Englewood Cliffs, N.J.: Prentice-Hall, 1980.

Garfinkel, Harold. "Conditions of Successful Degradation Ceremonies." *American Journal of Sociology* 61 (March 1956): 420–24.

Genego, W. J., et al. "Parole Release Decision-making and the Sentencing Process." *Yale Law Journal* 84 (1975): 810–902.

Gibson, James L. "Race as a Determinant of Criminal Sentences: A Methodological Critique and a Case Study." *Law and Society Review* 12 (Spring 1978): 455–78.

Goffman, Erving. *Asylums*. Garden City, N.J.: Doubleday, 1961.

Golde, Peggy. "Introduction." In *Women in the Field*, edited by Peggy Golde, pp. 1–15. Chicago: Aldine, 1970.

Goldstein, A. *The Insanity Defense*. New Haven: Yale University Press, 1967.

Goode, Steven J. "The Role of Counsel in the Civil Commitment Process: A Theoretical Framework." *Yale Law Review* 84 (June 1975): 1538–63.

Gove, Walter R. "The Relationship between Sex Roles, Marital Status, and Mental Illness." *Social Forces* 51(September 1972): 34–44.

———. "Labelling and Mental Illness: A Critique." In *The Labelling of Deviance: Evaluating a Perspective*, edited by Walter R. Gove, pp. 35–81. New York: Wiley, 1975.

Gove, Walter R., and Fain, T. "A Comparison of Voluntary and Committed Psychiatric Patients." *Archives of General Psychiatry* 34 (1977): 669–76.

Greeley, James R. "Alternative Views of the Psychiatrist's Role." *Social Problems* 20 (1972): 15–26.

Groethe, R. "Overt Dangerous Behavior as a Constitutional Requirement for Involuntary Civil Commitment of the Mentally Ill." *University of Chicago Law Review* 44 (1977): 562–93.

Gusfield, Joseph R. "Categories of Ownership and Responsibility in Social Issues: Alcohol Abuse and Automobile Use." *Journal of Drug Issues* 5, no. 4 (Fall 1975): 285–303.

Guttridge, Patricia. *Psychiatric and Non-Psychiatric Factors in the Hospitalization of Adolescents*. Ph.D. dissertation, University of Sourthern California, 1981.

Guttridge, Patricia, and Warren, Carol A. B. "Mental Hospitalization as a Resource Alternative as a Response to AB3121." In "Implications of California's Juvenile Justice Reform Law," by Katherine Teilmann and Malcolm W. Klein, chap. 5 (a final report submitted to the National Institute for Juvenile Justice and Delinquency Prevention, 1981).

Hagan, John. Extra-Legal Attributes and Criminal Sentencing: An Assessment of a Sociological Viewpoint." *Law and Society Review* 8, no. 3 (Spring 1974): 357–83.

Haney, C. Allen, and Michiellute, Robert. "Selective Factors Operating in the Adjudication of Incompetency." *Journal of*

Health and Social Behavior 9 (September 1968): 233–42.

Hardisty, J. L. "Mental Illness: A Legal Fiction." *Washington Law Review* 48, no. 4 (1973): 735–62.

Hart, Mark Allan. "Civil Commitment of the Mentally Ill in California: The Lanterman-Petris-Short Act." *Loyola of Los Angeles Law Review* 7 (1974): 93–136.

Helzer, John E., et al. "Reliability of Psychiatric Diagnosis: II. The Test/Retest Reliability of Diagnostic Classification." *Archives of General Psychiatry* 34 (1977): 136–41.

Herman, Robin. "Policy to Release Mental Patients Leaves Many to Face Harsh Fate." *New York Times* (November 18, 1979), p. 1. (a)
———. "Some Freed Mental Patients Make It, Some Do Not." *New York Times* (November 19, 1979), p. B1. (b)

Heumann, Milton. *Plea Bargaining: The Experiences of Prosecutors, Judges and Defense Attorneys*. Chicago: University of Chicago Press, 1977.

Hiday, V. A. "Reformed Commitment Procedures: An Empirical Study in the Courtroom." *Law and Society Review* 11 (Spring 1977): 651–66.
———. "Determinants of Judicial Decisions in Civil Commitment: A Multivariate Analysis." Unpublished paper, Department of Psychiatry, University of North Carolina Medical School, 1981.

Hiday, V. A., and Markell, S. J. "Components of Dangerousness: Legal Standards in Civil Commitment." *International Journal of Law and Psychiatry*, no. 3 (1980), pp. 405–19.

Hochschild, Arlie Russell. "The Sociology of Feeling and Emotions: Selected Possibilities." In *Another Voice: Feminist Perspectives on Social Life and Social Science*, edited by Marcia Millman and Rosabeth Moss Kanter, pp. 280–307. New York: Anchor, 1975.

Howard, I. "The Ex-Mental Patient as an Employee: An On-the-Job Evaluation." *American Journal of Orthopsychiatry* 45 (1975): 479.

Jeste, D. V., and Wyatt, R. J. "Changing Epidemiology of Tardive Dyskinesia: An Overview." *American Journal of Psychiatry* 138 (1981): 297–309.

Johnson, John M. *Doing Field Research*. New York: Free Press, 1975.

Kahle, L., and Sales, B. D. "Due Process of Law and the Attitudes of Professionals toward Involuntary Civil Commitment." In *New Directions in Psycholegal Research*, edited by Paul D. Lipsitt and Bruce D. Sales, pp. 265–92. New York: Van Nostrand Reinhold.

Kanter, Rosabeth Moss. "Women and the Structure of Organizations: Explorations in Theory and Behavior." In *Another Voice: Feminist Perspectives on Social Life and Social Science*, edited by Marcia Millman and Rosabeth Moss Kanter, pp. 34–74. New York: Anchor, 1975.

Kaplan, Harold I.; Freedman, Alfred M.; and Benjamin J. Sadock. *Comprehensive Textbook of Psychiatry, III*. 3d ed. Baltimore: Williams & Wilkins, 1980.

Katz, J. "The Right to Treatment: An Enchanting Legal Fiction?"

University of Chicago Law Review 36 (1969): 755–83.

Kaufman, E. "The Right to Treatment Suit as an Agent of Change." *American Journal of Psychiatry* 136, no. 11 (1979): 1428–32.

Kirk, Stuart, and Thierren, Mark E. "Community Mental Health Myths and the Fate of Former Hospitalized Patients." *Psychiatry* 38 (August 1975): 209–17.

Klawans, H. L., et al. "Tardive Dyskinesia: Review and Update." *American Journal of Psychiatry* 137 (1980): 900–908.

LaFave, W., and Scott, A., Jr. *Criminal Law*. St. Paul, Minn.: West, 1972.

Laing, R. D. *The Politics of Experience*. New York: Pantheon, 1967.

Lamb, H. R. "Roots of Neglect of the Long-Term Mentally Ill." *Psychiatry* 42 (1979): 201–7.

Lamb, H. R.; Sorkin, Alvin P.; and Zusman, Jack. "Legislating Social Control of the Mentally Ill in California." *American Journal of Psychiatry* 138 (1981): 334–39.

Leifer, Ronald. *In the Name of Mental Health*. New York: Science House, 1969.

Lelos, D. "Courtroom Observation Study of Civil Commitment." In *Civil Commitment and Social Policy*, edited by A. L. McGarry et al., pp. 141–81. Cambridge, Mass.: Laboratory of Community Psychology, Harvard Medical School, 1978.

Lemert, Edwin M. *Human Deviance, Social Problems, and Social Control*. Englewood Cliffs, N.J.: Prentice-Hall, 1967.

Lerman, Paul. "Trends and Issues in Deinstitutionalization of Youths in Trouble." *Crime and Delinquency* 26 (July 1980): 282–99.

Letters to the Editor. "Research Diagnostic Criteria" (Spitzer, Endicott and Williams), and "In Reply" (Overall and Hollister). *Archives of General Psychiatry* 36, no. 12 (1979): 1381–83.

Lipsitt, Paul D., and Lelos, D. "Decision Makers in Law and Psychiatry and the Involuntary Civil Commitment Process." *Community Mental Health Journal* 17, no. 2 (1981): 114–22.

Livermore, J. M., et al. "On the Justifications for Civil Commitment." *University of Pennsylvania Law Review* 117 (1968): 75–96.

Loftus, Elizabeth. *Eyewitness Testimony*. Cambridge, Mass.: Harvard University Press, 1979.

Los Angeles Times. "1 in 5 Adults Lack Basic Living Skills, Study Finds" (October 30, 1975), pt. I at 1.

———. "36 More Mental Hospital Deaths "Questionable'" (November 20, 1976), pt. I at 1.

———. "Psychiatry's Focus Turns to Biology" (July 21, 1980), pt. I at 1.

McGarry, A. L., and Schwitzgebel, R. K. "Introduction." In *Civil Commitment and Social Policy*, edited by A. L. McGarry et al., pp. 1–12. Cambridge, Mass.: Laboratory of Community Psychology, Harvard Medical School, 1978.

Mackie, J. L. *Ethics*. New York: Pelican, 1977.

Mackinnon, D. R., and Farberow, N. L. "An Assessment of the Utility of Suicide Prevention." *Suicide and Life Threatening Behavior* 6 (1976): pp. 86 ff.

Manning, Peter K. "Rules in Organizational Context: Narcotics Law Enforcement in Two Settings." *Sociological Quarterly* (Winter 1977).

Marshall, Gloria. "Field Work in a Yoruba Community." In *Women in the Field*, edited by Peggy Golde, pp. 165–94. Chicago: Aldine, 1970.

Mason, A. S.; Nerviano, V.; and DeBerger, R. A. "Patterns of Antipsychotic Drug Use in Four Southeastern State Hospitals." *Diseases of the Nervous System* 38 (1977): 541–45.

Massad, Phillip M. "Guardianship: An Acceptable Alternative to Institutionalization?" *American Behavioral Scientist* 24 (July/August 1981): 755–70.

May, P. R. A. "When, What and Why? Psychopharmacotherapy and Other Treatments in Schizophrenia." *Comprehensive Psychiatry* 17 (1976): 683–93.

Meehl, Paul E. "Psychology and the Criminal Law." *University of Richmond Law Review*, vol. 5 (1970).

Mendel, Werner M., and Rapport, Samuel. "Determinants of the Decision for Psychiatric Hospitalization." *Archives of General Psychiatry* 20 (March 1969): 321–28.

Menzies, R. J.; Webster, C. D.; and Butler, B. T. "Perceptions of Dangerousness among Forensic Psychiatrists." *Comprehensive Psychiatry* 22 (1981): 387–96.

Miller, Dorothy, and Schwartz, Michael. "County Lunacy Commission Hearings: Some Observations of Commitments to a State Mental Hospital." *Social Problems* 14 (1966): 26–35.

Miller, Kent S. *Managing Madness: The Case against Civil Commitment.* New York: Free Press, 1976.

Model Penal Code 4.01, Comment (Tent. Draft No. 4, 1955).

Monahan, John. "The Prevention of Violence." In *Community Mental Health and the Criminal Justice System*, edited by John Monahan, pp. 13–34. New York: Pergamon, 1976.

———. "Prediction Research and the Emergency Commitment of Dangerous Mentally Ill Persons: A Reconsideration." *American Journal of Psychiatry* 135 (1978): 198–201.

———. *The Clinical Prediction of Violent Behavior.* Washington, D.C.: Government Printing Office, 1981.

Monahan, John; Caldeira, C.; and Friedlander, H. D. "Police and the Mentally Ill: A Comparison of Committed and Arrested Persons." *International Journal of Law and Psychiatry* 2, no. 4 (1979): 509–18.

Monahan, John, and Splane, S. "Psychological Approaches to Criminal Behavior." In *Criminology Review Yearbook*, edited by E. Bittner and S. Messinger, pp. 17–47. Beverly Hills, Calif.: Sage, 1980.

Monahan, John, and Wexler, David B. "A Definite Maybe: Proof and Probability in Civil Commitment." *Law and Human Behavior* 2 (1978): 37–42.

Moore, M. "Some Myths about 'Mental Illness.'" *Archives of General Psychiatry* 32 (1975): 1483–97.

———. "Responsibility and the Unconscious." *Southern California Law Review* 53 (1980): 1563–1675.

Morris, Grant H. "Conservatorship for the 'Gravely Disabled': California's Nondeclaration of Nonindependence." *San Diego Law Review* 15 (1978): 201–37.

Morse, S. J. "The Twilight of Welfare Criminology: A Reply to Judge Bazelon." *Southern California Law Review* 49 (1976): 1247–61.

———. "Crazy Behavior, Morals, and Science: An Analysis of Mental Health Law." *Southern California Law Review* 51 (1978): 527–624.

———. "Failed Explanations and Criminal Responsibility: Experts and the Unconscious." *Virginia Law Review*, vol. 68 (1982), in press.

Murphy, J. G., and Dantel, W. E. "A Cost-Benefit Analysis of Community versus Institutional Living." *Hospital and Community Psychiatry* 27 (1976): 165–70.

Murphy, Jane M. "Psychiatric Labeling in Cross-cultural Perspective." *Science* 191 (March 1976): 1019–191.

Musgrove, Frank. *Margins of the Mind.* London: Methuen & Co., 1977.

Nader, Laura. "From Anguish to Exultation." In *Women in the Field*, edited by Peggy Golde, pp. 97–118. Chicago: Aldine, 1970.

Overall, J., and Hollister, L. "Comparative Evaluation of Research Diagnostic Criteria for Schizophrenia." *Archives of General Psychiatry* 36 (1979): 1198–1205.

Parsons, T. *Social Structure and Personality*. New York: Free Press, 1970.

Paul, G., and Lentz, R. *Psychosocial Treatment of Chronic Mental Patients.* Cambridge, Mass.: Harvard University Press, 1977.

Poythress, N. G., Jr. "Psychiatric Expertise in Civil Commitment: Training Attorneys to Cope with Expert Testimony." *Law and Human Behavior* 2 (1978): 1–23.

Psychiatric News. "Half of Patients in Study Improperly Detained" (November 18, 1977), pp. 20–21, quoting Lansing Crane, J.D., Howard Zonana, M.D., and Stephen Wizner, J.D., in *Hospital & Community Psychiatry* (November 1977).

Quinney, Richard. "A Critical Theory of Criminal Law." In *Criminal Justice in America*, edited by Richard Quinney, pp. 1–25. Boston: Little, Brown & Co., 1974.

Rabkin, J. G. "Opinions about Mental Illness: A Review of the Literature." *Psychological Bulletin* 77 (1972): 153–71.

———. "Criminal Behavior of Discharged Mental Patients: A Critical Appraisal of the Research." *Psychological Bulletin* 86, no. 1 (1979): 1–27.

Rachlin, T., et al. "Civil Liberties versus Involuntary Hospitalization." *American Journal of Psychiatry* 132 (1975): pp. 189–92.

Rappeport, J., ed. *Clinical Evaluation of the Dangerousness of the Mentally Ill.* Springfield, Ill. Thomas, 1967.

Reiss, Albert J. "Discretionary Justice." In *Handbook of Criminology*, edited by Daniel Glaser, pp. 679–702. Chicago: Rand McNally, 1974.

Rock, Ronald; Jacobson, Marcus; and Janopaul, Richard. *Hospitalization and Discharge of the Mentally Ill.* Chicago: University of Chicago Press, 1968.

Rofman, E. S., et al. "The Prediction of Dangerous Behavior in Emergency Civil Commitment." *American Journal of Psychiatry* 137 (1980): 1061–64.

Rose, Stephen M. "Deciphering Deinstitutionalization: Complexities in Program Analysis." *Milbank Memorial Fund Quarterly* 57 (1979): 429–60.

Rosenblatt, A., and Mayer, J. E. "The Recidivism of Mental Patients: A Review of Past Studies." *American Journal of Orthopsychiatry* 14 (1974): 697–706.

Rosenhan, David L. "On Being Sane in Insane Places." *Science* 179 (1973): 250–58.

Roth, L. H. "A Commitment Law for Patients, Doctors, and Lawyers." *American Journal of Psychiatry* 136, no. 9 (1979): 1121–27.

Roth, Sir Martin. "The Principles of Providing a Service for Psycho-Geriatric Patients." In *Roots of Evaluation*, edited by John K. Wing and H. Hafner. Oxford: Oxford University, 1973.

Rovner-Pieczenik, Roberta. "Another Kind of Education: Researching Urban Justice." In *The Research Experience*, edited by M. Patricia Golden, pp. 465–73. Itasca, Ill.: Peacock, 1976. (a)

———. "Labeling in an Organizational Context: Adjudicating Felony Cases in an Urban Court." In *The Research Experience*, edited by M. Patricia Golden, pp. 447–64. Itasca, Ill.: Peacock, 1976. (b)

Rubin, Jeffrey. *Economics, Mental Health, and the Law.* Lexington, Mass.: D. C. Heath, 1978.

Ryan, J. P. "Adjudication and Sentencing in a Misdemeanor Court: The Outcome Is the Punishment." *Law and Society Review* 15 (1980–81): 77–108.

Sainsbury, Peter, and Grad de Alarcon, Jacquelyn. "Evaluating a Service in Sussex." In *Roots of Evaluation*, edited by J. K. Wing and H. Hafner. Oxford: Oxford University, 1973.

Santos, Boadventure de Sousa. "The Law of the Oppressed: The Construction and Reproduction of Legality in Pasagarda." *Law and Society Review* 12 (Fall 1977): 5–126.

Sarbin, T. R., and Mancuso, K. "Failure of a Moral Enterprise: Attitudes of the Public toward Mental Illness." *Journal of Consultation and Clinical Psychology* 35 (1970): 159–72.

———. *Schizophrenia: Medical Diagnosis or Moral Verdict?* New York: Pergamon, 1980.

Scheff, Thomas J. "Decision Rules, Types of Error and Their Consequences in Medical Diagnosis." *American Behavioral Scientist* 8 (1963): 97–107.

———. "The Societal Reaction to Deviance." *Social Problems* 11 (1964): 401–13.

———. *Being Mentally Ill: A Sociological Theory.* Chicago: Aldine, 1966.

———. "Medical Dominance: Psychoactive Drugs and Mental Health Policy." *American Behavioral Scientist* 19 (1976): 299 ff.

Schofield, W. *Psychotherapy: The Purchase of Friendship.* Englewood Cliffs, N.J.: Prentice-Hall, 1964.

Schwitzgebel, R. K. "Survey of State Commitment Statutes." In *Civil Commitment and Social Policy,* edited by A. L. McGarry et al. Cambridge, Mass.: Laboratory of Community Psychology, Harvard Medical School, 1978. (a)

———. "Treatment and Policy Considerations." In *Civil Commitment and Social Policy,* edited by A. L. McGarry et al., pp. 36–69. Cambridge, Mass.: Laboratory of Community Psychology, Harvard Medical School, 1978. (b)

Scull, Andrew T. *Decarceration: Community and the Deviant: A Radical View.* Englewood Cliffs, N.J.: Prentice-Hall, 1977.

———. "A New Trade in Lunacy: The Re-Commodification of the Mental Patient." *American Behavioral Scientist* 25 (July/August 1981): 741–54.

Segal, Steven P.; Baumohl, Jim; and Johnson, Elsie. "Falling through the Cracks: Mental Disorder and Social Margin in Young Vagrant Population." *Social Problems* 24 (February 1977): 387–400.

Seidmann, R. R., and Chambliss, W. J. "Appeals from Criminal Convictions." In *Handbook of Criminology,* edited by Daniel Glaser, pp. 651–67. Chicago: Rand McNally, 1974.

Shah, Saleem A. "Some Interactions of Law and Mental Health in the Handling of Social Deviance." *Catholic University Law Review* 23, no. 4 (Summer 1974): 674–719.

———. "Dangerousness: A Paradigm for Exploring Some Issues in Law and Psychology." *American Psychologist* 33 (1978): 224–39.

Sharfstein, S. S., and Nofziger, J. C. "Community Care: Costs and Benefits for Chronic Patients." *Hospital and Commmunity Psychiatry* 27 (1976): 170–73.

Sheridan, E. P., and Teplin, L. A. "Recidivism in Difficult Patients: Differences between Community Mental Health and State Hospital." *American Journal of Psychiatry* 138 (1981): 688–90.

Shneidman, Edwin. "The National Suicide Prevention Program." In *Organizing the Community to Prevent Suicide,* edited by Jack Zusman and David Davidson. Springfield, Ill.: Thomas, 1971.

Shwed, H. J. "Protecting the Rights of the Mentally Ill." *American Bar Association Journal* 64 (1978): 564–67.

Siegler, M., and Osmond, H. "The 'Sick Role' Revisited." *Hastings Center Studies* 1 (1973): 41–58.

Simon, R., and Cockerham, W. "Civil Commitment, Burden of Proof, and Dangerous Acts: A Comparison of the Perspectives of Judges and Psychiatrists." *Journal of Psychiatry and Law* 5 (1977): 571–94.

Slovenko, Ralph. *Psychiatry and Law.* New York: Little, Brown & Co., 1973.

———. "Criminal Justice Procedures in Civil Commitment." *Wayne Law Review* 24 (1977): 1–44.

Sosowsky, L. G. "Explaining the Increased Arrest Rate among Mental Patients: A Cautionary Note." *American Journal of Psychiatry* 137 (1980): 1602–5.

Spece, R. G. "Preserving the Right to Treatment: A Critical Assessment and Constructive Development of Constitutional Right to Treatment Theories." *Arizona Law Review* 20 (1978): 1–47.

Spitzer, R. L., and Fleiss, J. "A Re-Analysis of the Reliability of Psychiatric Diagnoses." *British Journal of Psychiatry* 125 (1974): 341–47.

Srole, Leo, et al. *Mental Health in the Metropolis: The Midtown Manhattan Study.* Rev. ed. New York: New York University Press, 1978.

Staats, Elmer. Letter to Honorable Henry M. Jackson. In *Hearings before the Permanent Sub-Committee on Investigations, U.S. Senate,* June 1976, pt. 3, pp. 397–422.

Steadman, Henry J. "The Statistical Prediction of Violent Behavior: Measuring the Costs of a Public Protectionist versus a Civil Libertarian Model." *Law and Human Behavior,* in press.

Steadman, Henry J., and Cocozza, Joseph H. *Careers of the Criminally Insane: Excessive Social Control of Deviance.* Lexington, Mass.: Lexington Books, 1974.

Steadman, Henry J., and Keveles, G. "The Community Adjustment and Criminal Activity of the Baxstrom Patients: 1966–1970." *American Journal of Psychiatry* 129 (1972): 304–10.

Steadman, Henry J., et al. "Comparing Arrest Rates of Mental Patients and Criminal Offenders." *American Journal of Psychiatry* 135 (1978): 1218–26. (a)

———. "Explaining the Increased Arrest Rate among Mental Patients: The Changing Clientele of State Hospitals." *American Journal of Psychiatry* 135 (1978): 816–20. (b)

Stier, S. D., and Stoebe, K. J. "Involuntary Hospitalization of the Mentally Ill in Iowa: The Failure of the 1975 Legislation." *Iowa Law Review* 64 (1979): 1284–1435.

Stone, A. *Mental Health and the Law.* Washington, D.C.: Government Printing Office, 1975.

―――. "Psychiatric Abuse and Legal Reform: Two Ways to Make a Bad Situation Worse." *International Journal of Law and Psychiatry,* in press.

Stuart, Richard B. *Trick or Treatment: How and When Psychotherapy Fails.* Champaign, Ill.: Research Press Co., 1970.

Suarez, T. "A Critique of the Psychiatrists Role as Expert Witness." *Journal of Forensic Science* 12 (1967): 172–79.

Sudnow, David. "Normal Crimes: Sociological Features of the Penal Code in a Public Defender Office." *Social Problems* 12 (1965): 255–76.

Szasz, Thomas. "Psychiatric Expert Testimony: Its Covert Meaning and Social Function." *Psychiatry* 20 (1957): 313–16.

―――. *The Myth of Mental Illness.* New York: Harper & Row, 1961. (Rev. ed. 1974.)

―――. *Law, Liberty and Psychiatry,* New York: Macmillan, 1963.

―――. "Involuntary Psychiatry." *Cincinnati Law Review* 45 (1976): 347–65.

Talbott, John A. *The Death of the Asylum: A Critical Study of State Hospital Management, Services, and Care.* New York: Grune & Stratton, 1978.

―――. "The National Plan for the Chronically Mentally Ill: A Programmatic Analysis." *Hospital and Community Psychiatry* 32 (1981): 699–704.

Task Panel on the Nature and Scope of the Problem. Report submitted to the President's Commission on Mental Health, vol. 11, appendix, 1978.

Teilmann, Katherine, and Klein, Malcolm W. "Implications of California's 1977 Juvenile Justice Reform Law" (a final report submitted to the National Institute for Juvenile Justice and Delinquency Prevention, 1981).

Teknekron, Inc. *Improving California's Mental Health System: Policy Making and Management in the Invisible System.* Berkeley, Calif.: Teknekron (December 1978).

Temerlin, Maurice K. "Suggestion Effects in Psychiatric Diagnoses." *Journal of Nervous and Mental Diseases* 147 (1968): 349–58.

Test, M. A., and Stein, L. I. *Alternatives to Mental Hospital Treatment.* New York: Plenum, 1978.

―――. "Alternatives to Mental Hospital Treatment." *Archives of General Psychiatry* 37 (1980): 392–97.

Tolor, A., et al. "Altruism in Psychiatric Patients: How Socially Concerned Are the Emotionally Disturbed?" *Journal of Consulting and Clinical Psychology* 44 (1976): 503–7.

Torrey, E. F., and Taylor, R. L. "Cheap Labor from Poor Nations." *American Journal of Psychiatry* 130 (1973): 428–34.

Treffert, D., "The Practical Limits of Patients' Rights." In *Diagnosis and Debate*, edited by R. Bonnie, pp. 227–30. New York: Insight Communications, 1977.

Tribe, Lawrence. "Trial by Mathematics." *Harvard Law Review* 34 (1971): 1328–93.

Urmer, A. *The Burden of the Mentally Disordered Offender on Law Enforcement*. Chatsworth, Calif.: ENKI Research Institute, 1973.

Van Dusen, Katherine Teilmann. "Net Widening and Relabeling: Some Consequences of Deinstitutionalization." *American Behavioral Scientist* 24 (July/August 1981): 801–10.

van Praag, H. M. *Psychotic Drugs: A Guide for the Practitioner*. New York: Brunner/Mazel, 1978.

Vidich, A. J., and Bensman, J. "Academic Bureaucrats and Sensitive Townspeople." In *Reflections on Community Studies*, edited by A. J. Vidich et al., pp. 313–49. New York: Wiley, 1974.

Vonnegut, Mark. *The Eden Express: A Personal Account of Schizophrenia*. New York: Praeger, 1975.

Warren, Carol A. B. "Involuntary Commitment for Mental Disorder: The Application of California's Lanterman-Petris-Short Act." *Law and Society Reveiw* 11 (Spring 1977): 629–49.

———. "The Social Construction of Dangerousness." *Urban Life* 8 (October 1979): 303–11.

———. "Data Presentation and the Audience: Responses, Ethics, and Effects." *Urban Life* 9 (October 1980): 282–308.

———. "New Forms of Social Control: The Myth of De-institutionalization." *American Behavioral Scientist* 4 (July/August 1981): 724–40.

Warren, Carol A. B., and Johnson, John M. "A Critique of Labeling Theory from the Phenomenological Perspective." In *Theoretical Perspectives on Deviance*, edited by Robert A. Scott and Jack D. Douglas, pp. 69–92. New York: Basic, 1972.

Warren, Carol A. B., and Messinger, Sheldon L. "Women and Mental Illness: The Ambivalence of Housework." Paper presented at the annual meetings of the Society for the Study of Social Problems, New York, 1980.

Warren, Carol A. B., and Paul K. Rasmussen. "Sex and Gender in Field Research." *Urban Life* 6 (October 1977): 349–69.

Wax, Rosalie. *Doing Field Work: Warnings and Advice*. Chicago: University of Chicago Press, 1971.

———. "Gender and Age in Fieldwork and Fieldwork Education: No Good Thing Is Done by Any Man Alone." *Social Problems* 26 (June 1979): 509–22.

Weidman, Hazel Hitson. "On Ambivalence in the Field." In *Women in the Field*, edited by Peggy Golde, pp. 236–63. Chicago: Aldine, 1970.

Weinstein, R. "Patients' Attitudes toward Mental Hospitalization:

A Review of Quantitative Research." *Journal of Health and Social Behavior* 20 (1979): 237–58.

———. "The Favorableness of Patients' Attitudes toward Mental Hospitalization (Reply to Comment by Essex et al.)." *Journal of Health and Social Behavior* 21 (1980): 397–401.

Weisbrod, B. A.; Test, M. A.; and Stein, L. I. "Alternative to Mental Hospital Treatment II, Economic Benefit-Cost Analysis." *Archives of General Psychiatry* 37 (1980): 400–405.

Wenger, D. L., and Fletcher, C. R. "The Effect of Legal Counsel on Admissions to a State Mental Hospital: A Confrontation of Professions." *Journal of Health and Human Behavior* 10 (1969): 66.

Wenk, E. A., et al. "Can Violence Be Predicted?" *Crime and Delinquency* 18 (1972): 393–402.

Wexler, David B. "Mental Health Law and the Movement toward Voluntary Treatment." *California Law Review* 62 (May 1974): 671–92.

———. *Mental Health Law: Major Issues.* New York: Plenum, 1981.

Wexler, David B.; Scoville, Stanley; et al. "The Administration of Psychiatric Justice." *Arizona Law Review* 13 (1971): 38–51.

White, H. S., and Bennett, M. B. "Training Psychiatric Residents in Chronic Care." *Hospital and Community Psychiatry* 32 (1981): 339–43.

Whyte, William F. "The Slum: On the Evolution of *Street Corner Society.*" In *Reflections on Community Studies,* edited by A. J. Vidich et al., pp. 3–69. New York: Wiley, 1964.

Wing, J. K. *Reasoning about Madness.* Oxford: Oxford University Press, 1978.

Yarrow, Marian, et al. "The Psychological Meaning of Mental Illness in the Family." *Journal of Social Issues* 11, no. 4 (1955): 12–24.

Zander, Thomas K. "Civil Commitment in Wisconsin: The Impact of *Lessard* v. *Schmidt.*" *Wisconsin Law Review* (1976), pp. 503–62.

Ziskin, J. *Coping with Psychiatric and Psychological Testimony.* Vol. 1. 3d ed. Venice, Calif.: Law and Psychology Press, 1981.

Name Index

Subject Index

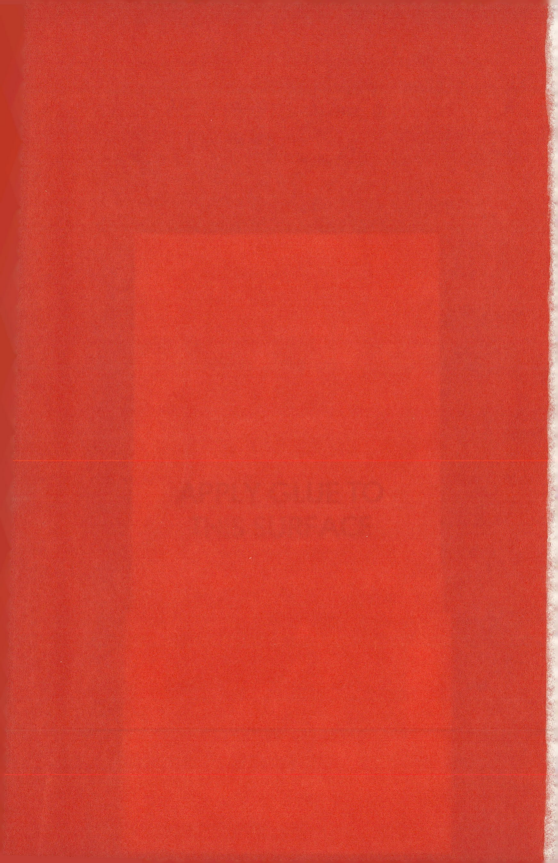